The Mahfouz Dialogs

The Mahfouz Dialogs

Gamal al-Ghitani

Translated by
Humphrey Davies

The American University in Cairo Press
Cairo New York

First published in 2007 by
The American University in Cairo Press
113 Sharia Kasr El Aini, Cairo, Egypt
420 Fifth Avenue, New York, NY 10018
www.aucpress.com

First published in Arabic in 2006 as *al-Majalis al-mahfuziya* by Dar El Shorouk

Dar el Kutub No. 13905/07
ISBN 978 977 416 127 8

Dar el Kutub Cataloging-in-Publication Data

al-Ghitani, Gamal
The Mahfouz Dialogs / Gamal al-Ghitani; translated by Humphrey Davies.—Cairo: The American University in Cairo Press, 2007
p. cm.
ISBN 977 416 127 0
1. Arabic literature—History and criticism 2. Mahfouz, Naguib, 1911–2006 I. Davies, Humphrey (trans.) II. Title
810.9

1 2 3 4 5 6 7 8 9 10 12 11 10 09 08 07

Designed by Andrea El-Akshar/AUC Press Design Center
Printed in Egypt

Contents

Introduction

The year 1994 may be regarded as a turning point in the life of Naguib Mahfouz and in my relationship with him, not in terms of the content of that relationship, but in its form and the circumstances surrounding it. In 1988, when he won the Nobel prize, does not compare in my opinion. When that prize was announced, on a Thursday, I went to his house. A large number of Egyptian, Arab, and foreign journalists had gathered in front of his home, which was on the first floor of a building that overlooks the Little Nile, the narrow branch of the river on the Giza side. I greeted his wife; she was having to deal with a situation such as she had never experienced in her life, which had passed in tranquility far from the spotlight, with only Mahfouz's most intimate friends visiting the small home in which the family had lived since the fifties. It was a small apartment, its furniture chosen with exquisite taste. Before the Nobel prize, I had had occasion to enter it only once, when I had visited the Master during a passing illness some years previously; from the time of our first acquaintance in 1959 our meetings had taken place in cafés. On that October Thursday afternoon of the Nobel prize, everyone else was asking where the Master had gone. I did not bother to inquire, but left the house and made for Casino Qasr al-Nil. I found him there and went up to say hello and congratulate him. He was sitting with his friends from the old 'Riffraff' group, including 'Adil Kamil, a lifelong friend who had set out on his own career as a novelist at the same time as Mahfouz, providing Arab readers with a beautiful work entitled *Mighty Millième (Millim al-akbar)* and a play, *Mistress Gulfidan (Gulfidan Hanim)*, before abandoning writing and turning to the world of business. The actor Ahmad Mazhar, God rest his soul, was there too, as was the director Tawfiq Salih. All three were old Riffraff members.

Thursdays were set aside originally for two gatherings. The first took place at 'Urabi's café in al-'Abbasiya, with friends from his childhood and youth. In the seventies, however, the café closed and was divided up into shops while at the same time most members of the 'Abbasiya clique had passed away, and those who were still living no longer left their homes because of ill-health or old age. By the eighties, therefore, this tradition had been abandoned. He had first permitted me to go see him at that café in the sixties. Every week, he would spend precisely two hours there, from six to eight. Then, when the time came for him to leave, he would go to a friend's house on Pyramids Road for a meeting with the Riffraff.

On Fridays, the site of the gathering was different at different times, settling in the seventies Café Riche. Then it moved to Casino Qasr al-Nil. Saturdays were for the family, and Mondays, Tuesdays, and Wednesdays for writing. During the summer months, Tuesdays were for a special meeting at Fishawi's café, attended only by Yusuf al-Qa'id and the writer of these lines. The Master stopped writing during the summer, apparently due to an eye allergy that began in the spring. He would spend one month of every summer in Alexandria, where he also had a symposium, and this also was an axis around which the littérateurs of the port-city and its summer visitors revolved; anyone who wished to attend was welcome, though he remained its most prominent member, taking his position in the most prominent place in the café. In the early nineties, when his sight declined and after an operation in London, he stopped going to Alexandria.

Even in 1994, even on that Friday, the Master was proceeding according to his rigorous 'Mahfouzian' schedule, which he maintained unvaryingly; the location of the gathering would change only if circumstances or unavoidable realities required it.

So it was until that fateful day that put an end to all the Master's customs and habits, to his going out among the people, to his daily early morning excursions and his progress to the café on al-Tahrir Square—that beautiful walk that he permitted me to take with him every day in the sixties, when I was working in an organization that had its headquarters in al-Duqqi and would meet him on al-Gala' Bridge, keeping him company as far as Qasr al-Nil Bridge. The Master lived among the people. He interacted with them. He treated them, as they did him, with love. And when the press campaigns that prepared the climate for that Friday were launched against him and books written by the scholars of darkness against *Children of the Alley (Awlad haratina)* appeared, he refused to accept bodyguards. He told me then that he could not picture himself walking in the street with a guard. He had a deep inner faith that no harm would come to him. Once he bent his head and told me, "Our days are in God's hands."

I, on the other hand, had intimations of fear due to my experience of the sixties, with their pursuits and fear of detention. I was, after all, part of a generation that had been born into fear and had plunged into clandestine action against the prevailing order, which many of us saw to be wrong—all of which had resulted in an acute sensitivity to security. From the start of the nineties, our meetings had become a fixture of Tuesdays, and when I became a chief editor at *Akhbar al-adab* and had my own car, provided by the Akhbar al-Yawm publishing house and driven by one of my driver colleagues, I took it upon myself to bring the Master to these meetings from his home.

At five to six I would be waiting, and at six precisely he would come through of the door of the apartment block. I would go toward him so as to walk next to him until he reached the car, and would open the door for him; he preferred the front seat, next to the driver. Then we would set off to the place where we usually met, which, during the seventies, had settled on the Farah Boat, moored, then as now, on the bank of the Nile.

Although I was unarmed—and had I been armed I still wouldn't have known how to use a weapon well—on my arrival in front of the house, I would check the place visually, imagining the possibility of some kind of assault. The Master's strict punctuality would make it easy for anyone who spied on him to pick the right time for an attack. I was expecting some such thing; I was on the alert following the rise in acts of violence by extremist groups that were, in essence, protests against corruption and vice, but which had lost sight of their true goals for reasons it would take too long to explain here.

After they published the photograph of the youth who had buried his knife in the Master's neck that Friday, I remembered him. Once I had been waiting for the Master and it was hot. My glance took in a young man wearing jeans sitting beneath the balcony that ran the width of the Master's home on the ground floor and was enclosed in thick glass and fenced with decorative iron bars, and which Madam 'Atiyyat Allah, the Master's lifelong companion, had filled with plants that formed a small but delightful garden.

I had looked at the youth, who had returned my look with a hard stare and then occupied himself with tearing papers he was carrying into small pieces, showing no other reaction; indeed, he remained crouched where he was. I thought that he might be seeking refuge from the heat, but his image leapt to my mind weeks later when the photograph was published. It was the same youth who went up to the Master later that Friday afternoon to shake his hand with one hand and with the other bury an old knife, its broken handle held together with strong string, in his neck—a blow that divided two extraordinary decades, each totally different from the other and the second of which continues today.

I return to the private papers in which I recorded the events of those days in 1994, and specifically those of Friday, 10 October. That day, I had been relaxing after my return the day before from a trip to Morocco. I had been arranging my library, which I had been absent from for a while, and listening to some recordings of the music of al-Andalus that I had acquired in the ancient city of Fez. The telephone rang. I heard the voice of my colleague and friend Mustafa Bakri saying, "Have you heard that they attacked Naguib Mahfouz? Please confirm the report."

I answered that I could not. I asked him to call me in a little while. I was taken aback. I froze. It was the moment I had been expecting and hoping would not happen. Now, it seemed, I would have to face it. It takes seconds for a blow to reach the pain centers in the brain. While I was in this state, I had a vision of the good-hearted man with his fatherly presence, and of my friendship with him. I called his home. His younger daughter answered. In a neutral voice and as though I had nothing special in mind, I said, "All's well? What's up?"

Pain and fear of the future in her voice, she replied, "I don't know what's happening now. Papa is in the operating room. Please pray for him, Uncle."

Then she said, "Mama and my sister are with him, here at the Police Hospital next door."

I uttered some short sentences that I hoped would reassure her and said a prayer for his survival. Then I acted. I called my colleagues at the *Akhbar al-yawm* editorial center. I was the first to inform them of the news. I called my friend Yusuf al-Qa'id. He was at home. He said that a friend of his had called him to ask what was going on. I called my friend 'Imad al-'Abbudi, the engineer and businessman. The Tuesday session was a small one at the time, and Imad was one of its pillars. He said he would go by Yusuf's, the two of them would come to my place, and then we would set off for the hospital. I went out into the street. I was confronted by the night and fear of what might happen, my memory springing to life and pelting me with a torrent of flashes, a condition with which I am familiar when reality threatens me with the loss of a friend. Moments I have known, moments I have heard about, flash before my eyes like lightning.

I waited in front of the house every Tuesday; what had happened today, when Dr. Fathi had been by his side, could have happened when I was there—listening to him, drawing close to his left ear, with which it was still possible for him to hear with the help of a hearing aid, raising my voice; his moments of silence; how his glance would wander; his 6 a.m. stroll along the Nile, which he loved, from the houseboat he lived in for a year after he married, then from the flat he had found close by (Mahfouz of the Nile and the Nile of Mahfouz); his stop to buy newspapers; his regular appearance at Café Riche, Groppi's café, the Ali Baba café, in all of which he would read the newspapers, write telegrams of condolence and congratulation, and record observations; his evenings at 'Urabi's café, the smell of tobacco rising from the waterpipe that I learned from him how to smoke and then gave up; his ringing laughter with childhood friends from the 'Abbasiya clique; our strolls in the lanes of al-Gamaliya; how I had respected his moments of companionship with its ancient cafés when he recalled his own past, when I would speak to him only if he spoke to me; people's affection for him; how he would walk among them returning a greeting from this person, shaking hands with that, rebuffing no one; amazing patience, vast modesty, tolerance the like of which I have never known; the moment when he would partake of food in our company—the food of an ascetic—a piece of white cheese, a slice of tomato, a bean patty, no more, no less.

What I had not experienced with him was what it was like to grow up in the Bayt al-Qadi neighborhood—the 'pasha's beard' tree, the fights among the neighborhood gang leaders, the love for al-Husayn, his games in Qirmiz Passage, the 1919 Revolution, the thirties, Cairo's golden age, the Second World War, the bomb shelters, the end of the era of the neighborhood gang leaders, having lunch at al-Agati's and al-Dahhan's, the kufta and kebab, evenings at Tout Va Bien, the Midaq Alley café, the ministry of religious endowments, the days when he worked in the office at the Mausoleum of al-Ghuri, the July 1952 Revolution.

Naguib Mahfouz—an entire epoch embodied in one man. He lived Egyptian society and gave it expression over seventy years of continuous writing, a unique achievement in the history of literature and writers. On that now far distant day, I came close to grasping the horror of what had happened and started to take it in that I should be wailing and crying out in tears, "My Master! My beloved!"

When we reached the hospital, which by divine providence and God's care was situated approximately thirty meters from his home, about two hours had passed since the blow had been delivered. We went into the waiting room close to the operating theater. Tharwat Abaza was there, sobbing like a child and repeating, "Naguib. Naguib. How could anyone hurt him? How could anyone do anything to him?"

We urged him to calm down, though ourselves in need of someone to calm us down. There, on the second floor, the Master lay stretched out on the operating table, with a team of skilled surgeons led by Egypt's most important blood vessel surgeon, Dr. Ahmad Samih Hammam. Once again, I was convinced divine providence had intervened.

The first time had been because the person responsible for accompanying the Master that day had been Dr. Fathi Hashim, a veterinary physician perhaps, but a physician nonetheless. When the Master got into the car and settled down next to him, the young man came up to him, shook his hand, and then drove his flick knife into the Master's neck and started trying to cut his throat. He had meant to cut the main artery that conveys the blood to the head and brain. As Mahfouz told us later, "After he shook my hand, I felt a fiery beast pressing against my neck."

What saved Naguib Mahfouz was the fact that he was old and, as a result, bent forward. This caused the knife to just miss the main artery. At that moment, when the car started to shake, Fathi Hashim noticed what was going on. He screamed, "What are you doing, you madman?"

He leaped from the car, and at this the young man threw the knife down and ran. Fathi started after him, but preferred to go back to the wounded Master, whose blood was spurting like a fountain. He quickly got back in the driver's seat, pressed on the wound with one hand, and with the other steered the little car backward, making for the hospital. He covered the few intervening meters and when he arrived at the main gate, rushed to the door shouting, "Open up! It's Naguib Mahfouz. They tried to . . . ."

The door opened quickly. Up to this moment, the Master was conscious. They got him out onto a stretcher trolley, and before he lost consciousness he said, "Be careful. I have diabetes."

In fact, he was treated with the utmost competence. After a rapid evaluation, the hospital's administration telephoned Dr. Ahmad Samih Hammam, and here again fate intervened. Cell phones were unknown in Egypt at that time. The call was made at the moment the celebrated doctor was standing in front of the elevator outside his apartment, preparing to leave for a dinner party. They caught him before he stepped into the elevator. He obeyed the summons immediately, it taking him no longer to get to the hospital than the time spent on the road, and he entered the operating theater at once. Brigadier Hasan al-Alfi, then minister of the interior, arrived, as did Dr. Mamduh al-Biltagi, then minister of tourism, and a number of senior officials from the national security forces.

"The bleeding has been stopped. The blood was spurting like a fountain."

"Eight liters of blood have been transfused, fourteen bags."

Intellectuals and ordinary people were gathered in front of the hospital. They had come in droves after the news spread, many volunteering to donate their blood to save the Master. After four hours, we heard that the operation had been successful. The Master was being transferred to the intensive care unit.

After midnight we walked through the corridors of the hospital, which were finally quiet now that the critical hours had passed. There were four of us—Yusuf al-Qa'id, Imad al-'Abbudi, Mamduh al-Laythi, and myself. We traversed the long passages without knowing exactly where we were going and eventually arrived at the intensive care unit, where there was more than one patient. Naguib Mahfouz was lying on his back. For the first time in my life I saw him without glasses. He seemed shaken; his voice was tremulous and hoarse. He shook hands with his left hand, and I thought of what Dr. Samih Hammam had said about the nerve leading to the right hand being affected: he had been reassured when he had seen the Master move his extremities, but it would need time.

I go back to the papers that I wrote during the week thereafter and find the following: "Today, Wednesday morning. I think about his right hand, the slowness with which it moves. This is the hand that dug a conduit for Arab creativity, the hand that wrote *The Cairo Trilogy (al-Thulathiya)*, *The Harafish (Malhamat al-harafish*, literally *The Epic of the Riffraff)*, and *Children of the Alley*. I contemplate the dark color of the skin, which I do not recognize as that of the hand that I have so often kissed. I think of him bedridden in the days after his recovery. I am confident that he will adapt to the new circumstances, just as he did after he began to lose his sight and hearing, even though I know that he changes his habits only with great difficulty. I dream now of those moments, which I keenly anticipate, when I shall accompany him as is our custom, and we explore the alleyways of historic Cairo, strolling through history."

His return to writing took place after four years of daily physical therapy. One day he leaned toward me to tell me in confidence, "Today I was able to write without slipping off the line."

During those four years since the attack, he had put his affairs in order and, by virtue of a strong inner will, adapted to the new circumstances—not just those resulting from the injury, but also those resulting from advancing age and weakness. Old age had affected his sight, so that he could no longer read. We offered to help him but he refused to be a burden to any of us. He arranged for some kind gentleman to come to him every day for an hour in the morning to read him the most important items in the morning papers, both government press and opposition. The important articles and literary texts, however, his friends would read to him at our evening gatherings, which followed a particular order. I, for example, usually read him old poetry, which he loved and which he usually used 'so as to start things on a sweet note' whenever he sat down to write or read. In a loud voice I would read him something I liked from the ancient poets, and sometimes he'd surprise me by completing the verses from memory. I have written down all the odes that it seemed to me he had memorized, and I consider these the equivalent of his personally selected anthology.

Sometimes I would read him passages of prose, and his expression as he concentrated to follow what I was saying would attract my attention; at the end, he would sometimes make some insightful comment on the text, for if time had affected his senses of hearing and sight, it had not affected his mind, which remained sharp and incisive, while his memory was amazing.

Sometimes one of us would raise some topic or other and ask his opinion, and he would answer with a couple of passing words, as when I asked him what he thought about the events of September 2001 about a year after their occurrence, and the first thing he said to me was, "Do they need an opinion?"

When I repeated the question, he said, "You know . . . ."

Then he stopped. We moved on to other subjects. Then suddenly after about half an hour he leaned forward and raised his finger. At this, we all listened attentively, knowing that he was going to say something he thought was important, to express an opinion. He said, "You know, about September 2001, I don't believe that an event more damaging for relations between East and West has ever occurred. The ones who committed the crime did grievous harm to Islam. Before that, there was the conduct of the Taliban, who also did harm to Islam and its image. We need a great effort to get back to the situation before September."

He fell silent for a little and then said, "I don't think the situation will go back to the way it was. We're still at the beginning of a phase whose features are unclear and whose outcomes are unknown."

Sometimes, discussions would arise on literary topics or those concerned with local or foreign politics. All he needed was to listen and absorb the discussion to come up with something wise. His capacity to make jokes was still at its height, and every week he would make us roar with laughter at some unexpected *qafsha* (witty wisecrack), some sudden sally that took us by surprise. The *qafsha* is a highly developed Egyptian art that goes back to better days, when public problems were less burdensome, when close friends could have good times together, when the world was less troubled. Naguib Mahfouz was one of the outstanding practitioners of the *qafya* (a kind of punning repartee) and the *qafsha*, both arts that depend on quick wits and a keen capacity for sarcasm.

For example, after receiving the check for a million pounds from Ibrahim al-Mu'allim, he said nothing for a while. Then he asked, "Know what I'm thinking about right now?"

We waited in silence. He said, "I'm thinking of making a run for it."

Naturally, we all roared. In those days, news of people who had taken loans of millions, and in some cases billions, and then fled with the depositors'—other people's—money, filled the newspapers. How perceptive, how revealing, how painful Mahfouz's joke seemed!

On another occasion, we were talking about a well-known dancer's statement to the press that she intended to retire. After a moment's silence, he said, "You'd better bring out a volume on her in *Holy Relics*."

Holy Relics (al-Dhakha'ir) was a book series put out by the Palaces of Culture that I supervised in which I presented important texts from the Arabic classics.

The 'Mahfouzian joke' is distinguished by intelligence, culture, precision, and a high dose of sarcasm. Just recalling the way he looked at the moment he threw out or gave birth to the joke, or pronounced the quip, makes me smile. Observing his features as we sat with him granted us a clear and accurate map of the human emotions. I always respected his silences, even before the attack and his advancing years. He would sit, straight-backed, gazing upward, with that expression on his face that cannot be described without resort to the Egyptian concept that is summed up in the single, extremely expressive, word *tayyib* (good-hearted; decent, honest, and kind). He looked magnanimous, brilliant, focused on the distance, yet still accessible. Now, with the advance of the years, his body was ruined, he bent over a little, and his silences would continue for long periods as he communed with himself. During our meetings with him, I would take care that we did not start up conversations on the margin. When he felt that those who were with him had left him out, and he could no longer follow what they were saying, he would retreat into himself, going back to his own private pasts. At such moments, I would come up with a question, or recount a piece of news or something amusing. Nowadays, the Master listens carefully most of the time, either to whoever is talking to him or to his internal dialog. He is most loquacious when recounting his memories of the city, of literary life, of past times.

I try to remember his features when angry and I cannot. He would get excited when expressing an opinion he was announcing for the first time or that he imagined would surprise us or was contrarian. Perhaps that moment during the summer of 1967 embodies what I'm talking about. It was when we had begun meeting at Fishawi's—the original café was still standing in those days—and the appalling June defeat was still fresh. He leaned forward a little and said, pronouncing his opinion, "If we don't have the capability to confront Israel militarily, settlement is a necessity."

Of course we argued, and that remained the focus of our discussions for many years. When he supported a settlement with Israel in the seventies, he was expressing his true position. In the special issue devoted to him by Raga' al-Naqqash in 1970, the Master says that when he sat down to write, he cared about nothing, that on matters related to his fundamental beliefs he never expressed anything at odds with his inner convictions, and that he did not keep petty accounts. Often I differed with him, and the passing of time proved that he had been the more far-sighted. He may not have sought to be provocative in his statements to the press, he may have been balanced in his positions concerning his relationship with authority, be it political or governmental, he may have been reticent, but he never made a statement at variance with his inner beliefs; and when he sat down to write creatively, he listened to nothing but his own voice and the demands of his conscience.

After the attack, I and others who loved him offered to set aside one or two hours a day so that he could dictate to us what he wanted to write, but he thanked us and gently declined. Writing, as far as he was concerned, was a highly private pursuit whose secrecy he had always maintained; how then could any person, no matter how close a friend, share with him the most private moments of his life? He had spent four years in physical therapy up to the moment at which he confided in me that he was able to keep to the line and not slip below it. In other words, Naguib Mahfouz learned to write twice in his lifetime: first in his childhood and a second time in his ninth decade, and the latter was the more tiring and difficult. How often I looked at his hand, at the large, jerky letters that he wrote when he signed his name on a copy of one of his works—the hand that had written his novels and his short stories, enlarging Arab and world literature, the hand that hatred, fanaticism, and ignorance had wounded.

Following the assassination attempt, I saw the young man whom I had caught sight of that day below the window. They asked him on television whether he felt any remorse for his attempt to kill Naguib Mahfouz, and he said that he felt none and that if he had the opportunity he would do the same again. When the presenter asked him if he had read anything by Mahfouz, he replied that he hadn't read a word but that his 'amir' had issued a decree declaring Naguib Mahfouz a blasphemer. In fact, the first accusation of blasphemy had been made by three leading shaykhs in a report to the president at the beginning of the sixties; from that time on, *Children of the Alley* had been banned in Egypt and declared contrary to religion, and things continued in this vein until they climaxed with the events of Friday 15, October 1994.

By the time Mahfouz had started to keep well to the line and write, his optical nerve had deteriorated. How then would the Master respond to these new circumstances?

It was not long after that the *Dreams* series began to appear in the pages of the magazine *Nisf al-dunya*—extremely concentrated texts that partook of both prose and poetry. He would write them first without ink, in his head. Then he would write them on paper with his eyes closed. He was not able to read them but, through strength of will and determination, he was able to embody what was in his mind on paper in a 'Mahfouzian' writing that I consider to be the most beautiful, the essence. This phase started with *Echoes of an Autobiography (Asda' al-sira al-dhatiya)* and reached its pinnacle with *The Dreams (Ahlam fatrat al-naqaha)*. They are texts of a poeticism that rises to the level of wisdom, evoking for me such similar works of human creativity as the poetry of Hafiz, the tales of Sa'di al-Shirazi, and proverb and wisdom texts. They possess the power of penetrating to the core of human experience and existence.

When, in December, we went out together for the first time after he had started to recover from the attack, winter was at its peak. We made for the Pyramids plateau with Yusuf al-Qa'id, Zaki Salim, and Dr. Yahya al-Rakhawi, who was in charge of organizing the days of his week and the last phase of his treatment and went on to become an essential member of the Riffraff meetings. We had lunch that day at the Mena House Hotel, and the Master was under police guard. It was a new situation, but one we would soon get used to; the members of the police guard in fact became friends of ours and like a new family for the Master and ourselves. It was not a situation he had sought, but one that put an end to the days of strolling through the streets of the city whose life he had lived and on some of whose districts he had bestowed immortality. All his life, he had been against mere appearances, including that of simplicity, but necessity has its rules. The days of wandering through the lanes and alleys of the old parts of Cairo had come to an end. I had often seen him, during the sixties and seventies, roaming through the districts where he had been born, the alleys and streets of al-Gamaliya. I was careful not to disturb him so that I would not cut short his meditations, his recapturing of the place.

The three of us (Mahfouz, al-Qa'id, and myself) resumed our meetings on the boat moored on the Nile, the Nile that he loved with passion and was careful always to stay close to, so that even if he could not see it with his eyes, he could see it in his imagination.

During our meetings of the last few years, I awoke to the value of the views expressed by the Master. I would be careful, on my return home, to record what had been said, either in full as I remembered it, or as a summary, in order to offer the Arab reader the texts that I have entitled *The Mahfouz Dialogs (al-Majalis al-mahfuziya)*. These make up Part One of this book. Part Two of this book contains the text of sessions that took place every Monday over the course of summer 1978 and which appeared earlier in the book *Naguib Mahfouz Remembers (Nagib Mahfuz yatadhakkar)*. Part Three contains texts relating to my wanderings with Mahfouz through the old districts of Cairo and to gatherings devoted to specific events. The three parts conjure up and record the distinguishing features of a companionship extending for more than forty-four years with our great writer, may God prolong his life, in the hope that they may shed some light on his world, his views, and his thoughts.

I must mention with gratitude our Tuesday friends and the fixed pillars of these gatherings, each of whom has his own special relationship with and pure affection for the Master—my brother Yusuf al-Qa'id, Eng. Hasan Nasir, Maître Magdi Sa'd, and Prof. Yasin al-Tuhami, each of whom surrounds the Master with his fondness. To them, then, thanks and goodwill. We pray, from the bottom of our hearts, that Naguib Mahfouz may experience a long life, good health, and the same happiness that he has brought all of us.

November 2004

Part One

These conversations, of which I was accustomed, especially in later years, to record a summary, took place during the gatherings that extended from the days of the Café Opéra in 1960 to the appearance of this book in 2004.

Dialogs

Café Opéra, 1960

The café has three floors. The first looks directly over the beautiful square dominated by the elegant old wooden opera building, which provided a focus for the place and contributed to the special atmosphere of the city's downtown area, with its European layout and architecture. The first floor was a café distinguished by its elegance, where both men and women sat, and where waterpipes with authentic 'Persian' tobacco were available; to my amazement I would observe women who had passed middle age smoking waterpipes at a time when it was unusual to see women smoking in public.

One ascended to the second floor via a side entrance with a narrow spiral stairway that gave onto an oblong hall containing a European-style café, where there were no waterpipes, only hot and cold drinks. Here the weekly symposium that Naguib Mahfouz had initiated in 1954 (the year in which I was born) held its meetings. Entire generations passed through this group, and here the writers of the sixties discovered one another. In other words, this weekly encounter abbreviated long stretches of time that might otherwise have ended without my meeting Mohamed El-Bisatie, Yusuf al-Qa'id, Ibrahim Aslan, Sabry Hafez, the late Galal al-Sayyid, and others.

On the third floor there was a nightclub run by Artiste Safiya Hilmi. The third floor was open for business after ten o'clock in the evening, and Hilmi, who was a celebrated performer from Badi'a Masabni's troupe, gave her name to the entire building.

In the first-floor café, I listened to the conversations of those present, who arranged themselves around Naguib Mahfouz—conversations which, had it been possible to preserve them for posterity, would have provided an extraordinary record of the discussions that took place among the intellectuals of the period. The symposium began at ten and ended at half-past one. The Master, with his customary discipline, provided the continuity of regular hours to the group. He was always the focus of the group. Even when the talk turned away from him and those present starting discussing things among themselves, he remained the center around whom everyone else was in orbit.

One morning I arrived early and was startled to find myself alone, face to face with the Master. I sat in silence while he observed me with sparkling eyes.

Suddenly he asked me, "Gamal, why do you write?"

I was taken aback by the question but replied immediately, "I write because I want to write."

He nodded. When I recall that brief conversation, it opens up for me all our other conversations, conversations that were to continue throughout the succeeding years. When I recall his tone of voice, I am almost certain that he was asking himself why he wrote, why the writer writes. Once in later years, he told me that writing was like an instinct, like sex, like the desire for life, like eating, hunger, repletion.

It may be that what he said then was an answer to the question he had asked me that morning long ago during the sixties of the last century.

Settlement!

Fishawi's

AUGUST 1967

The events of June dominate our thoughts, our spirits, and our moods. Against his normal practice, he had expressed a desire to meet us at Fishawi's, and this provided another opportunity for a private encounter with him, as only a very limited number of his friends attended.

We were three: Yusuf al-Qa'id, Isma'il 'Adli, and myself. We talked about what was happening and what might happen. Suddenly, he said, "You know, everyone . . . ."

We looked at him.

"I'm going to tell you my opinion and I know it may upset you."

We listened even more attentively. He said, "If we don't have the capability to confront Israel militarily, we have to try and find a means to bring about a settlement."

We looked at him in stupefaction.

This was in August, 1967.

Sadness

Café Riche

NOVEMBER 1980

I was sad, grief-stricken, the wound still fresh, hot, and bleeding. It started following the unexpected passing away of my father when I was far from home. I told him that I would never be able to get over my father's sudden departure, that I would never ever see him again, never meet him again.

He said, "How do you know, Gamal? Just as matter is transformed into other forms, maybe the consciousness lives on in some form. Who are we to insist that a meeting is impossible?"

Fishawi's

A WINTER'S MORNING, 1988

I am listening to him speak of his memories of Cairo, and from this I realize how its former landmarks were and know what it has become.

He said, "There used to be a cinema called Je Sais where the Benzion department store now stands on 'Imad al-Din Street. That was where I heard Umm Kulthum. She used to put on her concerts in the cinema theater and she could make herself audible throughout a hall filled with three thousand people without a microphone."

After a few moments of silence, he added, "I would listen to Umm Kulthum in the flesh and then listen to the same song recorded and I'd find a great difference. Of course, the real thing was much better."

Fishawi's

Wednesday, a winter's morning, 1989

He said, "'Ali al-Gharbi was one of the famous neighborhood gang leaders, a famous procurer, and, at the same time, one of Cairo's most famous homosexuals. When the police caught him, there were lots of scandals. It was one of Cairo's big incidents."

The Ali Baba Café

A spring morning, 1989

I asked him, "Which is dearer to your heart, *The Harafish* or *Morning and Evening Talk (Hadith al-sabah wa-l-masa')*?"

He said, "I think *The Harafish*. . . . Sometimes one is influenced by other people's opinions."

I asked him, "What about the unpublished novels?"

He said, "There are three. A novel whose hero is a soccer player, which I wrote in the forties and tore up, a novel about the countryside which I didn't publish and whose whereabouts now I don't know because I don't keep drafts, and another social novel, the draft of which may be with the director Khayri Bishara."

Farah Boat

Summer 1991

He said, "When a woman got into difficulties and started down the path of deviant behavior, she'd go to the police to register her name and she'd say to the officer, 'I want to "walk in *al-wa'd*"' (meaning, 'accept God's promise *(wa'd)* for me,' or 'accept my fate'). This was how she'd obtain a license to practice prostitution. Once the English judge bent over to the Egyptian assistant judge sitting on his right and asked him, 'Where is this place called al-Wa'd, my friend?'"

Farah Boat

Tuesday 27 October 1992

The birthday of Director Tawfiq Salih, former member of the Riffraff. Mahfouz recalls his memories of the cinema:

"The first cinema I knew was at the Egyptian Club Hotel, near the mosque of Our Master Husayn. It was a revelation to me. We looked out from it over an amazing world of the imagination. All the films were foreign. The translation was on an oblong screen to one side and if it was out of sync with the scene we'd shout, 'Correction! Correction!' and the man running the cinema would adjust the translation to fit the scene. The music was live, with a clever musician playing the piano next to the screen. Sometimes a bunch of us would go and we'd wake the owner of the cinema up to put on the movie for us."

He said, "I knew the Cinéma Olympia in 'Abd al-'Aziz Street. On the same street there were also the Cinéma Idéal and the Cinéma Royal. The Cinéma Olympia used to print a magazine called *News of the Stars*. Mary Pickford was my favorite. I read that she had married Douglas Fairbanks. On al-Gaysh Street were Cinéma Ramses, Cinéma Misr, Cinéma Hollywood; there were also Cinéma Suhayr close to al-'Abbasiya, Cinéma al-Belvédère and Cinéma Plaza in al-Zahir, Cinéma al-Fath in al-Gamaliya, and Cinéma Je Sais for French films on 'Imad al-Din Street."

He asks, "How many of these movie houses are left now?"

I say, "Only Cinéma Olympia and Cinéma Hollywood."

(On Tawfiq Salih's birthday we broke with tradition and didn't have dinner on the Farah Boat, which was unusual, even unique. We went instead to Christo's Restaurant at the end of Pyramids Road, which specializes in fish and where Mahfouz used to take the family every Friday.)

He said, "I only started liking fish at an advanced age. I went to Ra's al-Barr where a friend invited me to a meal of fish. He asked me what I'd like and I said, 'Perch, catfish, eels.' They all laughed and my friend said, 'Those fishes that you like are what we feed to our fish.'"

I asked him laughing, "And what about rabbit?"

He said, "I used to be afraid to eat it because one day I saw my mother skinning one after it had been slaughtered!"

Farah Boat

October 1992

Earthquake Jokes

The following jokes were told on Tuesday evening:

- They caught the guy who caused the earthquake and he confessed.
- These days, when they walk in procession with the bride, they sing, 'Quake your hips, you pretty one, you cute one.'
- They said, 'The town's shaking and dancing!' We said, 'We'll take up a collection for the musicians!' (Meaning that the government was profiting from donations in aid of the victims.)

Sheraton Coffee Shop

Summer 1995

It was our first time in this place, which is designed for the meetings of lovers and businessmen. Everyone talks in low voices. We, on the other hand, had to talk loudly, which was out of the question there. We sat down and fidgeted. In front of us sat a man from the Arabian Peninsula, wearing a robe and a pointed beard. He started to exchange conversation with us as he drank his cold beer. He began with the American elections.

"That Bush, I swear he's a nice guy."

Then he started lamenting the fate of Islam and how little respect it got from its own followers. He said that Islam had "arrived as a stranger and would leave as a stranger"—"Yes, by God!"

He'd say that phrase and follow it with a swig of beer. Our session didn't last long. We got up and left.

Farah Boat

Fall 1992

He said, "I read some examples of the anti-novel and came out of the experience no wiser than I went in. Marguerite Duras, however, is a different proposition: in her work I found a story, an issue, and human beings."

Yusuf al-Qa'id spoke of the ranking of writers in France according to public opinion surveys. Duras was the first and Ben Jelloun the twenty-eighth.

Mahfouz said, "It's the media. They can help to get a writer known for a certain period even if he doesn't have any real value. The media don't add any real value. Take, for example, the novel *Ulysses*: every author and reader is bound to nod in admiration, but the number of people who have actually read it remains very limited."

Farah Boat

11 NOVEMBER 1992

The earthquake, which had taken place at one in the afternoon, dominated the gathering. For me, the main feeling was one of dejection: that is the way I face events of universal purport. A joke or two could not dispel the tyranny of my mysterious, hidden melancholy.

I don't know why I asked him about beginnings; perhaps because yesterday I looked through the first story of his to be published, in *al-Risala* magazine in 1937.

He said, "My dealings with the magazine were few. I used to go to its main office in 'Abdin where I would see major writers dealing with Ahmad Hasan al-Zayyat, but I didn't form any relationships with them. I saw Shaykh Mahmud Shakir. He was extremely short-tempered and he had such a loud voice it seemed to me even the king in 'Abdin Palace next door must hear him. However, I did form relationships with members of my own generation—al-Siba'i, who used to publish in the magazine *Musamarat al-gayb*, and Ihsan 'Abd al-Quddus and 'Ali Adham. I earned my first pound from the magazine *al-Thaqafa* and I spent it on a night out with my friends in al-'Abbasiya. We ate kebab and kufta. Boss 'Belly' clapped with delight and said, 'I swear, you can make money out of literature, boys!' I took *al-Thaqafa* another story, called 'The Air Raid' *(Fi-l-ghara)*, about a mother who returns to her house to find the headless corpse of her son. The censor got wind of it and gave the magazine a warning: 'How can you allow the publication of such stories, stories that sow terror among people?' When I went to get the second pound, I was taken aback to find that the magazine's secretary received me with extreme distaste. He asked me disparagingly, 'What's this you've gone and done?'

"It became clear to me to just what he must have been subjected to. I left the pound and never went back to *al-Thaqafa*."

He said, "I published a lot in *al-Riwaya*, but I didn't get any money. *Al-Risala* published the work of new writers free. Al-Zayyat used to say that *al-Risala* had brought him a printing press and a farm; he'd say it quite openly, unlike the other publishers, who always claimed to be living in poverty."

He said, "When 'Abd al-Hamid al-Sahhar set up a publishing house called The Publishing Committee for Academics, he chose just three stories from the collection *Whispers of Madness (Hams al-gunun)*. My other stories had not yet come out in book form and were still only in magazines. Al-Sahhar asked me to invite all the writers who had, like me, received prizes to participate, and that was how Bakathir and others were published. The memoirs of Sa'id Gawda al-Sahhar are inaccurate: he even forgets the role of his brother 'Abd al-Hamid al-Sahhar, and his version of the publication of *The Cairo Trilogy* is incorrect.

Talk of the story "The Air Raid" seems to have led us to talk about the air raids of the Second World War.

He said, "We used to go to the shelter. Each group of families had a particular shelter. With time, these turned into something like cafés: we would talk, laugh, discuss everything, and during the periods when the guns were silent, we'd go out to get a breath of air. We knew the sound of the anti-aircraft guns, but with the entry of the Italians into the war we heard for the first time the sound of explosions, to which we'd not been accustomed before. We said to ourselves, 'Well, now things are getting serious to be sure. They've got us where they want us now.' Every night there was a raid. Once we were at the Qushtumur café. We were playing Monopoly, a game that had cities and stopping places and the winner was the one who took these over; one of our friends had traced it out for us and we finished it. We finished the game and went home. After just half an hour, a bomb fell that made a hole in the roof and went down to where we had been sitting. Radio silence was the sign of approaching danger. We used to take the game with us and finish playing in the shelter."

He said, "The Qushtumur café belonged to the son of the musician Dawud Husni. His brother went to Israel and became a broadcaster. I heard that the owner of the café became a Muslim, but I'm not sure."

Farah Boat

TUESDAY 17 NOVEMBER 1992

For the first time we're sitting on the lower deck of the floating restaurant, in a room in the English style.[1] The 'umda, or village mayor, as the Master calls him—Eng. 'Imad al-'Abbudi—has issued his orders to the administration that they are to get the place ready to receive us. The chairs are of luxurious leather, the walls paneled in wood.

The talk started with the subjects of terrorism, the storm created by the dissolution of the Labor Party (Hizb al-'Amal), and the closing of the newspaper *al-Sha'b*.

He said, "My view is that the cure for the situation is more democracy. Everyone is bound to stand up against those who bear weapons in an atmosphere of democracy, but closures and confiscations will only make the matter worse."

We spoke about social justice, the need to provide society with hope, and the dignity of the state. We spoke about other things.

A TUESDAY IN 1995

He said, "I saw Muhammad 'Abd al-Wahhab twice. The first time was in the thirties. I was returning from the huge amusement park that had been built where Sphinx Square is now, in al-Muhandisin. It was a very spacious park and very diverse; I don't remember seeing any larger. In the streetcar on my way back, Muhammad 'Abd al-Wahhab got on at al-Zamalik. I said, 'Good evening, Master' and he said, 'Hello.'

"He sat in the corner wearing his tarboosh. I was delighted to see him because I loved his 'rich' voice, but we didn't exchange another word. In the sixties, I was invited to the home of Dr. Mustafa Mahmud. I met him over lunch and we still didn't exchange more than a few words."

A TUESDAY IN 1997

He said, "If the Islamic Salvation Front had come to power in Algeria through the elections that were held, if they had come to government through those elections, what happened in Algeria would not have happened. However, the intervention against the elections—

whose probity Western observers testified to—led to the tragedies that took place.

Al-Qa'id said, "But if they had acquired power they wouldn't have allowed democracy."

He said, "I can see no justification for the cancellation of the results of the elections by force. The results are worse, as you can see."

An Evening, Summer 1993

When we were on our way back to the gathering after going to the toilet, he suddenly stopped and asked me, "By the way, why didn't al-Qa'id come tonight?"

I said, "He must have had something to take care of."

He laughed and said, "Or maybe he went to see Naguib Mahfouz!"

Of course, I roared.

A Tuesday, Summer 1998

He said, "Despite our hatred of British colonialism and our resistance to it, we observed in them a number of positions that were admirable. During the case of the murder of Sirdar Sir Lee Stack, an Egyptian journalist launched an attack against the accused Egyptians. The British judge showed his displeasure at this, asking in distaste, 'How can anyone launch an attack against an accused man who is not in a position to defend himself?'"

Investigation

August 1991

"I was working at the ministry of religious endowments when an article containing a review of the novel *A Scandal in Cairo (Fadiha fi-l-qahira)* was published in the magazine *Akhir sa'a*. The writer described the events of the novel without revealing that it was fiction until the last line. I was surprised to be summoned to meet with the undersecretary, Shaykh Ahmad Hussein, brother of Dr. Taha Hussein. He asked me about the events to which the *Akhir sa'a* writer alluded. I told him the book was a novel and that they were fictitious events that did not target specific individuals. Then he asked me, 'Are you a student of Shaykh Taha Hussein?'

"I answered that I had studied philosophy at the College of Humanities and considered myself one of his students. At this point, Shaykh Ahmad seemed to soften toward me. He said, 'Why write about the scandals of the pashas and make trouble for yourself? You'd do better to write about love, and it would be safer for you.'

"I looked at him and didn't answer, and the investigation was shelved."

Taymur and al-Balamiti

SEPTEMBER 1992

"When my novel *Rhadopis of Nubia (Radubis)* was published in 1943 by the Publishing Committee for Academics, I gave copies to numerous people. Only four answered and thanked me. These were Mahmud Taymur, Ahmad Bakathir, Zaki Tulaymat, and Ahmad Kamil, God grant him long life. Mahmud Taymur invited me to lunch at the 'Ali Hasan Restaurant close to Opera Square. Zaki Tulaymat, who was a friend of Taymur's, was with us; he had an enormous appetite and could have eaten the 'Ali Hasan Restaurant and everything in it.

"Taymur was of noble birth. His father Ahmad Taymur Pasha was a well-known scholar and a major researcher, but Mahmud tended to prefer the company of ordinary people. He was known to be in love with a new singer of those days called Malak, who was a little snub-nosed and would enter the theater carrying a goat, at which we would all ask, 'Which of them is singing—her or the goat?'"

We laughed heartily and he joined in and then went on: "He wrote pioneering stories that opened up the path. He liked to write about the streets and the passersby, though his view was that of a passing tourist. One morning I went early to Fishawi's. In the early hours of the morning, the café was beautiful and quiet, and I found Mahmud Taymur sitting with an ironer, a man call al-Balamiti. Al-Balamiti was huge with a coarse voice and went barefoot, and they were having a breakfast together of stewed beans and green onions and talking as though they'd been friends all their lives. My attention was caught by the way Mahmud Taymur greedily devoured the onions, so I went up to him and asked, 'No meetings with "The Angel" *(al-Malak)* today?'"

Al-'Aqqad

SEPTEMBER 1992

We asked the Master, "Did you know al-'Aqqad?"

He said, "Not personally. In the forties I wrote an article in which I responded to something he'd written and it was published in *al-Risala*. It was about the art of the novel, which al-'Aqqad compared unfavorably to the art of poetry, but we never met. Once I saw him. I used to go to the Anglo-Egyptian Bookshop every week to buy the new books that had arrived from London. As I was entering, Subhi the manager whispered in my ear, 'Al-'Aqqad is here. Would you like to speak to him?'

"However, I thanked Subhi and went on in to look at the books. I caught sight of him sitting looking at the books and leafing through the volumes in front of him. I wasn't eager to talk to him or to attend his symposium, I don't know why. I was fine on my own, and he knew me because I used to publish stories on the literature page of *al-Gihad* newspaper, which was owned by Muhammad Tawfiq Diyab and which he edited, and it had reached me that he had said, 'Naguib Mahfouz is good.' One of my friends offered to go with me to his symposium, but I declined. Later, however, after I left my position as film censor, it happened that he phoned me at home. He was furious because he'd heard that a director and a screenplay writer had presented a story that mocked him personally. I told him that I was no longer responsible for the censorship department and had left the post, but he continued to be angry, asking how such a movie could be permitted. When I found that he could not be convinced that I had left the department, I told him I would speak to the censor who had succeeded me, and I did in fact speak to him and discovered that the movie had never been made."

Al-Rafi'i

OCTOBER 1992

I asked him if he had read anything by Mustafa Sadiq al-Rafi'i.

He shook his head and said no.

Then he asked me, "Have you read him?"

I answered yes.

"How did you find him?" he asked.

I said he was a unique case in Arabic prose and that his language was authentic and had a special modernism and stateliness.

He said, "I remember that Taha Hussein used to admire him, especially his book *The Miraculous Nature of the Qur'an (I'jaz al-Qur'an)*. If his prose is the way you describe it, it's a pity I haven't read him."

I asked him again why he hadn't, and he said that the newspapers he usually read had always attacked al-Rafi'i.

He was silent for a while and then he said, "Al-Rafi'i lived in Tanta. He was self-taught, a clerk at the court, and he had a sharp tongue."

I talked to him about al-Rafi'i's book *Skewered ('Ala al-saffud)*, in which he attacks al-'Aqqad. The late Shaykh Amin al-Khawli had read some chapters to us at the Custodian's Symposium. This was in 1963, after the fierce battle between al-Rafi'i and al-'Aqqad that had broken out in the pages of *al-Akhbar* newspaper. From a sense of outrage, it seems, Shaykh al-Khawli read us chapters that I consider to be among the most disgusting exercises in defamatory literature I have ever heard.

"You really think so?" asked the Master.

I said yes.

Taha Hussein

December 1992

We asked him, "Did you know Taha Hussein?"

He said that he had read him before entering university and had met him twice. The first time was when he joined the College of Humanities; at the test that was administered to applicants, he was surprised to find that the examiner was Taha Hussein in person. The Master said, "He asked me, 'Why did you choose the philosophy department?' I started my answer by talking about my desire to know the secret of the universe and the mysteries of existence. He listened to me carefully and then said sarcastically, 'You're well suited to philosophy because what you say is incomprehensible.'

"The second time was in the sixties, when a television program with him was recorded—the only one, I think."

He was silent for a short while. Then he said, "Taha Hussein was not only a great thinker and writer. He played a role too."

Where Are the Drafts?

We asked the Master what happened to the manuscript of *Echoes of an Autobiography*. He said, "I sent it to *al-Ahram*."

We showed our disquiet. *Echoes* had been published in a jumbled version in *al-Ahram*, its arrangement disturbed and numerous sections omitted, and the idea of republication in *Akhbar al-adab* had been mooted. He said, "There's a copy of the manuscript."

We asked him again, "But the original?"

He said he'd sent it to *al-Ahram* and didn't know what had happened to it.

At another evening gathering, he told us that he wasn't used to keeping his drafts. He had a handwritten original of a novel about a soccer player, but he didn't know where it was now—likewise of an unpublished novel about the countryside. But he remembered that the movie director Khayri Bishara had taken possession of it and maybe the manuscript was still with him. Maybe.

At another evening gathering we spoke about the handwritten original of *The Cairo Trilogy*. The *Trilogy* was in reality just a single novel, entitled *Palace Walk (Bayn al-qasrayn)*. It took up about 1,800 foolscap pages in Naguib Mahfouz's handwriting, and there was only one copy. Copying machines were unknown at the time, and Mahfouz used ordinarily to pay the printer by giving him his handwritten originals. He took the trilogy to al-Sahhar and was surprised to hear the publisher tell him, "What in God's name is this? How am I supposed to publish it?"

Mahfouz went out onto the street in a sad mood, talking to himself and leaving the manuscript with the publisher. After about a year, Yusuf al-Siba'i called him and told him that a literary magazine called *al-Risala al-jadida* was coming out and he offered Mahfouz the chance to publish the trilogy as a serial. Mahfouz immediately hurried to al-Sahhar, and fortunately the man had kept the unique original. Mahfouz took it back and started to publish *Bayn al-qasrayn* in installments. This is the story of how *The Cairo Trilogy* made it to the public. However, every one of us will be shaken when we think, just think, that this great work might have been lost or mislaid for some reason. As to the original manuscript of *Echoes of an Autobiography*, God alone knows where it came to rest, just like all the other originals that he didn't preserve.

The Public Eye!

After suffering the grievous attack, he stopped writing. The hand that had penned for Arabic literature the most wonderful short stories and novels had been injured as the result of a stab wound in his neck from a knife aimed at him by a misled youth who hadn't read a word he'd written. He received regular physical therapy and can now sign his name, in gross, ill-formed letters.

The magazine *Nisf al-dunya* regularly publishes some of his short stories. Every time the magazine announces a new story, we ask him hopefully, "Was it written recently?"

"No," he says sadly—a long, melancholy "No." Then he goes on, "It's from my stock. Every now and then I send them a story to keep myself in the public eye."

I ask, "Are you worried about keeping in the public eye, Uncle Naguib?"

He stares and then says, "Somewhat."

I know that he doesn't want us to continue—I have learnt his reactions by heart—but still, I ask myself privately, is he really concerned about keeping in his readers' eye when he has become a permanent presence in the minds of all?

The First Articles

NOVEMBER 1992

I told him that I had come across an early article that a reader of *al-Risala* magazine had written about the novel *Khufu's Wisdom ('Abath al-aqdar)* on its publication.

He looked up, gazed into space, and nodded.

"I don't remember it. But I remember the first article Sayyid Qutb wrote about me. It was about the novel *Thebes at War (Kifah Tiba)*. It's an excellent article that was followed by years of silence, until Anwar al-Mu'addawi wrote another article, which was again followed by years of silence. Sayyid Qutb was a talented critic and had it not been for his tendency to extremism, he would have become the most important critic in Egypt."

I asked him if it was really true that he had written about Sayyid Qutb in *Mirrors (al-Maraya)*.

He told me immediately, "Yes. Some friends discovered the original models for the characters in *Mirrors* but unfortunately mixed up the real elements with the fictitious elements that I had added from my own imagination. This bothered me a lot."

I reminded him of the days when we used to sit in 'Urabi's café in al-'Abbasiya in the sixties, when he spoke to me of his intention to invite some of the characters whom he had known in his life and to write about them. He had said that he didn't have any particular project for a novel to write that year. It was one of the very few, rare, occasions on which he spoke of a literary work he intended to write.

Democracy

NOVEMBER 1992

The discussion was on the subject of terrorism, the position of the Labor Party, and the rumors that were flying about about the closure of *al-Sha'b* newspaper, which supported terrorism. Naguib Mahfouz said angrily, "The cure for the situation lies in increased democracy. We have to take a position against the closure of any newspaper, or the dissolution of any party, as long as our experience is still at its beginning. If democracy is deepened, then everybody will have to take a stand against any who bear arms."

We talked of society, social justice, the young people who suffer from unemployment, the climate that backs and indirectly supports terrorism, and the dignity of the state, comparing Egyptian society before and after the July 1952 Revolution. He said, "Before the July Revolution, the state's role was limited to security and defense. After the Revolution, however, the state got involved in all fields and in all areas of life and it was a different situation."

In more than one discussion and on numerous occasions, his faith in democracy appeared as absolute, unbudgeable.

Hamam

DECEMBER 1992

After a silence, he asks us suddenly, "Do you know the poet Mustafa Hamam?"

Laughing, he says, "He used to write articles for a Wafdist newspaper in the mornings and for an anti-Wafdist paper in the evenings, where he'd answer himself using an assumed name. The odd thing was that both newspapers knew about it."

We laugh. The loveliest memories are the ones that surface unexpectedly, the ones that he tells in summary form and with an amazing capacity for telling a story, and which generally end with a smile.

Criticism

December 1993

The Master said, "After *Khan al-Khalili* came out, someone wrote an article from a religious perspective whose central point was, 'How could the hero be stricken with tuberculosis after Ahmad 'Akif had sought refuge with Our Master Husayn, son of the daughter of the Prophet?'"

Boutros Boutros-Ghali

November 1996

Despite his calmness, his reactions could be violent. After listening to the news that Yusuf al-Qa'id had brought of America's opposition to the election of Boutros Boutros-Ghali, he immediately said, "This is a challenge to the whole world and it reveals the fraudulent nature of American democracy. If the Great Powers behave this way against a single individual, how are we ever to have justice? I tell you that Egypt has won the battle. It's enough that fourteen states have taken a position against the United States. It's a true victory."

Tuesday 20 November 2001

I said, "What do you think of Bin Ladin's situation as a human being?"

He listened closely, as witnessed by the signs of his interest—his moving closer to his interlocutor and the look of attention on his features. I said, "I don't think any human being in the history of mankind has been pursued as Bin Ladin is being pursued now. It's a global pursuit, with the most modern means known to science and every power we can imagine against one individual. I think about his circumstances: How does he move about with his family, with his wives? How do they sleep? How do they hide themselves in the wilderness? Certainly, he's a terrorist and promotes mistaken notions such as his insane division of the world into unbelievers and believers, but all the same . . . I think about him as a human being pursued as none other has been before."

After a few moments silence he said, "Of course, you're right. The fuss that's been stirred up these days does not allow such thoughts. The Taliban have harmed Islam as no other power has done before. They have presented the worst model of the worst type of government that the world can know. Despite this, I believe that their subjection to this terrifying bombardment calls for pity, just as their insistence on not handing over Bin Ladin despite all the material inducements and terrifying threats turns out, if you take a fresh look at it, to be a principled position."

TUESDAY 28 NOVEMBER 2001

I asked, "Why have you chosen dreams as the axis of your recent work? Does it form one big mosaic?"

He said, "The fact is that, since my faculties weakened, it has been as though a thick curtain had descended about me and cut me off from the world. My eyesight is no longer fit for reading, my hearing has gotten poor, I can't talk on the telephone, whether landline or cell phone, I can't watch television. I can no longer practice the pleasure of walking and I can no longer go to the area of al-Husayn and meet people and roam through the sites of my memories. When a person is cut off from the world, he looks within. He goes over what he has lived through. Dreams take the place of reality. I dream of events that occurred and events that did not occur, of books I have read and poetry I have memorized. As for the dreams that I remember, they have become provisions and helpmeets for the journey.

"Sometimes I wake up and I find the dreams that I have seen are very clear. I record them the same day. The material of which dreaming is made is very fragile. Sometimes one remembers it and then, suddenly, one forgets it. What I wrote under the title *The Dreams* are the texts of dreams as I saw them, fragments of dreams that I saw and added to, and imaginary dreams.

I said, "The language of *The Dreams* reminds me of that of *Echoes of an Autobiography*—a language close to poetry."

He replied, laughing, "Dreams are themselves poetry."

I said, "Have you published everything you have?"

He replied, "I don't publish everything I write at one go, but over time, so that I continue to keep myself in the public consciousness. The dreams that I have on hand now are enough to cover me for several months."

I said nothing, asking myself once more: Is he still worried about staying in the public eye by producing new material? He is present through his creativity and his own physical presence.

Tuesday 27 August 2002

Last Saturday's earthquake imposes itself on the conversations that are taking place. I think of the earthquake of 1992 and the pall of dejection that it cast over our session, apart from the jokes that we exchanged then. In such circumstances, everyone gives an account of where he was, how he felt, what he did. The mere fact of telling the stories means that the danger has passed without harm: since we are talking about it, we must have survived. We spoke of the repeated occurrence of earthquakes in recent years and I said, laughing, "Even nature is dissatisfied with the situation we're in."

The epicenter of the most recent earthquake is something new to us. It was more or less under Cairo, at Abu Za'bal and Qalyub, which is why people heard the roar of cosmic explosions accompanying the earthquake, which only lasted twenty-five seconds. Zaki Salim said, "The announcement said that the tremor measured 4.5 on the Richter scale, but I think it was more."

We agreed it was more—we have come to doubt even the announcements of the Hilwan observatory. However, the Master, who had been listening for a long time, took us by surprise with his lighthearted attitude when he said, "When the earthquake struck, I was sitting in the reception room. I felt it strongly and looked at the ceiling waiting for it to fall and for the actress Barlanti 'Abd al-Hamid to appear and come down from upstairs."

Barlanti lived in the same building, on the top floor, and the Master lived on the ground floor.

Tuesday, September 2002

We were talking about surgical operations and associated matters and he said, "After I had my operation in London, the English doctor asked me, 'Do you feel like eating anything in particular?'

"I said, 'What I've got an appetite for doesn't exist here.'

"He asked me, 'What is it?'

"I said, '*Ful*, of course.'

"The doctor smiled and said, 'They have *ful* near the hospital, at a restaurant called Ali Baba.'"

And indeed the Master sent out for some and the *ful* came and it was a very enjoyable meal.

I said that the management of the hospital in Cleveland had noticed that most Egyptians wanted to eat *ful* after the successful completion of their heart operations and had as a result added *ful* as a breakfast dish in the hospital's main cafeteria: genuine stewed beans, with different kinds of oil—linseed and olive and cottonseed and flax.

I said that after a person survives a danger, he clings to memories, especially those of foods that he's used to or loves. "*Ful* I've found. What I still haven't found in the United States is molasses with sesame paste."

Molasses with sesame paste is a dish that the poor of Egypt have devised. It delivers a high dose of calories and is considered the most delicious meal in the prisons, especially with hot local-style bread.

Tuesday 3 September 2002

I returned to the Master's relationship with al-'Aqqad. I wanted to clarify it more. Why didn't he go to al-'Aqqad's weekly symposium?

He said that he didn't "know a specific reason but I used to consider him close to me. It was at his hands that I learned advanced ideas about democracy and liberalism, through the articles he used to write in *al-Garida*, which I used to read in my early youth. For a long while I thought he was strictly a political writer, and I was taken by surprise when I read his literary works."

I asked him, "But you saw him at the Anglo-Egyptian Bookshop and it didn't occur to you even to shake his hand?"

"That's true," he said. "Maybe it was because I'd heard that he had an unattractive personality."

"But things were different with Taha Hussein," I said.

He elaborated: "I met him numerous times. It was at the university, when I attended his classes at the College of Humanities. Then I visited him at his house, sometimes on my own and sometimes with Tharwat Abaza.

I asked him whether he'd met Shaykh Amin al-Khawli.

He said, "He was a teacher of mine at the university but I never met him personally."

I said that the symposiums Mahfouz had convened starting in 1945 were a basic element of literary and cultural life. The Opera symposium began in 1945 and has continued in various guises and places up to today. Mahfouz was always at the center, with many people surrounding him—some talking, some silent, some staying in one place, some moving around or merely passing by, but Naguib Mahfouz was always the axis. How had his relationship to these symposiums begun, especially the Opera symposium?

He said, "Before the Opera group, the literary symposium in a café was unknown to Egypt's literary life. There were literary salons, of which Mayy Ziyada's was of course the best known, but I was of a later generation; I only read about it. I remember that I once went to a salon run by a lady of the wealthy classes, but I never went back." (He tried to remember her name but could not.) "I didn't feel at ease in the atmosphere of the salons."

"So how," I said, "did the Opera group start?"

He replied, "It happened that five writers received literary prizes."

"Which prizes?" I asked.

"Either those of the Arabic Language Academy or of the ministry of public education."

I said, "The first prize you got was the one awarded by Qut al-Qulub al-Dimardashiya. Then you got the Arabic Language Academy prize."

He said, "The Academy prize I won along with four others—'Abd al-Hamid al-Sahhar, 'Ali Ahmad Bakathir, Yusuf Gawhar, and a poet who wrote like Tagore and was a judge."

"Husayn 'Afif, perhaps?"

"Maybe. 'Abd al-Hamid al-Sahhar proposed that the Publishing Committee for Academics be established and start by publishing the winning works. All of us accepted except for Yusuf Gawhar, who rejected the idea of publication without remuneration. We started meeting at 'Urabi's café, but the owners of the café told me, 'Those literary friends of yours are a nuisance and they talk too loudly. Find yourselves somewhere else.' That's why we moved to Café Opéra and it was there our weekly meetings started, every Friday, from 1945 on. They continued in the same place until they came to an end in the way you know" (referring to the security forces having put an end to the symposium in 1961.)

I said that the group had had a major beneficial influence on cultural life through its regularity and the fact that it was patronized by different generations. As far as our generation was concerned, it had brought us together sooner than might otherwise have been the case. It is possible that my encounters with Mohamed El-Bisatie, Ibrahim Aslan, Yusuf al-Qa'id, or others would have been delayed for periods at which I can only guess were it not for Naguib Mahfouz's symposium, to which different generations made, and still make, their way. The late Tawfiq al-Hakim had a symposium at Shepheard's Hotel and another in Alexandria, but the people who went to al-Hakim's were pashas and leading figures of society and only a few young writers dared to attend. In my own case, when I made for Petro's café overlooking the Mediterranean one summer in the sixties, I was on my way to a meeting with Naguib Mahfouz, who sat in silence most of the time while Tawfiq al-Hakim talked non-stop. He was a great storyteller, speaking as though he were acting, his hands giving expression to what he was saying. I asked Naguib Mahfouz how he had come to know al-Hakim.

He said, "After *Midaq Alley (Zuqaq al-midaq)* came out, he asked me to meet him. When I started going regularly to his weekly group in Cairo and the daily one in Alexandria (during the summer months), the former pashas were disturbed by my presence. Among them were Shams al-Din 'Abd al-Ghaffar, Burhan Nur, Ibrahim Pasha Farag of course, and Ibrahim Tal'at. They told al-Hakim that they were afraid of me because I wrote for *al-Ahram*, whose editor-in-chief was Muhammad

Hasanayn Haykal, who was close to Gamal Abd al-Nasser, the leader of the Revolution. But al-Hakim told them, 'I guarantee him!' I remember that one of them asked Shams al-Din 'Abd al-Ghaffar, after he'd been quiet for a long time, what he was thinking about, and he replied in terror, 'I'm not thinking! I'm not thinking at all!'"

The Master laughed his pure, ringing laugh and after a few moments of silence resumed his narration.

"Al-Hakim used to talk for long periods, but most of what he talked about was personal. For example, we'd begin the conversation on a literary issue, but he'd digress and talk about people, telling us about his father or his memories of Muhammad 'Ali Street. Once I asked him about this, and he said that his theoretical views were in his books and anyone who wanted to become acquainted with them could read those."

The Master had a special affection for Tawfiq al-Hakim. Al-Hakim's office on the sixth floor was open, I never saw it closed, and in his last years he'd sit on his own, saddened by the loss of his only son, Isma'il. On Thursdays, Naguib Mahfouz would move from his own office, which was nearby, to sit in front of al-Hakim's desk. Sometimes Tharwat Abaza would appear, or Dr. Zaki Nagib Mahmud, Ihsan 'Abd al-Quddus, or Yusuf Idris. After al-Hakim passed away, *al-Ahram*'s management assigned the room to Naguib Mahfouz, but he never sat in al-Hakim's place; he always sat in the same place in front of the desk, and al-Hakim's chair remained unoccupied, as though he were expected to arrive.

In the Master's house there is a small cupboard for the decorations and the commemorative gifts that were dear to him because of his high regard for the person who had given them to him. I saw a black fountain pen that his wife told me he'd put among the decorations he'd received because he was so fond of it. It was a present from Tawfiq al-Hakim. The Master always describes *The Return of the Spirit ('Awdat al-ruh)* as a breakthrough for the Arabic novel.

The writer Zaki Salim asked whether it was true that an exam had been held under the management of *al-Ahram* but supervised by al-'Aqqad for a number of writers, and that all of them had failed. The exam was on the Arabic language.

The Master knit his brow and said, "I don't remember such an exam. The exam that I remember was announced and run by a leading British diplomat at the British embassy. His post was that of what they called 'Oriental secretary,' I believe. I don't remember the subject of the exam but I remember the prize. It was a month's vacation in the Oriental secretary's house in Alexandria. I think he was called Mr. Smart. The winner was a public prosecutor and he used to publish writings in a dignified style like al-Jahiz. Unfortunately I've forgotten his name."

Talk of the public prosecutor must have led to talk of the judiciary, and he said, "The fact is that the Egyptian judiciary was very well respected. I remember someone who shot and killed a chief of police, the reason being that the police chief had insulted his manhood when he had raped the man with a broom handle in front of people. The man was condemned to death, and when the time came for the appeal, the judge gave him life imprisonment instead of execution because the killing was the result of a physical humiliation."

I asked him, "Do you remember the judge's name?"

"It was 'Abd al-'Aziz Fahmi, one of the great judges of Egypt," he replied.

Yusuf al-Qa'id asked, "How do you take the news about public corruption that's been announced—the case that was apprehended at the ministry of agriculture recently, and the people who absconded with billions of the banks' money. Where do they stand in comparison with the corruption described in *A Scandal in Cairo*?"

The Master replied quietly, "The corrupt of the thirties and forties look like saints next to those of today." Then he said, "I remember an employee working in the university administration who was charged with embezzling three pounds. We viewed him as we would someone who'd committed a major crime, and after the Revolution he left under the 'cleansing.'"

After a moment's silence, the Master said, "My oh my! Time!"

Tuesday 10 September 2002

The Master loves the River Nile. His favorite place to walk is beside it; his favorite place to sit is next to it. The ancient river has a unique quality, as though it were a person who understands and absorbs and responds. Probably not many people know that he lived on the Nile, in the days when living on a houseboat was quite common in Cairo. When he got married, he rented a houseboat near al-Gala' Bridge and he lived in it for more than a year. It came about that the child of the family living in the houseboat next door drowned, so the Master's wife, who had just given birth to her first child, a girl called Umm Kulthum, insisted on moving, and they rented the apartment that the family still lives in on al-Nil Street in al-'Aguza.

I asked him about his relationship with the Nile and he said, "It started on outings with my mother. Just as she took me to visit the ancient monuments, so she would take me to walk beside the Nile or on the bridges—Qasr al-Nil Bridge and Abu al-'Ila Bridge. When I grew older, I loved to walk or sit by the Nile. I used to take a small cushion with me and I'd go to a circular garden in front of the house that Anwar al-Sadat lived in when he became president of the republic. (The garden was converted into a landing pad for helicopters.) I would sit on my own on the edge of the Nile for several hours, up to midnight, contemplating and thinking. Then I'd go back to al-'Abbasiya after midnight. It was in this garden that the Riffraff met for the first time. I named it 'the pessimist's symposium.'"

"Why?" I asked.

"Because," he replied, "we were pessimistic about the future of literature and reading. We used to discuss and laugh, and one night a police private came and asked us to keep our voices down because Yusuf Rashad, King Faruq's physician, was living close by."

Mahfouz told me, "The place that inspires me to meditate, where numerous scenes in my novels have been completed, is the bank of the Nile. I only have to feel that I am next to it, even if I cannot see it."

"As we are now," I said.

"Exactly!" he said.

TUESDAY 17 SEPTEMBER 2002

He is very reticent when we mention other writers or ask him for his opinion of any of them. He listens carefully and answers with short sentences. I asked him about the writers of his generation, especially those who started with the Publishing Committee for Academics, such as the late Muhammad 'Abd al-Halim, Yusuf al-Siba'i, 'Ali Ahmad Bakathir, 'Abd al-Hamid al-Sahhar, and Ihsan 'Abd al-Quddus. My question was about the difference between a writer who merely tells a story and one who has an overall vision of the universe and mankind.

He said, "There is no fixed relationship between the writer and what he writes, meaning that he may be talented and not cultured. Shakespeare, for example, didn't receive a regular education, but he read what was available to him in his time, acquainted himself with the stories that were current. He must have known about Greek drama. Lots of the subjects of his plays had been dealt with before, but his extraordinary talent allowed him to present them in a different way."

I said, "Certainly, he must have had a vision. But most of the writers of your generation were merely narrators of stories that had happened. For example, Yusuf al-Siba'i, Muhammad 'Abd al-Halim, Ihsan 'Abd al-Quddus, and Sa'd Mikkawi were merely storytellers. The works of such writers may achieve some fame for a limited time, but later they disappear from view."

"Why do you say that they disappear?" he asked. "Do you know anything about their sales figures?"

"According to the information available to me," I replied, "the only one whose books still have some circulation is Ihsan 'Abd al-Quddus. The other names aren't comparable."

"Is that so?" he said.

"Yes," I said.

He made no comment and lapsed into his usual silence.

TUESDAY 17 SEPTEMBER 2002

I asked him, "In the novel *Morning and Evening Talk*, you mention the Bannan family. Did you know any of its members?"

He replied, "Of course. They lived on Qirmiz Road. But take care—the Bannan family who were our neighbors was not the same as the

Bannan family of al-Husayniya. The Bannan family of Qirmiz Road was an old family that traded in coffee."

"Then the Bannan that I mean is one of them," I said. "I knew the name Bannan from a big famous café on the corner of Habs al-Rahba and Qasr al-Shawq streets. It had two levels. The inner one was a little raised and I saw a billiard table there. It was the first time in my life that I had seen such a table, but I never saw anyone play billiards. Of course, I came to know the game later, but it wasn't widespread until the eighties. There was a billiards club above the Cinéma Rivoli, and later the game appeared in a lot of cafés. But the significance of the presence of that table in the Bannan café was that, once upon a time, there was someone who played billiards in al-Gamaliya."

His face showed great surprise. After a few moments I asked, "Tell me about the Bannan family from al-Husayniya."

He said, "The Bannan I knew was one of the 'Abbasiya set. He didn't complete his education with us. His father stripped him of his school uniform and made him put on a *gallabiya* and turban. He put him to work supervising their coffee factory. We used to walk in front of the factory and see him and laugh. The odd thing is that later on, his father beat the father of Kamal Salim the director, who was a Wafdist, because of 'Urabi, the neighborhood gang leader. Bannan the father also held Wafdist principles, but the Wafd leadership was leaning toward Kamal Salim's father. One day, Sa'd Pasha Zaghlul decided he was going to go and lend support to Kamal Salim's father in al-Husayniya. When Sa'd Pasha's car appeared, 'Urabi's men surrounded it, hoisted it onto their shoulders, and made off with it toward al-Bannan's marquee instead of the one set up by Kamal Salim's father. That's how 'Abd al-Hamid al-Bannan came to win and to enter parliament as a representative of the Wafd party."

We laughed, of course and the conversation moved on to the legendary figure of 'Urabi. He said, "One day, 'Urabi and his men occupied the quarters of al-Dahir and al-Sakakini. They got trucks and loaded them with stones and bottles and made for al-Sakakini. What happened was that a young friend of ours, called al-Birri, had ogled a girl from al-Husayniya. 'Urabi called out his troops and launched a disciplinary campaign against al-Birri's men and everyone who had anything to do with al-Sakakini. He also occupied the Dahir police station and stripped the British constable of his clothes. The man went into the interior ministry naked, made for Harvey Pasha, the Cairo chief of police, and told him, 'See what the gangs did to me?' This incident may be considered the end of the era of the neighborhood gangs. The police launched a fierce campaign against 'Urabi. They put him in prison for a year, after which he came out a different person, meek as a mouse, and if anyone made a complaint against him they hauled him off to prison. I don't know what they did to him."

I asked him, "Was the story of the movie *Gang Leaders of al-Husayniya (Futuwwat al-Husayniya)* written specially for the movie, or was it written as literature and then the movie taken from it?"

"No," he replied. "It was written for the cinema. I remember that I met the director, Niyazi Mustafa, and he told me, 'I want something with a traditional neighborhood feel.' I wrote the story especially for the cinema and the movie was a big success."

I said, "I saw the movie in the fifties. I remember scenes from it. The acting, by Mahmud al-Miligi, Huda Sultan, and Farid Shawqi, was outstanding, but I haven't seen it again since, and it's only been on television once in the last twenty years."

After a few moments he said, "After the 'Urabi incident, the gang leaders had a hard time of it in al-Husayniya. The police harassed them a lot. They moved out to the slaughterhouse district, where they became butchers and took their beating and throat-cutting out on the cows and sheep. 'Urabi's café closed. His children sold it."

He seemed moved. I remember passing through al-Gaysh Square. The café vanished in the seventies and was converted into a collection of ill-matched shops. It was one of the most beautiful places that I ever formed an association with and meant, for me, my youth, and the friends of that beautiful period of my life.

Tuesday 24 September

There was discussion of the book by Thierry Meyssan, the French author who questions that a plane crashed into the Pentagon and likewise has questions about the Pennsylvania plane. The talk went on to include the article by the American ambassador published in *al-Ahram* the previous Friday, in which he demanded that the editors-in-chief of Egyptian newspapers carefully check and review their writers' articles dealing with the events of 11 September, the storm caused by the article, the violent statement by intellectuals issued the same day, and the relatively calmly worded statement by the journalists' syndicate.

After a few moments silence, he said, "What the ambassador wrote is not appropriate and is not worthy of the spirit of the United States, but I don't believe that the Americans struck the World Trade Towers or the Pentagon for political goals."

I told him about what an eyewitness had told me during my visit to Washington: He lived in Virginia and worked in Washington D.C., like many others, because the rents are cheaper in the state of Virginia. He was on the long road that passes by the Pentagon; the traffic was heavy, and movement slow, when he noticed a plane flying low in the direction of the building. Usually the planes make for the airport in the center of Washington, which is located close to Congress, the White House, and the federal institutions. My friend said that what attracted his attention about this plane was that it was so low. After he had watched it for a few seconds, the sound of a terrible explosion rang out, and he felt that his car had risen and been slammed back on the ground. He got out and was surprised to find everyone looking in the direction of the Pentagon and an awful ball of black smoke ascending into the sky.

Mahfouz listened in silence. I asked him whether he had lived through any period similar to the one we were living through then. After a little thought, he said no. I asked him, "Not even the economic crisis of 1929?"

After thinking again for a little, he said, "No. The effects of the crisis of 1929 were limited to the big cotton merchants and certain private economic projects, but we as a people didn't feel them. The Egyptian pound was strong, well established—stronger than sterling. It never occurred to me that its value would be shaken. The idea that it might lose value was not on the table, wasn't even imagined in fact until the start of the Second World War, when I started to become aware that my salary was no longer enough to cover basic needs. What, then, to do? We government employees started trying to save money on this and that, but things kept getting more difficult—up to the time when al-Nahhas Pasha took over the government after the celebrated 4 February Incident. He brought in what he called 'the cost of living increase,' which was a financial supplement added to one's salary that was equal to the percentage of inflation. In addition, he started what was known as 'fair treatment,' meaning the fair treatment of government employees whose promotions from one grade to another had been delayed. As a result, I was promoted from Grade 7 to Grade 5 at one go. Along with the cost of living increase, this meant a decent increase in my salary and it produced an affluence such we'd never seen before. I remember that on the day the increase and the fair treatment policy were announced, the office messengers and custodians jumped onto the desks and started dancing for joy."

"How much was your salary after the increase and the promotion?"

"About twenty-five pounds."

At this point, the lawyer Magdi Sa'd and Eng. Hasan Nasir started calculating the value of the amount in terms of the Egyptian pound today, in September 2002. They concluded that the amount was equivalent to 18,000 pounds today. When this was communicated to him, he laughed his pure laugh and said, "Just think! I was up there with the insecticide guy!"

He was alluding, with his customary intelligence and sarcasm, to a public employee who had recently been accused of allowing the import of carcinogenic insecticides, whose total salary and bonuses had amounted, according to the press, to 400,000 pounds per month. I returned to al-Nahhas Pasha and asked if he had ever seen him.

"Many times."

He usually responds with a single word when the answer is positive. Then, after saying nothing for a while, he returns to the subject in detail. On this occasion, he said, "I used to listen to him at public meetings. He was a powerful orator and hugely popular. I used to go to the marquee. The meetings were organized by youth members of the party, who would stand at the entrances and check the identity of certain arrivals. A Wafdist didn't need to fill in a form or carry a card to say that he belonged to the Wafd. It was enough for a person to proclaim his membership of the Wafd party. Naturally, there were rich people who contributed to the party and there were some who worked for the party full time, but most people considered buying the party's press organs enough to proclaim one's allegiance."

After a short silence, he returned to al-Nahhas Pasha.

"Along with the fair treatment policy and the cost of living increase, he announced free education up to the secondary level. In the cabinet, Taha Hussein demanded free university education. Al-Nahhas Pasha told him, 'The day you tell me you have a place for every student, research tools, and a sufficient number of professors, I will issue a decree making university education free forthwith.'"

I asked him if he had walked in al-Nahhas's funeral procession.

"Yes," he replied, "but I didn't go all the way to Our Master Husayn's tomb, where they said prayers for him. You know, of course, what happened."

I laughed and told him that at the Tura Farm detention center in 1966, I'd seen more than thirty Wafdists who'd been detained immediately following the funeral. The crime for which they'd been detained without trial was that at the demonstration they'd shouted, "No leader after you, al-Nahhas!" Some of those whom I met at the detention center had indeed shouted this slogan, as they informed me. One of them was Mustafa Nagi, God rest his soul—a tall man with a dark complexion, who told me that he had indeed shouted that slogan, and that some people had walked alongside him and asked him his name and address and that he hadn't been scared off. It was the same with Hafiz Shiha.

At this he asked me, "Hafiz Shiha was with them too?"

"Yes," I said.

He said, "Hafiz Shiha was a Wafdist student leader. I used to know him. He informed me that he'd organized a strike at the law school. The then president of the university, Ahmad Lutfi al-Sayyid Pasha, had called him in. He was tall, from Upper Egypt, and went he entered the office it seemed huge to him. Walking toward Ahmad Lutfi al-Sayyid was like crossing a street, and when he reached him, the latter told him, 'Do sit down. Do you take your coffee with or without sugar?' He asked for coffee with sugar. After he had drunk it, Ahmad Lutfi al-Sayyid stood up and told him, 'You are dismissed from the university without possibility of reinstatement.'

"In 1954, Muhammad Naguib entered the March crisis. Hafiz Shiha was with Naguib. Gamal Abd al-Nasser's men seized him and took him to the military prison. He entered a wide, spacious room at one end of which an officer was seated. Suddenly, someone gave him a kick and he was pushed forward. He crossed the room and reached the desk without his feet touching the ground. He became an important and respected lawyer, so clearly he must have returned to the university after being dismissed and finished his law degree."

I said, "When I saw him in the detention center he was composed. With them too was Yasin Sirag al-Din, who looked elegant even in the white prisoners' clothes and spent all his time with us. The halls where the Wafdists were kept were opposite ours and there were about thirty-six of them who were victims of the arrests at al-Nahhas's funeral. Of course, it was a fatuous thing and there was no need for it at all. I remember one Wafdist detainee whose name was Hasan Husan. He was a huge man, good-hearted, and he worried about his two sons. He would weep from the fear that they might go astray when he was so far from them. In those days, 'going astray' meant, at the worst, smoking cigarettes and drinking beer. When I saw their photographs, I beheld two very manly young men. There was a hall in the detention center set aside for the people they called 'Hostile Activities,' and these were a mixture. Some of them had told jokes or had spoken out loudly and someone had written a report on them. Such people didn't have a clear political allegiance and each had a different reason, usually trivial, for being in detention. Some spent several years there. Most of the center, however, was occupied by Muslim Brothers, who numbered about 2,500. There were about five hundred 'Hostile Activities' and we Communists were seventy-five. The halls were of equal size. The Muslim

Brothers' halls each held 150 or more. They used to sleep in turns, half of them standing for the first half of the night while the others lay down; then they'd change places. Of course, the living conditions were inhumane, but for all their awfulness the Tura detention center was a paradise compared to Abu Za'bal, the military prison, and the Citadel. Those were set aside for torture, which is to say, for investigation using the methods of those days."

Dialog in Celebration of His Ninety-Third Year

(9 December 2003)

It is only in Naguib Mahfouz that I have experienced wisdom personified. In recent years (may God prolong his life), he has appeared before us at his appointed time (six o'clock exactly) followed by his personal bodyguard—he who had spent his entire life wandering freely through the streets, marketplaces, and cafés. Things had changed, however, after 1994 and the hideous attempt on his life. But that incident revealed to us Naguib Mahfouz's true nature. Despite the closeness of our companionship with him, and though we had been aware of its presence and significance, it was only now that we saw it personified. The essence of this true nature may be summarized in two words: Mahfouzian will. I have never known a will so strong. It takes on the challenges of pain, sickness, incapacity, and the deterioration of the faculties, and its goal is to be able to go on writing, which, for him, means to go on living.

Despite the fact that he was nearing his ninety-third birthday, and even though we were in continuous communication, I had a desire to engage him in a dialog—one, however, that would involve posing specific questions and thereby allow me to show the reader his preoccupations, his visions of the world from the perspective of this time and place. In recent years, I had been solicitous of the privacy of our relationship and especially concerned to keep it away from the media.

When he is able to hear a question, he answers in one of two ways—either rapidfire or after a long or short pause. Sometimes it seems to me that he doesn't want to answer, but he then surprises me after a while. In either case, he speaks with wisdom. Sometimes I imagine that he's said everything he has to say, but then after a while he returns to the subject I had asked him about and I know immediately that his mind has been busy with the question.

To start with, I asked him about an opinion he had uttered some weeks earlier when commenting on certain cultural events: he had said that the discussion of literature was dominated by politics.

He said that he had noticed the preponderance of judgments on literature that sprang from political visions, and not from a literary perspective. He said, "My point of view on this may not be absolute, but I'm thinking of Sonallah's refusal of the state prize for the novel. It was a political position, and people's reaction to that position was likewise from a political standpoint. No one, however, gave any thought to treating him as a writer."

I asked him what he thought of Sonallah Ibrahim's position.

He said that he admired the position in and of itself, and that a writer who was bold enough to refuse a hundred thousand pounds because of his vision deserved to be appreciated and was exemplary. With regard to the statement that Ibrahim made in justification of his refusal, each one might agree or disagree according to his own perspective. For himself, he would be capable of such a refusal in order to maintain a certain position.

I inquired what he though about literary life, in terms of what he saw of it.

He said, "Don't forget you're talking to a person who lives in isolation and who cannot keep up with everything that comes out."

I wrangled with him. "Are you the only person living in isolation?"

He asked me what I was getting at.

I explained that there are many works of literature, some of them excellent, that come out and are then enveloped in a thick cloud of silence, and there are others that fall into oblivion for lack of a critical movement. "How," I asked, "do you see the literary movement when you look back over seven decades during which you have practiced writing without interruption?"

He replied, "There can be no doubt that the balance between literary creativity and criticism has given rise to an active and healthy movement that has lasted through successive generations. However, I agree with you that the absence, for many reasons, of a critical literature has had an effect on literature. I think our generation was luckier. Your generation is lucky too, but what I'm thinking about is the young writers who suffer from critical and media neglect."

I asked him, "How do you view your journey with literature now, God grant you long life?"

"It was very tough," he said, "and fruitful. I got my reward."

"What kind of reward?" I asked him. "Do you mean that negatively or positively?"

"Positively, of course," he answered immediately.

I asked him, "Do you think your job held you up or helped you?'

"It held me up and it helped me," he replied.

"How?" I asked.

He said, "Of course, it took a lot of my time, time I could have devoted to literature, but from the other side it gave me the opportunity to become acquainted with numerous human situations and types that had an impact on what I wrote. It also provided me with the wherewithal to deal with life."

I said, "I remember that when you reached retirement age at the beginning of the seventies you were joyfully happy. You told me you could now walk as you wished without the restrictions of set times for starting and leaving work and that you had lots of ideas that you'd now be free to write up. *The Harafish* was written after you retired. If we were to suppose that you were to go back in time, or that time were to take you back, and you had the easy financial circumstances that became available following the Nobel prize—I mean, if time could be turned back and you had the Nobel money—would you still have chosen that job?"

"Of course not," he replied. "It would be unthinkable for me to make a career as a government employee. I wouldn't have continued as a government employee."

I asked him, "Did having the job create some kind of dichotomy within you? Meaning, you were a very dedicated government employee—your service record may be the best for any Egyptian government employee—and at the same time you were writing *A Scandal in Cairo* and *Adrift on the Nile (Tharthara fawq al-Nil)* and courageously facing reality in your writings."

"That was natural," he replied. "A job is a job, and writing is writing."

"Nowadays," I asked him, "do you think about some of the major writers whom you knew personally and had relationships with?"

He answered, "There were no special relationships between me and the major writers in my generation."

"What about Salama Musa?" I asked.

"It was a relationship of respect and discipleship from my side, but there was no personal relationship," he replied.

"What about Taha Hussein?" I said.

"The relationship of a pupil to his teacher," he replied.

"Who, then," I said, "is most in your thoughts now?"

He said, "Those who have remained in my memory you know—Taha Hussein, al-'Aqqad, Tawfiq al-Hakim, and Salama Musa."

"But I have noticed," I said, "that you treat Tawfiq al-Hakim with special respect, and when he presented you with a pen on your birthday, you kept it among your decorations and medals."

"Because he was an artist," he said.

"And the others?" I asked.

"Some of them were both thinkers and artists and some were thinker-artists, or pure thinkers," he replied.

I said, "Despite your deep respect for al-'Aqqad, you didn't strive to form a relationship with him, and when you saw him at the Anglo-Egyptian Bookshop you didn't respond to the manager's desire to introduce you to him."

"Al-'Aqqad was a great person," he said. "A thinker, daring, strong-willed. But I didn't know the way to his weekly symposium and didn't feel any desire to form a personal link. The spiritual relationship was enough."

"And what about the ones you couldn't stand?" I asked him.

He was silent for a little and I asked him jokingly, "The discreet government employee takes over?"

"No," he said. "Not at all. As you know, I'm broad-minded and don't bear grudges. The people I've loved are still with me until now. For me, now, al-Manfaluti is the Manfaluti I loved when I was young. As for the ones I couldn't stand, I don't remember them."

I said, "After your long experience in literature and public life, do you think it's better for the writer to announce his positions on public issues publicly, whatever that may cost him, or should he express these positions through his literature?"

"There is no escape from public life," he said. "The writer does not live in isolation, he is a citizen. In other words, if he has a political position—if he's a member of a party or belongs to some group—he's going to make that public."

"Let us suppose a different situation," I said. "Suppose a writer witnesses corruption and errors, should he respond to this by writing articles and through public activism, or reserve his position for his creative writing?"

He said, "If his circumstances permit him to announce his position via articles and taking a stand, he should not delay, but should follow his conscience in what he says. In other words, if he's working as a journalist like you, he should raise his voice as high as he can. If he's not a journalist and has no pulpit, then creative literature is his area of practice. The writer has to follow his conscience whatever the price. Creativity does not accept half measures. For myself, I both spoke and wrote."

I said, "After the novel *Cairo Modern (al-Qahira al-gadida)* as the publisher called it, appeared, you were investigated at the ministry of religious endowments concerning the contents of the novel, but fortunately the investigator was Taha Hussein's brother, so he dealt gently with you and asked you to write about love and keep away from social criticism and topics that could cause headaches. What effect did that have on you at the time?"

Laughing, he asked, "What do you think?"

I said, "I think that it had no effect on you and that you made no compromises in your creative work." At this point, he leaned forward a little and said, "After I wrote *Adrift on the Nile*, it was serialized in *al-Ahram*. That was thanks to Muhammad Hasanayn Haykal. The fact is Haykal was the one who provided space for creative literature that was critical of the situation in the sixties. Do you remember al-Hakim's *Anxiety Bank (Bank al-qalaq)* and *The Perplexed Sultan (al-Sultan al-ha'ir)*?"

"Yes," I said, "and I remember *Children of the Alley*, *The Thief and the Dogs (al-Liss wa-l-kilab)*, *Miramar*, *The Beggar (al-Shahhadh)* and your short stories, which we used to wait for and would interpret on the basis of information we couldn't own to knowing. I remember a wonderful story that you wrote after your return from Yemen, expressing your opposition to sending the Egyptian army there."

He said, "Field Marshal 'Abd al-Hakim 'Amir, as I am informed, when they told him what was in *Adrift on the Nile*, or perhaps he read it himself, said, 'The boy's really asking for trouble. He's going to have to be taught a lesson.' An acquaintance of Dr. Hasan Sabri al-Khuli, who was close to Gamal Abd al-Nasser, told me."

"Al-Khuli held the position of 'personal representative of President Gamal Abd al-Nasser,'" I said.

"Exactly," he said. "Exactly. A friend we had in common who was part of my 'Abbasiya circle informed me that a decree had been issued for my detention and that Dr. Tharwat 'Ukasha had intervened personally with Abd al-Nasser and that Abd al-Nasser had intervened to stop the process. It was Tharwat 'Ukasha's view that it was inappropriate to subject a novelist to harsh treatment for a novel, and on who's say-so? On Abd al-Nasser's!"

I said, "But you were banned under Anwar al-Sadat."

"Yes," he said, "when I signed the declaration of 1972 in support of the student demonstrations and calling for a resolution of the no peace–no war situation. The late president dismissed more than a hundred writers and journalists from their posts. You were one of them."

I laughed and said, "Indeed. I coined the term 'the 4 February Incident' for it because the decree was published in the newspapers on the morning of 4 February 1973. I woke up to find myself a 'deviator': the headlines said 'Resolute Measures against Deviators' and stated that it had been decided to terminate our membership of the Arab Socialist Union; it followed that we were dismissed from the institutions of the press. The curious thing was that I wasn't a member of the Arab Socialist Union or of any government party, nor have I ever joined one."

"Nor I," he said.

"They dismissed you secretly, along with Tawfiq al-Hakim" I said. "Your names weren't published in the list."

"That was at the suggestion of Dr. Kamal Abu al-Magd, who was minister of information at the time, and an intelligent man."

I said, "All your novels and stories were published in *al-Ahram* under the editorship of Haykal but after he left *al-Ahram* you had two novels published elsewhere—*Love in the Rain (al-Hubb fi-l-matar)* and *Mirrors*. Was that because Yusuf al-Siba'i had taken a position against you?"

He said, "No. It was because of the opinion of Dr. Luwis 'Awad in his role as cultural advisor to *al-Ahram*. He objected to the publication of *Mirrors*, so Raga' al-Naqqash published it in the magazine *al-Idha'a wa-l-tilifizyun*. He published it with great fanfare and the characters were drawn by the artist Sayf Wanli. Luwis 'Awad also objected to *Love in the Rain*, and *al-Shabab* magazine was just starting at the time, edited by the late Salah Jahin and that was how . . . ."

"It seems," I said, "that Luwis 'Awad didn't have a positive opinion of your writing."

Naguib Mahfouz fell silent for a little. I know that silence, which is the one he uses when he doesn't want to be explicit. After a while he said, "God rest his soul." I had forgotten whom we were talking about so I asked, "Who?" "Luwis 'Awad," he said.

I asked him once again, "So your view is that the writer has to give his opinion, given the lack of effective political forces?"

He replied decisively, "Of course he has to speak, to give his opinion."

After a silence he said, "I believe that the *Point of View (Wighat nazar)* column that I write every Thursday has given me the opportunity to say what I think on everything that preoccupies me and my readers."

"That's true," I said. "But in the seventies, when you used to write a full page under title *The Notebook (al-Mufakkira)*, you used to anger the government. They didn't like your views."

He nodded but didn't say anything. Then I asked him, "Why did you start to write articles after Haykal left *al-Ahram* in 1974?"

"Look," he said. "Haykal never asked for anything from me or from Tawfiq al-Hakim. As far as I was concerned, I would publish my novels and my short stories. But when Yusuf al-Siba'i came, he met with us and said it didn't make sense for us to have a presence in *al-Ahram* and not write articles. He asked us to write and set aside one day for each of us, under the title *al-Mufakkira*.

I said, "See what a novelist will do to his friends!"

Once more his response was, "Hmm" and I didn't understand whether this "Hmm" was meant to convey agreement or to show that he had heard what I said. Knowing the tones of his voice, I'd say the second was the more likely.

I said, "Of course, writing articles of that size must have been a very exhausting matter."

"Naturally," he replied.

At this point I preferred to move on to another topic.

I said, "Professor Naguib, you lived through the revolution of 1919, when you were a boy, and you lived through the world economic crisis in 1929, and you lived through the signing of the Anglo-Egyptian Treaty in 1936 and its abrogation in 1951, and the Second World War, the war of 1948, the revolution of 1952, the tripartite aggression of 1956, and the war of 1967. Now, when you scrutinize all these events that Egypt has witnessed, how do you view Egypt today?"

After a brief moment of silence, he said, with extreme deliberateness, "Egypt today is in a crisis, Gamal, a very grave crisis. It is not possible to predict the future from the situation that we are passing through at present."

He fell silent for a moment, and then he said, "One always likes to be optimistic . . . ."

"Have there been circumstances even more difficult than the ones we are going through now?"

After a few minutes, he said, "No. The economic crisis at the beginning of the thirties was cruel, but we government employees didn't feel it and nor did the rest of the ordinary people of the middle classes and the poor. It was the big merchants and especially the cotton merchants who were affected by it. We government employees didn't feel it: one's salary at the end of the month was guaranteed and it was quite enough. As government employees, we were living in luxury. If you went to Cicurel or Chemla's, they'd treat you like kings even though, as a government employee, you'd only be spending pennies. Still, you were spending; you had a fixed salary after all. Now, you know what government employees have to manage on, and the middle classes too."

I said, "When you reached fifty, in 1961, *al-Ahram* put on a big party for you and Haykal invited Egypt's important and iconic personages to fête you. You were at the forefront of the cultural scene and honored at the highest levels even before you turned fifty. When you compare your situation with that of the members of our generation, wouldn't you agree that we've been marginalized?"

With amazement, and perhaps a touch of sarcasm, he inquired, "You're marginalized?"

"Until the mid-eighties," I said, "the term that was applied to us was 'the youth writers.' This term was first applied in the mid-sixties and didn't change for twenty years."

"You are the ones who hold the reins now, and the keys to cultural life," he said. "You yourself are the editor-in-chief of a major literary review."

"It's a delicate situation," I said. "As far as I'm concerned, I'm an editor-in-chief in my professional life, and I learned from you and from Yahya Hakki not to use that platform to promote myself. That was your position when you took over the post of film censor. Over the past twelve years, I have published in the review only a very limited number of short stories, few enough to be counted on the fingers of one hand. It's unthinkable that I should publish an article about myself or even a news item. My relationship with the institution for which I work differs from your relationship and that of the great writers with *al-Ahram*. I'm a professional journalist, not a full-time writer."

"But your generation controls the cultural apparatus now," he said.

"That's true," I replied, "if we consider 'generations' to be a matter of age. But the climate that we live in is different. Members of this generation manage the cultural establishment with all its apparatuses, but they are heavy-handed, and in a society that is supposed to have adopted a free economy and political freedom, we find that the cultural establishment takes positions with regard to writers according to their allegiances. Loyalty must be to the undersecretary of the ministry and not to the regime!"

"Culture now seems to be more governmental," he said. "What you are describing now is the impact of the bureaucratic spirit."

"Let's look at it from another side," I said. "In the first half of the last century, Egyptian culture flourished, especially in the form of publishing houses and non-governmental organizations. State intervention was very limited. For example, the culture administration in the ministry of public education used to buy a few copies of cultural magazines as a form of subsidy, and the educational process was a basic part of the cultural movement. Do you prefer that culture arise and continue through efforts of this type, or do you prefer the current situation, where the cultural apparatuses interfere in the tiniest details of cultural reality, spending millions on showy activities that do not lead to any genuine cultural production?"

"Certainly," he replied, "the former is better because it leads to a natural cultural life that in turn leads to the creation of a genuine climate for culture and the winnowing of the chaff from the grain. It's better that the state practice its cultural role from a distance."

"And you have to add to all that," I said, "the impact of the media, for whom the insistence on publishing news about certain writers or government servants is more important than cultural output or activity."

"Perhaps the media can be a support for culture if they are managed with pure intentions and integrity," he said. "The media are an important element in the creation of a sound climate."

After a few moments of silence, I asked how his writing was going now.

He replied, "My current writing is limited to the *Dreams*. I think about the dream, I memorize it thoroughly, then I write it down as it comes, meaning from memory. I've written ninety-seven dreams that way, but I dictated the last three dreams to Hagg Sabri because my hand will no longer obey me."

"It's the first time you've dictated a text to someone else," I said.

"That's correct," he affirmed.

I became aware of the sorrow in his voice and sought to change the subject.

I asked, "Are the *Dreams* in fact derived from your real dreams or are they made up?"

"No," he said. "They're real dreams. The dream has taken the place of reality."

"But the stuff of which dreams are made is fragile and one forgets them quickly," I said.

He replied, "I write what I remember. My focus now is on my dreams. I derive the material from them. It seems I jinxed myself when I wrote *I Saw as the Sleeper Sees (Ra'aytu fima yara al-na'im)*," and the famous Mahfouzian laugh rang out.

I asked him again, "But you have lots of ideas that you haven't written?"

He replied, "Most of my material is from my dreams. That is what I can do at the moment. I can't do more than that."

"But the earlier dreams in *I Saw as the Sleeper Sees* weren't real," I said.

"Precisely," he said. "They were made up."

"So the real dreams," I said, "are the ones known as *The Dreams*, a hundred of which have been published so far in *Nisf al-dunya* magazine?"

"Exactly, exactly," he replied.

"But aren't you sometimes taken unawares by an idea for a short story?"

"That's not possible," he replied. "The idea needs to be made operational through writing and I don't write now. All I can manage is the dreams."

"The dreams are very concentrated," I said. "They're closer to poetry."

After a period of silence, I asked him once more about when he started dictating.

"It was a few weeks ago," he said. "I was talking to some friends about my dreams and they asked me to write them down so that I wouldn't forget them."

"But you're normally very secretive about your writing," I said.

He replied, "The fact is they were asking me about how I was doing so I told them how my dreams were doing."

I said, "I remember the only book you gave me any hint about was *Mirrors*. That was in the days when we went to 'Urabi's café. After you had retired, you used to bring the morning session to a close quickly and tell me, 'I'm writing about something that intrigues me.' Later, I discovered that it was *The Harafish*."

Here Yusuf al-Qa'id made an observation about the disjointed nature of the relationships in *Mirrors*, that all of the relationships remain incomplete.

Naguib Mahfouz laughed and said, "So you want me to explain my dreams to you?"

Zaki Salim intervened and said, "I believe that it is of the nature of dreams that the relationships in them are never completed, that they come to a sudden stop. That's the nature of life too."

Again Yusuf al-Qa'id asked, "Do you dream in color or black and white?"

He laughed and said, "Technicolor!"

"Which are the novels that you remember clearly now?" I asked him. "Meaning, after a long life as a reader."

"*War and Peace*," he said. "*Remembrance of Things Past*."

"What about *Ulysses*?" I asked.

"To be honest, it really makes no difference whether one remembers it or not."

Everyone laughed loudly.

"It's in the new things," he said, "that the accummulated influence of these readings shows through. I've read the new literature, but I've used it in its place, in its context."

After a few minutes, he went on, "Once the former minister of culture of Spain came to see me. He informed me that he had read my story *Qismati wa-nasibi (My Fate and My Destiny)*, in translation of course, but his strange interpretation of the story drew my attention. He interpreted it as being about the Arab–Israeli conflict and as saying that the one who gets the better of the other will kill him and dispose of the body."

I said, "That's a very strange interpretation."

"Indeed," he said.

"This raises the issue of reception," I said. "A writer may write a story, and when it reaches a different reader, in another place or time, the latter may interpret it in a way that had never occurred to the writer."

"That's true," he agreed.

After a few minutes of silence, he said, "But you haven't asked about what I do when I'm alone during the day."

I said, "I'm afraid of tiring you with my questions."

"No," he said. "To tell the truth, I want to tell you how I spend my time. Do you know what I do?"

We all looked at him enquiringly, and after a moment of silence he said, "I sing."

I asked him what he meant.

He said, "I go over the songs that I've learned by heart going back to the days of Sayyid Darwish, 'Abd al-Wahhab, and Umm Kulthum."

"Where did you get the idea of doing that?" I asked him.

"Just like that," he replied.

I asked him, "Do you remember things in detail?"

"I remember very many details," he replied. "Most of them from the early days."

I asked him, "Do you drink tea or coffee during the day?"

"Neither," he said. "Just the couple of sips of coffee that you see before me."

"Cigarettes?" I asked him.

"Just two," he replied.

I said, "I have the impression you smoked three today."

"Impossible," he replied.

I asked him once more, "Which songs do you remember and sing when you're alone?"

"Lots," he said.

"'How Long Ago Were We Here? A Month, A Year?' by 'Abd al-Wahhab?" I asked.

"For example," he said. "I'm very fond of that one."

"What do you remember of Munira al-Mahdiya's?" I asked.

"'A Brown-Skinned Boy Has Seized My Soul,' and 'After Dinner, It's Fun To Joke And Make Merry.'"

"What about 'White Dove'?"

"That's by Dawud Husni," he said. "It's lovely!"

"Did you hear Munira live?" I asked.

"I heard her at Ramses Entertainment City. It was the most beautiful of the entertainment parks, in what is now the Muhandisin district. I also heard her at the Majestic Theater on Alfi Street, but at this last concert her voice was weak and she sounded hoarse. I was very sad."

"And Umm Kulthum?" I asked.

"At the beginning I almost quarreled with a friend of mine when he told me that there was a new singer whose voice was better than Munira's, but when I heard her I fell in love with it."

"What was the difference between them?" I asked.

"'Abd al-Wahhab described it very accurately," he replied. "He said that both voices were extremely powerful, but Umm Kulthum's had better brakes, by which he meant the way she brought the song to a close."

After a silence, he continued, "Munira had many admirers, including Husayn Rushdi Pasha, who was prime minister in the twenties. A famous story says that he once held a meeting of the cabinet on her houseboat."

Jokingly I ask him, "On her houseboat? Whatever could he have been doing there?"

He laughed and replied, "How should I know what kind of hanky-panky he was up to?"

I asked him, "Have you ever loved anyone or wanted to be their friend but couldn't?"

"What do you mean?"

"Let me give you an example," I said. "I was very fond of Hagg Ibrahim Nafi', Mahmud al-Sa'dani's friend. He was a wonderful guy, a true gentleman, but circumstances didn't allow it."

Here Zaki Salim interposed, "I know what you mean. I believe the Master was very fond of al-'Aqqad but never became his friend."

The Master agreed with Zaki Salim. When I asked him why, he said, "I didn't attend his symposium, but he was a great person."

I asked him, "I've noticed that you're more at ease with people who aren't intellectuals."

"Intellectuals are such worriers. Maybe some of the Riffraff characters are different."

"Which of your works is the closest to being autobiographical?" I asked.

"*Fountain and Tomb (Hikayat haratina)*," he said.

After a silence, he started going over some of his memories of Qirmiz Passage, which ran beneath the Amir Mithqal mosque. Then he laughed and said, "I remember there were stories about a female afreet whose name was Zurumbeiha, and when I was a child at home I used to sing a song that had the name Zurumbeiha in it. The neighbors heard me and sent a message to my mother asking her to stop me from singing it so the afreet wouldn't appear to them."

Zaki Salim said, "Zurumbeiha occurs in *The Thousand and One Nights*."

We went back to talking about al-Gamaliya and stories he'd heard when he was a child. To my amazement, I'd heard the same stories when I was a child too, four or five decades later—such as the afreet in Qirmiz Passage who appeared to people in the form of a policeman. He'd stop someone walking through the passage and ask the time. After listening to the answer, he'd turn and walk away, and the person who'd answered him would look round, perhaps because of the strange sound made by his footsteps, and be horrified to discover that his upper half was that of a man but his lower half was a goat's.

We spoke of Cairo in the thirties, about the streetcar routes, which he remembered in detail—No. 15 to Giza and the pyramids, No. 33 to Imbaba (this was the one on which he ran into 'Abd al-Wahhab), No. 4 from al-Imam al-Shafi'i to al-Sabtiya, No. 22 from al-Madbah to al-'Abbasiya; he used to take it when returning from the old parts of Cairo. We spoke of Shaykh Zakariya Ahmad, of the ecstasy of listening to music, of his friends from al-'Abbasiya, all of whom had passed away, and we prayed that the Master live a long and beautiful life.

Tuesday 6 July 2004

I noticed that the Master was having to make an effort to hear. I asked him, "Has the battery run low?"

"I think so," he said.

Zaki Salim commented that this was something new that had only started two days ago.

We suggested he try a new, digital, type but he just waved his hand, a gesture well known to me, which I can imitate perfectly and which means "It's not important." After a few moments of silence, he said, "A year ago, a doctor suggested that I have an operation. 'Which is worse,' he asked me, 'a quarter of an hour's pain or hours of inconvenience?' I told him I only had quarter of an hour left to my life and he smiled and said, 'God grant you long life, Master!'"

Tuesday 6 July 2004

For Zaki Salim's sake, the Master agreed to change the place and time of our meeting, which normally took place in one of the café-restaurants overlooking the Nile but which on this day was at the Heliopolis Sheraton, close to the airport. Zaki Salim had booked a room furnished in the English style and invited a group of professors of philosophy, headed by Dr. 'Atif al-'Iraqi, who had supervised Salim's doctoral dissertation on "Critical Thought in the Work of Shaykh Muhy al-Din ibn 'Arabi," which he had defended the week before. Of Mahfouz's Thursday friends, 'Imad al-'Abbudi came, and Yusuf al-Qa'id, and the painter Muhammad al-Shirbini.

The presence of Dr. al-'Iraqi and the other professors caused the talk to turn to the Master's memories of his studies of philosophy and of university life. Before that, however, there was a long conversation about the expected change of cabinet following the return of President Mubarak the previous day from a trip to Germany for medical treatment.

When Naguib Mahfouz learned that Dr. 'Atif al-'Iraqi was a 1957 Cairo University graduate, he said, "Heavens! He's very recent."

Of course, he himself had graduated from the same department in 1934. He mentioned that when he applied to the College of Humanities, the examiner was Dr. Taha Hussein, and when the latter had asked him his reasons for choosing the department of philosophy, he had answered by expressing some of his ideas and Dean Hussein had said, "You talk incomprehensibly. Go do philosophy!"

Mahfouz said that the department of philosophy had only four students, and these made up the class of 1934. They were Tawfiq al-Tawil, 'Abd al-Hadi Abu Rayda, and 'Ali 'Isa. He said that he had been very close to Tawfiq al-Tawil, and that when al-Tawil died, he had cried with emotion. The department consisted of these students only. A few students from other departments would visit to listen to the lectures, among them Rashad Rushdi. The phenomenon of the vast numbers that now crowd the university did not exist then. He stopped a little and smiled before starting to talk again, which we knew meant that he was going to tell an anecdote.

He said, "The social studies department had only one female student. Her name was Ihsan—I don't remember her last name. About twelve professors and teaching assistants gave her instruction. There were more teachers than students. Ihsan was very elegant. She'd come to the university in a dress that revealed her arms, and one of the professors called her in and asked her to cover her arms. She started coming in a dress that had two sleeves attached that were held in place by buttons. As soon as she left the lecture, she would remove these."

Al-Qa'id commented, "No doubt they were very beautiful sleeves."

"Certainly!" he replied. "Extremely!"

Tuesday 13 July 2004

"Did you see Tal'at Harb?" I asked him.

"From a distance," he said. "I used to go to the Cinéma Ezbekiya, and he used to come sometimes in the company of certain young men! I saw that everyone treated him with respect, despite the things that were known about him."

I asked him what he meant by "The things that were known about him."

He fell silent and didn't answer. I realized that he didn't want to speak clearly, so I turned away from the topic by asking him, "Was there a cinema in Ezbekiya in those days?"

"Yes," he said. "There was a cinema in the middle of the garden belonging to the Bank of Egypt where you could enter for two piasters and sit at a table and eat steeped dried apricots and smoke a waterpipe if you wanted while watching the movie."

He was silent for a little and then he said, "Those were the days."

Tuesday 20 July 2004

He laughs without preamble, remembering an anecdote.

He says that he was listening to Umm Kulthum at one of her concerts, and she was singing a poem set to music and performed by Shaykh 'Ali Mahmud, one of the best known and most powerful voices among singers of praises to the Prophet and Sufi poetry. Overcome with ecstasy, he cried out joyfully, addressing Umm Kulthum, "Bravo, Shaykh 'Ali!"

TUESDAY 15 JUNE 2004

A while ago, he informed us that he was no longer able to write on his own. He had trained at length after the incident but he was no longer able to do so. He had started to dictate his new work, *The Dreams*, to Hagg Sabri.

Zaki Salim asked him, "Does that lead to any change in the text?"

Mahfouz replied, "The dreams plus the dictation call for a great deal of concentration. I fear that this may cost them some of their poetry."

Silence reigned. I tried to imagine Naguib Mahfouz sitting down with Hagg Sabri in the mornings and dictating to him whatever new dreams there might be—Mahfouz who used to consider writing an intimate secret, one that no one else should observe. Despite this, his desire to write, his instinctive desire to create, allowed him to bend the most intractable circumstances to his will.

TUESDAY 13 JULY 2004

Today the new cabinet was announced, headed by Dr. Ahmad Nazif. I asked the Master about cabinets before July 1952 and he answered, "They were party-based. When a party won the elections, it would bring in an entire new team with its own particular perspective. This was true even for the minority cabinets, such as that of Isma'il Sidqi—he brought in a team that had a vision. Naturally, the cabinets came after elections, and the only free elections were those that elected the Wafd; when the elections returned minority cabinets, they were fraudulent. The fixing of elections came about because of the king's intervention."

I asked him if he remembered the phase before the Revolution, when a number of cabinets followed one another in quick succession over a short period. Yusuf al-Qa'id commented, "There's an excellent book by Musa Sabri about that period—*A King and Four Cabinets (Malik wa-arba' wizarat)*."

Mahfouz noted that this period had witnessed the decline of the king's image among the people and had greatly hurt his reputation. He said that the Wafd Vanguard, which was considered the left of the Wafd party and included Muhammad Mandur and Ibrahim Tal'at, had started to move in the direction of a popular revolution, but the army's move had come and initiated a different course.

I asked him how he viewed the new cabinet that had just been formed that day under Dr. Ahmad Nazif. He thought for a little and said, "I can only hope for the best."

Once again, I asked him about the Wafd. It was well known that he took a Wafdist line. Had he been a member of the party itself? He answered quickly, "Of course not. I was not a member of the Wafd Party. Membership of the Wafd was more important than being in the cabinet, but I was one of the Wafdist masses."

"What's the difference?" I asked.

"There's a big difference. The party had its structure—the Higher Committee and the Governing Assembly, followed by the governorate-level committees. The Wafdist masses, of whom I was one, did not have official membership, meaning that we didn't fill out forms or attend meetings. But we would hold demonstrations in support of the Wafd and sympathize with it."

Here al-Qa'id commented, "There were two large families in our village of al-Dahriya that were known for their allegiance to the Wafd. They contributed large sums of money to the party. Whenever the Wafd got into power, a number of telephone lines would be installed in the houses of the two heads of the families and whenever they were expelled from power, the telephone lines would be cut off."

Eng. Hasan Nasir said, "The telephone used to be the symbol of authority in the countryside. A telephone meant power, especially among the village mayors."

Tuesday 27 July 2004

The talk turned to philosophers. Zaki Salim asked, "Dr. 'Atif al-'Iraqi says we have no philosophers, just professors of philosophy. Would you agree?"

Mahfouz replied, "Yes. The age of the great philosophers is over. I believe that the German, Hegel, was the last of them. After that, there is no one of his stature."

Zaki said, "Dr. al-'Iraqi considers Ibn Rushd to be the last philosopher of the Arabs and the Muslims."

I said, "In fact, there is one great philosopher after him, but he's not known in the Arab World. His name is Mulla Sadr al-Din al-Shirazi, who combined the philosophy of Ibn Sina with the wisdom of the Illuminati."

"But he was Persian," objected 'Imad al-'Abbudi.

"He has works in Arabic," I said, "and Ibn Sina was from Transoxania. In fact, most Muslim philosophers came from there. Mulla Sadr al-Din is acknowledged to have been the last of the great philosophers, and Shaykh Mahmud 'Abd al-Fadil, who is now vice-dean of the College of Religious Fundamentals at al-Azhar, wrote a doctoral thesis on him."

"Will you read us some of his ideas next week?" said Mahfouz.

"God willing, Master."

Revisions

A Tuesday in July 2002

Yusuf al-Qa'id asked Mahfouz, "Do you not make revisions of your literary and creative output every so often?"

"No," replied the Master. "I don't make such revisions. I imagine that a thinker would have to do so, but I don't. Novelists and poets are continuously reviewing themselves, but stopping and revising for the sake of revision—I don't think so."

I asked, "Do you devote special attention to language, in the sense that you try to develop it from one work to the next? Your language has passed through a number of important stages. Anyone who reads *Khufu's Wisdom* and *Thebes at War* would never imagine that the person who wrote those novels would go on to create the works from *The Harafish* to *Echoes of an Autobiography*."

The Master said, "I don't deliberately develop the language. Language as far as I'm concerned is like a living being: it grows through experiment and experience, and experience is provisioned by reading. Sometimes the work imposes the use of a language with a special rhythm."

Tuesday 27 August 2002

I spoke about a book newly published in Cairo called *Scientific and Technological Research in Israel (al-Bahth al-'ilmi wa-l-tiknoluji fi Isra'il)* that compares scientific research in Israel to scientific research in the Arab world. The most important thing it says is that

640 patents were registered last year in Israel versus twenty-four in all the Arab countries.

He expressed his surprise, nodding twice. When the silence lengthened, I realized that he was turning the matter over in his mind and that he would deliver his opinion after a few minutes or many, or perhaps forget the matter altogether.

I resumed what I was saying.

I said that Muhammad Hasanayn Haykal had data that might seem strange to those who were not familiar with them but because of his careful follow-up . . . .

Mahfouz appeared to be listening with the greatest attention.

I mentioned that a few weeks previously I had been visiting Haykal and the conversation had turned to Israel. He said that what was attracting his attention now in Israel was not the army, which was a sort of crucible in which all the different elements from all over the world were melted down, but rather the scientific progress in the universities. The Hebrew universities had advanced research centers that were in contact with other advanced research centers all over the world. I said that Haykal's words had seemed strange to me at the time, the army being the pillar of the Hebrew state, but after reading this book I realized how true his words were and just how clear his vision had been.

After a few moments' silence, he asked me, "How many patents in Israel?"

"Six hundred and forty."

"And among us?"

"In the whole Arab world, twenty-four."

After a few more moments of silence, he said, "What will be the destiny of these inventions?"

I looked at him in silence and he continued, "Ultimately, they will become contributions to human welfare. Meaning, we shall benefit from them."

I listened to his words with their expression of a holistic human view that went beyond the current timeframe within which we live and didn't give voice to a query that I was turning over in my mind: And what of us?

Tuesday 20 July 2004

I asked whether he remembered Fr. Jacques Jomier. Immediately he replied, "Of course. He was the first foreigner to write about me, and I was acquainted with him personally."

I told him that I had become acquainted with the man when he was living at the Dominican Fathers' monastery in al-Darrasa, where he'd read me numerous pages from his doctoral thesis on the *mahmal*, or decorated camel palanquin, that was formerly sent every year from Egypt to the holy cities of the Hegaz as a symbol of the authority of the rulers of Egypt. He had also written a study of the Friday sermon, but unfortunately neither of this nor his thesis had been translated into Arabic from the French. I said that he was an extremely modest man and was still living in Toulouse, though he must be almost a hundred now.

Mahfouz remarked that his study of the *Trilogy* was pioneering.

I mentioned that we had read it in Arabic when it had been published by Misr Bookshop.

"I visited him at the monastery with Yahya Hakki," said Mahfouz. "I found an amazingly rich library there and read their copy of the second part of the collected verse of Hafiz al-Shirazi, translated by Dr. Ibrahim al-Shawarbi, of which I owned only the first part."

"Once," I said, "—and this was very rare, as you were anxious to keep it in your library, which contained only a few books—you lent me the same part to photocopy."

"Did I lend you the first part?" said Mahfouz.

"Yes," I said.

"I don't remember . . . ." he said.

After a silence, he said that he used to see Jacques Jomier passing 'Urabi's café, wearing the white robes of the Dominicans and apparently going to or from the monastery to shop or carrying a few things.

Tuesday 27 July 2004

I asked him whether Mustafa al-Nahhas had kissed the king's hand.

"I don't think so," said Mahfouz. "I asked Ibrahim Pasha Farag, but he was emphatic that it was not true. He said it was Husayn Sirri Pasha who had spread the rumor."

I said that Mustafa al-Nahhas's true worth as a national leader was great and only came to light many years after the July Revolution. I belong to the generation that came to awareness after the Revolution, and our image of al-Nahhas Pasha was negative. He was seen as a sort of buffoon who had inherited the leadership of the 1919 Revolution. However, when I'd absorbed the history of the epoch through the writings of al-Rafi'i, Tariq al-Bishri, and Latifa Salim (author of an important book on King Faruq) I saw a totally different picture. I found that he had been a strong national leader and an opponent of the king. It is enough to mention his opposition to the coronation of the king at al-Azhar when Shaykh Mustafa al-Maraghi tried to impose that.

Mahfouz said, "I remember what the oriental secretary said once at the British embassy: that the problem with Egypt was that the prime minister wants to exercise the king's powers and the king wants to be prime minister!"

Tuesday 27 July 2004

I asked whether ministers before the Revolution used to submit declarations of financial obligations.

He said, "Yes. But they didn't publish them."

I told him that I recalled looking at his government service file and that it included a declaration of his financial obligations dated 1952. At that time, he had had 620 pounds in the bank.

He smiled. After a few moments, he said that he submitted a statement of his financial obligations each year until he retired. After another silence, he returned to the subject and said that before the Revolution, the budget had been distinguished by its transparency. The king's allowances were known. He remembered well the debate over the budget in which five thousand pounds were allocated for the upgrading of the yacht *al-Mahrusa*, which belonged to the state. It was a fierce debate—an example of the best parliamentary performance—and we hadn't seen its like since.

Part Two

These dialogs were recorded in 1978
at Casino Cléopatra on al-Gabalaya Street and
at Fishawi's café and took place every Monday,
starting in June and ending in October.
They involved only the Master and myself.

Mahfouzian Memories

How fast the passing of the days!

More than a quarter of a century has elapsed since that hot Cairene summer. These were the months during which Naguib Mahfouz abandoned his writing because of an allergy, which began in June and continued until the end of August—or this at least is what we know as the publicly stated reason; perhaps there were other reasons too, such as a deliberate abandonment of writing in favor of meditation and a closer scrutiny of what was and would be. That particular summer, however, the summer of 1978, was unusual, especially for him. Mahfouz had announced his support for the visit to Jerusalem undertaken by President Anwar al-Sadat. In response, the Arab states, in the shape of the Arab Writers' Union (headed by whom at that time I don't remember—perhaps it was the Syrian, 'Ali 'Uqla), had decided to boycott him on both the personal and the literary level. Thus all his writings, both those written before the visit to Jerusalem and those written after, were banned from use in Arab movies, and producers were obliged to remove his name from films for which he had written the screenplay or story or in which he had participated in any way. It was a kind of literary death sentence for the greatest Arab writer, as well as an opportunity for some of those possessed by narrow regional jealousies hidden behind hyper-Arab-nationalist slogans to try to cut Egypt's cultural role down to size. Was Naguib Mahfouz's expression of certain political opinions to become the tool that a few would use to remove him *in toto* from the shelves? How could *Midaq Alley*, *The Cairo Trilogy*, *The Harafish*, or *Children of the Alley* be impounded?

It was a strange decision. Here, I must clarify that my own political position differed from that of Naguib Mahfouz. However, I, along with others who loved him and were his friends, had discussed the issue with him and engaged him in dialog, and as far as I am concerned, Mahfouz proclaims his political positions out of conviction and after long thought, and not, as certain writers do these days, for opportunistic reasons. Nor did his position come as a surprise to me. I remember that he had been frank with us in the summer of 1967, when the defeat was still a fresh and open wound. It was at Fishawi's café in historic Cairo and we were three—the novelist Yusuf al-Qa'id, the writer Isma'il al-'Adili, and myself. We were talking about what had and would happen when he surpised us with his view that if there was no possibility of defeating Israel militarily, we should resort to peaceful political methods and look for the possibility of a settlement.

This point of view, at that time, was a shock to us. Later, we had many discussions and many disagreements, but the link was never broken and our admiration for his beautiful creative output never ceased. It was in this context that the strange decision to boycott him was issued, a decision that was applied with exaggerated fanaticism. The Arab cultural conscience could not, however, accept such a decision, and the great Arab artists and intellectuals disavowed it and worked to end it and get around it in practical ways. In this unpleasant atmosphere, 'Imad al-Din Adib, the editor-in-chief of *Asharq Alawsat* newspaper, contacted me and proposed that I publish a long dialog, in non-traditional format, with Naguib Mahfouz, which would appear in installments. When we met in person, I probed the issue of publication, and he assured me that he had put the idea to the editorial staff and they were enthusiastic, and that everyone agreed that a creative and literary boycott of Naguib Mahfouz was impossible.

This is how it began.

Naguib Mahfouz had not yet started his summer vacation, during which he went to Alexandria. He had retired six years before and devoted his life entirely to writing, and during those years he had written *The Harafish*. He was in excellent health, took daily walks morning and evening, and would wander the streets of the older parts of Cairo every Wednesday in quest of the sites of his memories and the times for which he fondly yearned. When the matter was put to him, he was very enthusiastic and suggested that we meet someplace quiet and unfrequented by our acquaintances. Our choice fell on a European-style café or 'casino' that overlooked the Nile from the bank opposite his house in al-'Aguza. He would cross via the long Sixth of October Bridge, whose full extent runs from al-Muhandisin to Bab al-Hadid Square, traversing the smaller section that goes to the bank of the Little Nile and descending the steps to the café's entrance. I requested that we start a week later, and we so agreed.

Despite the length of our acquaintance, which went back to 1959, I was still awed by the assignment. This led me not to rely simply on the length and depth of our relationship, but to go back to the important interviews that he had given; I thus spent hours in the *Akhbar al-yawm* archives. The two main references that I pored over were his discussion with Fu'ad Dawwara, included in the latter's *Ten Writers Speak ('Ashara udaba' yatahaddathun)* and the special issue of *al-Hilal* magazine issued in 1970 and edited by Raga' al-Naqqash, who was then editor-in-chief. In my estimation, this is one of the best and most important of the special issues that have been published on Naguib Mahfouz; it remains a reference of great wealth both for its content and for its pictures, and one to which recourse must be had when anyone is thinking of doing anything on the great writer. I also listened to a two-hour-long discussion that was broadcast in the sixties and issued on cassette by the Radio and Television Union's Voice of Cairo company, as well as going over my own private observations.

In this way, I was able to prepare a precise, organized program, which gave me good insight into Mahfouz's capacity for self-discipline. The conversation covered a number of critical issues:
Childhood, upbringing, and literary formation.

Place, and especially the old parts of Cairo, for I grew up in the same area: I lived for thirty years on al-Tablawi Road, which branches off Qasr al-Shawq Street—in other words, only a few steps from Bayt al-Qadi Square and the house in which Mahfouz was born. Place is a cornerstone not just of Mahfouz's works, but also for his daily life and his literary formation. In addition, Mahfouz is himself a living repository of memories of Cairo, old and new, and it is through him that I have come to form an image of what was and of what has changed. Before starting my conversation with him, I had published a study of Cairo on site and in reality, and as depicted by Mahfouz. Through my familiarity with the place, I was able to compare the original with the creative facsimile. I included this study in the second edition of *The Face of Cairo over a Thousand Years (Malamih al-Qahira fi-alf 'amm)*.

Writing and connected matters. Naturally, it was not a matter here simply of questions and answers. It was rather a God-sent opportunity for me to explore dimensions of the creative world of a writer who did not speak much about this world or his writing practice, and of his relationship with language and modern forms of fiction.

Political opinions. This was an important topic during that specific period, especially after Mahfouz published his novel *Karnak Café (al-Karnak)* and announced his support for al-Sadat and his journey to Israel.

His relationship with the cinema: how it started, and how he came to write the screenplay or dialog for seventy-seven movies.

His job, or more precisely the relationship between the work the writer performs to make a living and the impact of this on his creative life, his formation as a writer, and his career. Naturally, I was trying to get at aspects of the similarities between what I live and what he had discovered.

Finally, his family life, love, and marriage. Where love was concerned, I was affected by his experience as expressed in *The Cairo Trilogy* through the love of Kamal 'Abd al-Jawad for 'Ayda Shaddad, that unique relationship that obsessed me for no small time. Through my extended conversations with him over many years, I had discovered various details of his private life, and I had lived close to the friends of his childhood or what he calls 'the 'Abbasiya gang.' To these he was extremely loyal, setting aside the evening of each Thursday to meet with them until ill-health and Cairo's traffic jams came between them. In time they all passed away, God rest their souls. Despite all this, I had only ever published what he wanted published and had suppressed anything that might upset him, for even today the conditions of our society do not permit the revelation of secrets in the European manner.

Thus it was that we began, and the work took up more than twenty hours over a month during which we worked ceaselessly, only Thursdays and Fridays excepted. When I started writing, I deleted the questions. It is thus the voice of Mahfouz's memory alone that is the narrator. I recall with nostalgia those burning days, the grueling journey in the extreme heat, for this was the longest opportunity ever granted me to be alone with the great writer who was, and still is, a friend, a helper, a companion, and a guide to me.

When I finished working on these dialogs, they were published first in installments in the *Asharq Alawsat* newspaper. At the end of the year I went to Beirut, where the Masira publishing house had prepared a program on them. I will always be proud of the fact that Mahfouz wrote a preface to these dialogs when they appeared as a book entitled *Naguib Mahfouz Remembers*, in which he says, "This book has relieved me of the need to think of writing an autobiography because of the essential and basic data that it contains concerning the course of my life, not to mention the fact that the author is himself a pillar of the latter."

Childhood

When I travel in memory to the most distant beginnings of my life, to my earliest childhood, I remember our house in al-Gamaliya as almost empty. My father had had six children before me, who had followed one another in quick succession, four girls and two boys, after which my mother had no more children for nine years. Then I came along. When I reached the age of five, the difference between me and my next oldest brother was fifteen years. All the girls but one, of whose life in that house I remember nothing, had gotten married. My two brothers also had married, and one of them had entered the military college and gone off to serve in Sudan. This is why I remember only my father and my mother in the house. I can't remember that any other person shared the house with us unless they were guests, such as my aunt on my father's side and her daughter, or people from outside the family. For most of my life in that house I was like an only child, though of course we would visit my siblings in their homes; this is why, if I try to recall my memories of the latter, I remember them in their houses and not in ours. My relationship with them was that of a child with adults, its foundation politeness and good manners. I didn't know them as siblings whose daily lives I shared, with whom I played or laughed. Consequently, the sibling relationship is one of those that I have followed with interest throughout my life.

Later there were siblings among my friends, and I would observe them, asking myself: I wonder, if my brothers and sisters had been closer to me in age, how would my relationship with them have gone? Among my friends were three siblings who always played together. They went to the park together, they laughed together, and I would observe them and ask myself: Would I have become like them? I was deprived of the feeling of being a brother.

This is why you will notice that I am always picturing brotherly relationships among siblings in my works: it is a result of my being deprived of such relationships, which appear in *The Cairo Trilogy*, in *The Beginning and the End (Bidaya wa-nihaya)*, and in *Khan al-Khalili*. I never experienced that kind of relationship in my real life. I always regarded it as something forbidden or unknown. I wanted to have that same relationship with my friends—that of brotherliness.

Play

Naturally, the house is always linked in my mind with play, especially the roof where there was lots of space for playing. There was the family's stock of household provisions; there were duck, chickens, geese, and little chicks. Planted in flowerpots were hyacinth, bean, and basil. And then there was the wide sky. We lived in a freestanding house—what they used to call in the common parlance, 'a house with its own door,' or what in modern terms we might call a 'vertical' house, each story consisting of a small and a large room, with the roof space on top. There you would find a summer room, where we slept on hot days. The house added its necessary components as it went up, meaning that on the bottom floor was the reception room, on the second a dining room, and so on, maybe because the area of the plot was so small. We used to play in the street too, with the sons and daughters of the neighbors. The house stood opposite the Gamaliya police station and looked out over Bayt al-Qadi Square, but we belonged to the quarter of Qirmiz Road.

Author's Note: The house that witnessed the birth of our great writer was demolished and its place is now occupied by a modern three-story house with a café on the ground floor. The Qirmiz Road quarter remains as it was, and the passageway which extends under one of the historic mosques is still there.

In those days, the quarter was a strange world, one where all classes of Egyptian society were represented. There was, for example, a tenement in which simple people lived, of whom I can recall a police private, a minor official in the water company, a poor woman who went about selling radishes or pumpkin seeds, and her blind husband. They had a room in the tenement. Directly in front of the tenement you would find a small house that was inhabited by a woman who was one of the first to receive an education and take a salaried job. Then you would find the houses of major families of notables, such as those of the Sukkari, the Muhaylimi, and the Sisi families, and ancient houses whose owners were merchants or lived off the return on an endowment. You used to find the richest categories of society, then the middle class, and then the poor. I don't know what the quarter looks like now, but maybe you know it because you lived in the area until the seventies. Everyone mingled in Ramadan. The rich houses opened what were called *manadir* for the poor, where anyone from the quarter could come in and eat, even strangers. I witnessed the disappearance of the social structure of the Egyptian *hara*, or semi-enclosed city neighborhood, in the thirties. The rich families moved out to West 'Abbasiya while the middle-class families, to which I belonged, moved to East 'Abbasiya.

There was a hostelry for dervishes in the quarter too, with people from Persia and Turkey whom we would see from a distance. Certain outstanding social features of the neighborhood have stuck in my memory, the most prominent of which perhaps is the *futuwwat*, or the gangs and their bosses, whose presence was recognized by the government itself. We used to wake up to the hullabaloo in Bayt al-Qadi when quarrels broke out among them, and they played a major role in the 1919 Revolution. I saw the *futuwwat* with my own eyes when they sacked and occupied the Gamaliya police station. As I told you, there was a room on the roof, and it had a window that looked out over the square. From that window, when I was a child, I saw all the demonstrations that passed in front of Bayt al-Qadi.

Author's Note: The passageway, the dervish hostel, the futuwwat, *and the ruined lot, were fixed landmarks for Naguib Mahfouz, and when he speaks to us of the Persians and the Turks we should no doubt recall those mysterious chants in* The Harafish *that emanated from behind the hostel's walls. Some of what our writer saw from the window during his early childhood of the takeover of the Gamaliya police station by the* futuwwat *and the demonstrations he recalled in* Fountain and Tomb. *Let us look at Story Twelve:*[2]

What is happening to the world?

Floods sweep over it, earthquakes shake it, fire burns its skirts, slogans explode from its throat.

Thousands—more than ever before—burst the great square, and their screams as they threaten with clenched fists rattle the walls of our alley and deafen our ears. Now even women ride in the rows of carts and take part in the frenzy . . .

Over the wall along our roof, I watch and ask myself what is happening to the world . . .

Speeches, electric and passionate, smash through the air and pour down a deluge of new words: Saad Zaghloul, Malta, the Sultan, the Cresent and the Cross, the Nation, sudden death . . .

Flages wave above shops, posters of Saad Zaghloul plaster walls, the imam of the mosque appears in the minaret to call and preach. And I tell myself that what is happening is strange but exciting and entertaining, truly magnificent.

Except that I witness a chase.

People rush into our street, throw rocks, and flatten themselves against our alley walls for protection.

Horsemen with tall hats and thick mustaches crash down our alley. Fierce, frightful voices ring out, then screams. Someone yanks me away from my lookout and pushes me into the house where terrified faces peer out at me and say, "It is death."

We strain our ears behind closed shutters but hear only voices in strife, footsteps, neighs, the buzz of bullets, a scream of agony, raging chants.

This lasts several minutes, then silence falls on the alley.

The uproar starts again, now at a distance . . . then total silence.

And I tell myself that what is happening is strange and terrifying and dreadful.

I know only a little about the new words Saad Zaghloul, Malta, the Sultan, and the Nation, but I know a lot about the British cavalry, bullets, and death.

Um Abdu, extremely wrought up, comes to tell tales of heroes and martyrs. She eulogizes Ilwa the baker's apprentice and swears the soldiers' horses became headstrong and uncomfortable in front of the takiya and threw their riders to the ground . . .

And I tell myself that what is happening is an exciting and unbelievable dream.

Here the story ends and Naguib Mahfouz continues his memories.

Lost in Time

Among the other characters whom I shall never forget were the women who used to visit our house to make amulets and perform spells. I used to watch them when they came to my mother, with whom they would sit and talk. Another landmark of my childhood was the *kuttab*. The educational system then in place required that we go to the *kuttab* first, then enter First Elementary. The *kuttab* taught us how to be naughty, but it also taught us the principles of religion and the principles of reading and writing. It was mixed. The *kuttab*'s premises were situated in Kababgi Alley, close to Qirmiz Road; I don't know what they house now. Perhaps you knew it. I went when I was four years old, but the strange thing is that I started seeing things outside the quarter at that early age. Do you remember that I told you before of my mother's passion for the ancient monuments? We would often go to the Egyptian Museum or the pyramids, where the Sphinx was. I don't know how to explain her fondness for them even now! We used to go out on our own or sometimes with my mother, who would pull me along by the hand,

and we would visit the Egyptian Museum, especially the mummy room. We went there a lot. My mother enjoyed a relative freedom, unlike Amina in *The Cairo Trilogy*, who wasn't allowed to go out without the permission of Ahmad 'Abd al-Jawad. Where, then, you will ask me, did I get the inspiration for the character of 'Abd al-Jawad?

I remember a family that used to live opposite us. The house was always closed, the windows were never opened, and the only person who ever came out of it was its master, a Levantine called Shaykh Radwan, a man of imposing appearance. My mother would take me to visit this family and I would see that the man's wife was forbidden to go outside. We used to visit them but she never visited us. She used to implore my mother to come and see her. I had lots of friends among the children and later on, when we moved to al-'Abbasiya and I was twelve, I kept up contact with them. Then I lost sight of them all in the rush of life—all the friends of my early childhood, with the exception of one, whom I ran into twenty or twenty-five years ago in al-Gaysh Square when I was on my way to 'Urabi's café. Many long years had passed during which we hadn't seen each other, but we recognized one another. Then he disappeared and I never saw him again.

My mother would always take me with her because there was just me. She would take me with her on her visits to relatives and neighbors, and that is how I saw many of the districts of Cairo, such as Shubra and al-'Abbasiya. Many of the areas that are now located in the center of Cairo were gardens and fields then.

The Father

At home, my father would speak constantly of Sa'd Zaghlul, Muhammad Farid, and Mustafa Kamil, and follow their news with great concern. Whenever my father mentioned the name of one of these men it was as though he were speaking of genuine holy relics. He would discuss household matters in the same breath as those of the nation, as though they were one and the same. Every event in our daily lives, great or small, was associated with some public matter. Thus such and such an event happened because Sa'd had said so and so, or because the Palace . . . or because the British . . . . My father spoke of them excitedly, as though he were talking of personal enemies or friends. My father was a government employee, and when he reached the age at which he was supposed to retire, he resigned. He worked for the government under an ancient sytem which is entirely unfamiliar to us now. After he retired, he worked with an old friend of his who was a merchant. His friend was a big merchant and used to travel all the time to Port Said.

Author's Note: We note here that Ahmad 'Abd al-Jawad in The Cairo Trilogy *traveled once outside Cairo, to Port Said, for trade. It was during this visit that Amina disobeyed his instructions not to leave the house and suffered the consequences.*

The house gave the impression that no one with any connection to art could possibly emerge from it. The only culture to be found in the house was of a religious nature, and the only thing to connect it to public life was of a political order. My father was a friend of al-Muwaylihi's and the latter had given him a copy of his book *The Tale of 'Isa ibn Hisham (Hadith 'Isa ibn Hisham)*, a copy that I remember very well.

Author's Note: Naguib Mahfouz reminded me here of certain traces of his father in The Cairo Trilogy *but there are other, even clearer ones in* Fountain and Tomb, *namely in stories 14, 15, 18, 19, and 23. Let us review Story 23:*[3]

> One morning I awaken with sudden harshness. A dark grip grabs and jerks me from the land of dreams. A flood of jangling noise engulfs me. My hair stands on end with horror: voices wail from the hall. Terrible thoughts rip at my flesh and the specter of death rises up before my eyes.
>
> I jump out of bed and dash to my closed door, hesitate a moment, then throw it open to face the unknown.
>
> My father is seated, my mother leans against the sideboard, and the servant stands in the doorway. They are all crying.
>
> My mother sees me and comes to me. "We scared you . . . Don't be afraid, son."

Through a dry throat, I ask, "What . . . ?"

She whispers hoarsely in my ear, "Saad Zaghloul . . . . May he live on in you!"

I cry from my soul, "Saad!"

I go back to my room.

Gloom hangs everywhere.

What Remained

I don't remember even a single one of my companions in the *kuttab* or in the elementary school, which was located opposite the mosque of al-Husayn, inside which there was a historic clock. I saw the demonstrations from this school. Much blood flowed in the area. You might say that the biggest thing to undermine my child's sense of security was the revolution of 1919. We saw the British and we heard the shooting and I saw the bodies and the wounded in Bayt al-Qadi Square. I saw the attack on the police station.

How do I view my childhood now? My life as a child is reflected to some extent in *The Cairo Trilogy* and even more in *Fountain and Tomb*. It was an ordinary childhood. I didn't experience divorce or polygamy or being orphaned. An ordinary childhood in the sense that the child grew up with parents living a quiet, settled life. My father wasn't a drunkard or addicted to gambling. He wasn't unusually authoritarian. Such things had no place in my life. Anything that might even cloud it was kept from me. The atmosphere in which I grew up spoke of my parents' affection and my family's affection, and I regarded my parents and my family as sacred. The only vein of culture in the family was religious. In 1937 my father died, at sixty-five years of age. I was living with my mother in al-'Abbasiya, to which we had moved in around 1924, but the place to which I remained attached, to which I always look back, is al-Gamaliya.

Between al-'Abbasiya and al-Husayn

We left the Gamaliya area for al-'Abbasiya when I was twelve years old. Our move to al-'Abbasiya had a major impact on my life. The 'Abbasiya to which I moved at that early age did not resemble today's 'Abbasiya. Now there are buildings everywhere and streets intersect and run parallel to one another, but the ʻAbbasiya of my early days contained a lot of green space and few buildings. The houses were small, consisting of a single story, and each house was surrounded by its garden. Beyond the houses, the fields extended to the horizon. My father would accompany me, with my mother, to the Qubba Gardens area, on the other side of Gardens Bridge, and there we'd ride a little trolley car that ran on rails and took us deep into the gardens. The quiet was profound and the area very large, with only a small number of villas. All that has gone. The gardens have disappeared and buildings have filled the place. Despite all that, al-ʻAbbasiya was not completely cut off from the older districts. I discovered the district of al-Husayniya, and ʻUrabi, the famous *futuwwa*—all the same traditions. I said that my move to al-ʻAbbasiya caused a major shift in my life, and the strange thing is that I have maintained my relationship with my friends—my friends from al-ʻAbbasiya, the friends of my boyhood—up to this moment, those who have passed into God's mercy excepted. Even when we have become divided geographically, one going to al-Maʻadi, another to al-Haram when we meet, even if it's after a long separation, it's as though we were resuming a gathering that was interrupted only yesterday. My ʻAbbasiya friends were a diverse bunch and contained every human type, from the most sublime to the most debased. Among them are people who have assumed the most important positions in their professions—doctors, engineers, and accountants—and among them are thugs, people who lead dissolute lives, and gang leaders. Our relationship was benign. Even the wicked among them practiced his wickedness far from the rest of us. There was more than one group, but I was friends with them all. All of them were unforgettable characters and the relationship has never weakened, even at a distance, which is strange.

An unavoidable authorial note: Our great writer derived numerous characters in his novels from his ʻAbbasiya friends, but I will refer here to just one work, in which he wrote about a number of them directly: Mirrors. *See the chapters devoted to Gaʻfar Khalil, Khalil Zaki, Rida Hamada, Hanan Mustafa, Zahran Hassuna, Saba Ramzi, Surur ʻAbd al-Baqi, Sayyid Shuʻayr, Shaʻrawi al-Fahham, Safaʼ al-Katib, Taha ʻAnan, ʻAdli Barakat, ʻAshmawi*

Galal, 'Isam al-Hamalawi, and 'Id Mansur. From the late sixties on, I used to attend the weekly meetings of our great writer with his 'Abbasiya friends every Thursday evening at the old 'Urabi café. There, with his boyhood friends, he appeared at ease, unconstrained. I became acquainted with most of the 'Abbasiya friends, but then the meetings stopped because of the crisis in the public transportation system, which prevented our writer from traveling from his home on Nile Street to al-'Abbasiya.

A Strange Character

I didn't forget al-Gamaliya.

My nostalgia for it cast a powerful shadow. I always felt a desire to go back to al-Gamaliya, to my friends there. What was it that made this easy for me to do, and on a regular basis? We had a friend from the 'Abbasiya clique who abandoned his studies and went to work with his father in a small fabric store in al-Ghuriya. We were on vacation during the school recess, which was more than four months long, and he used to say to us, "You have to come and see me every day." In those days we used to cover the distance on foot, starting from Faruq (now al-Gaysh) Square and then going via al-Husayniya Street, al-Futuh Gate, and al-Mu'izz Street. We had to walk as far as al-Ghuriya so that I could enjoy the area. When we got to him, we'd stay with him until the store closed and then we'd move on to his two favorite places to sit—the Midaq Alley café and Fishawi's café. I discovered Midaq Alley thanks to this friend of ours. The fact is there was a strange bond between the area, the people there, the historic monuments, and myself, a bond that stirred up heartfelt emotions and obscure feelings from which I was to find relief in later years only by writing about them. To return to that friend of mine, he was an adventurous person. He worked with his father, but when the crisis of the thirties arrived, he abandoned him and disappeared. He went to glean a living in Upper Egypt. He was very daring. He let his beard grow, said he was coming from 'Illumined Medina,' and sold people dust from the Prophet's tomb. He would treat sick people and got into lots of scrapes. Once, he caused a man to hemorrhage while pulling out one of his molars and had to flee the town. He was an excellent salesman despite that. Then he married and settled down. He was the perfect smooth talker. In fact, he was the one who taught us the way to the various parts of Cairo. Where is he now? I don't know. He used to come and visit me when he came to Cairo. He'd take me by surprise at the ministry of religious endowments, and later at the ministry of culture. Then he disappeared. I don't know whether he's still alive or has passed on into God's mercy. If he were living in Cairo, he would certainly visit me. He was an adventurer. I remember that after he abandoned his father in the wake of the crisis of the thirties and then got into financial difficulties, he wanted to go back to his father and he asked me to act as his go-between. I went to his father. He was a neighbor of ours, living on the same street. The man received me very cordially, but when I mentioned his son's name, the whole household flew at me, even his mother, because he'd abandoned the family at a difficult time. This friend of mine had no understanding of the principles of loyalty and family attachment. One might even say he had no principles, or was ahead of his time. In any case, what matters is that he was an adventurer, and his personality and his experiences opened up for me numerous worlds that I have written about many times and that are scattered through many of my novels. As for that friend of mine himself, I don't know where he is now.

My Starting Point

Among my friends from al-'Abbasiya who have passed into God's mercy are Fu'ad Nuwayra and Ahmad Nuwayra, both of whom belonged to the 'Abbasiya clique. They were brothers of the musician 'Abd al-Halim Nuwayra. My friendship was with Ahmad, the older of the two. 'Abd al-Halim Nuwayra used to join us from time to time. He was the youngest of the family. Both Ahmad and Fu'ad died young, God rest their souls. We always spent our evenings around the mosque of al-Husayn. I used to visit the area with boundless fascination. Our nocturnal outings would reach the peak of their beauty in Ramadan, when we would go to the mosque to listen to Shaykh 'Ali Mahmud and spend the whole night there until morning. This was while I was studying and then when I was a government employee. You know, I kept going to the Husayn area until the beginning of the seventies, when I used to meet you there.

However, my advancing age and the deterioration of public transport made me stop going regularly. In addition, the place itself had changed. The old Fishawi's was demolished. The nights I spent at Fishawi's until morning were among the most enjoyable hours of my life. These nights brought many different types together. Not to go to al-Gamaliya saddens me greatly. Sometimes one may complain of a certain aridity of the soul—you know those moments that every author goes through—but when I walk in al-Gamaliya, images flood my mind's eye; most of my novels came to me as living ideas while I was sitting in this area smoking a waterpipe. It seems to me that there has to be some link to a specific place, or a specific thing, that is the starting point for one's feelings and sensations. Take, for instance, our writers who lived in the countryside, such as Muhammad 'Abd al-Halim 'Abd Allah or 'Abd al-Rahman al-Sharqawi; you'll find that the countryside was the cornerstone and the wellspring of their works. Yes indeed. The writer needs something that shines and inspires.

First Love

I returned to al-Gamaliya as a government employee when I worked in the Ghuri Library and supervised the Good Loan project. That was at the end of the forties and the beginning of the fifties. I was working in the minister's office, the minister of religious endowments, and it happened that there was a cabinet reshuffle and they asked me to choose a different place to work, and I chose the Ghuri Library in the Azhar district. Naturally, they were astonished since it's a place no government employee would normally choose to go to because of its distance from the ministry and the neglect that surrounded it, but I had a different goal in mind. I spent some of the most enjoyable months of my life in the Ghuri Library. It was during this period, for example, that I read Marcel Proust's *Remembrance of Things Past*. I used to go regularly to Fishawi's café during the day, when the ancient café was almost empty. I'd smoke a waterpipe, think, and observe. I'd walk in the Ghuriya area too. This area is reflected in my works. Even when, later on, I shifted to treating intellectual, or symbolic, topics, I would also return to the world of the *hara*. What engages me is the reality of that world. There are some whose choice falls on a real, or imaginary, place, or an historical period; my preferred world is that of the *hara*. The *hara* came to be the background to most of my works, so that I could go on living in the area that I love. Why does *The Harafish* take place in a *hara*? I could have had the events take place anywhere—in some other place of a different nature. The choice of the *hara* came about here only because when you write a long work of fiction, you have to be careful to choose an environment you love, that you feel at home in, so that you 'have a good time.' As for the open space that appears within the world of the *hara*, I drew on al-'Abbasiya for that. When I was living in al-'Abbasiya I often used to go out to the edges of the desert, to the area of the springs where they customarily used to celebrate the Prophet's birthday. There I would find myself alone, especially given that this empty area was bordered by the tombs. It was a limitless space. It was in al-'Abbasiya that I suffered my first real love. Before that, I'd become aware of beauty in al-Gamaliya in so far as such feelings can seduce a boy of eight or ten; but in al-'Abbasiya, I knew my first love of the other kind. It was an experience devoid of any relationship, in view of the difference in age, and class, which meant that it could have no aftermath. If it had, it might be that the experience would have lost much of the emotion that I invested in it. The effects of this relationship would show up later in Kamal 'Abd al-Jawad's experience in *The Cairo Trilogy* and his love for 'Ayda Shaddad. I knew al-'Abbasiya as good times and irreplaceable friends. I used to play soccer with my friends. I was a good player.

Author's Note: In the words of the celebrated physician Dr. Adham Ragab, one of Mahfouz's 'Abbasiya friends: "Naguib Mahfouz was a soccer player of rare quality. When we were boys in al-'Abbasiya, he was a weaver and a dodger, a maneuverer of the ball who, had he continued, would have rivaled Husayn Higazi, al-Titsh, and, in the following generation, 'Abd al-Karim Saqr. I tell you, as history is my witness, that never in my life so far—and I speak as a soccer addict and thus an impartial witness—never in my life have I seen anyone who could run as fast as Naguib Mahfouz. He was like a rocket shot across the pitch, and this was appropriate to the game when we were boys, for when he is very young, the player's mind is in his feet and the talented player is the individual player who shoots off with the ball toward the goal like an unswerving arrow."

The Introverted Extrovert

You're asking me if I was an introvert?

Perhaps that's because you've known me at a different stage of my life, but the introvert is a different type altogether. One of the members of our clique was introverted. He'd sit on his own in silence and we used to hover or circle around him, asking him his opinion, trying to 'get a rise' out of him but he never responded to us, he'd just leave us and go home. Was I introverted? Never, at any period of my life, have I lacked for friends. In al-'Abbasiya I was with my friends all day long but, from another angle, you wouldn't find me exchanging visits with relatives. I only mix well with the friends with whom I feel completely myself and with whom I can spend time as I'm doing with you now—in a café, on the street, sitting on the ground. But if you come and tell me there's a meeting, or a wedding, or . . . that I can't stand; I can't stand any gathering that constricts me. I don't even go to family weddings. Yes, certainly I perform my social obligations, but within limits. At five o'clock, for example, you may find me with them at the formal reading of the bans, but then I leave. But official visits and things like that, no. My friends don't visit me at home for one simple reason: I'm with them all day long. With my friends I can be quite natural. I can't bear stuffiness; I can't stand it. The only thing I like is sitting with my friends as though I were on my own—you may remember our sessions with my old friends at 'Urabi's café.

A final authorial note: In the words of Dr. Adham Ragab: "Naguib was—and still is—loyal, with that mythic loyalty that you only read about in stories and fantasy novels."

His dear friends are the ones whom he got to know and who got to know him in his early boyhood, in the twenties and at the beginning of the thirties.

Anyone he has met after that is a mere acquaintance or colleague. His dearest friends were Mukhtar Nuwayra and Fu'ad Nuwayra, God rest their souls, 'Abd al-Hayy al-Alfi, the undersecretary at the ministry of finance, the writer of these lines, and another relative of his who died—he used to type out Mahfouz's early novels for him and I've forgotten his name. Naguib Mahfouz wasn't loyal only to people, he was also loyal to ideas and customs. He had a

Thursday program from which he didn't deviate, whatever the circumstances: he left his office at noon to have lunch with his mother, his brothers, and his sisters. One of his brothers, Prof. Ibrahim 'Abd al-'Aziz, was the principal of my old school; Naguib Mahfouz held him in near holy awe. When Naguib Mahfouz finished his Thursday lunch with his mother and his siblings, he would go at six o'clock to 'Urabi's café to meet his very old personal friends, and at eight o'clock he would go to the Riffraff, who are a recently formed set of friends, unlike the 'Urabi set, who are the set he's had his entire life.

Literary Formation and the Struggle between Literature and Philosophy

One day I saw one of my friends, Yahya Saqr, reading a book—a detective novel called *Son of Johnson (Ibn Junsun)*. Yahya is a relative of 'Abd al-Karim Saqr, the famous soccer player. I asked him, "What's that?"

He said it was a very enjoyable book.

I borrowed it from him, read it, and enjoyed it immensely. This was when we were in Third Elementary. I looked for other novels in the same series. Then I asked myself: If this is the son of Johnson, what about Johnson himself? I looked and found another series of novels in which the father was the hero. These were the first novels I read in my life. I was about ten and, as I told you, there was no atmosphere of culture in my family; the only work of fiction I ever saw in my father's hands was *The Tale of Hisham ibn 'Isa* because the author, al-Muwaylihi, was a friend of his. I used to read the Johnson novels as though they were real, which meant that I would be close to crying, or laughing, according to the developments. From novel to novel, from detective novel to historical novel, my reading proceeded, and I started writing books when I was an elementary school student. It was a strange sort of writing, though. I would read a novel and then rewrite it, with the same characters, but with minor modifications. Then, on the cover of the exercise book, I'd write

"Written by Naguib Mahfouz" and make up the name of a publisher. I rewrote novels by Sir Ryder Haggard and Charles Jarvis. I always wrote my books in the vacations. This is how I started my novel writing, with, naturally, the introduction of additions from my own life—from my relationships and my quarrels with my friends. After this, I started moving on in my reading until I reached al-Manfaluti and then the innovators. I also read the works of certain intellectuals—intellectuals being, during this period, the ones who were respected—such as Taha Hussein, al-'Aqqad, and others. I thought of literature as a hobby on the side. My respect was reserved for thought, articles, criticism, and reviews, and not for stories. This orientation raised philosophical questions. Al-'Aqqad raised questions on the origins of existence and on aesthetics, and it was from this that my interest in philosophy came. The literary form that was accorded respect was the article. Stories were not respected, and that is why I didn't think about devoting myself to literature, to writing stories. Moreover, my best marks were in math and science.

The Secret of Existence

The direction I would go in was already known—it would be either engineering or medicine. This is why, when I started thinking of philosophy, my father got extremely upset, as did my teachers, because I was weak in literary subjects. One of my teachers—his name was Bishara Baghus, God rest his soul—asked me disparagingly, "Why are you hurting yourself? What are you doing to yourself?"

The teachers in those days knew their students well because the class did not contain more than fifteen or sixteen. They would place bets on the students and take pride in the ones who shone. At the beginning, all I thought about was getting a job through soccer, meaning that I wanted to get a job that would allow me to remain in Cairo so that I could continue to play soccer. After I gave up soccer, I started to think about becoming a doctor or an engineer because I was strong in math and science—that was the only reason. But when I started reading articles on philosophy by al-'Aqqad and Isma'il Mazhar and others and my reading started to grow more profound, philosophical questions began to raise themselves within me. I discovered that it was these that concerned me, and I imagined that by studying philosophy I would find the true answers. Doesn't the one who studies medicine become a doctor and the one who studies engineering an engineer? In the same way, my study of philosophy would answer the questions that tortured me. I imagined that I would discover the secret of existence and the destiny of man, meaning that when I graduated I would do so taking with me the secret of existence. I used to be astonished to think that people could ignore the secret of existence at the philosophy department and go study medicine or engineering. Of course, my father put his foot down, and when met by my intransigence, he told me, "Go into law like your cousins, and graduate as a judge or a lawyer." But what sort of judge or what sort of lawyer? I wanted the secret of existence. Do you see the naiveté of the idea? Just as you could learn medicine, so you could learn the secret of existence. . . .

Literature and Philosophy

I proceeded in life without a guide. The members of my family were professionals—a doctor, an engineer, a judge—and none of them was interested in literature. Who was to direct me? The question itself was meaningless: to whom should I address it? To al-'Aqqad, for example? There was a dimension of introversion in this. I had grown up reading al-'Aqqad but never seen him. I had never even met Taha Hussein, except the one time when the late Yusuf al-Siba'i invited us to meet him at the Story Club. I believed that literature was a solitary pursuit, a pursuit that I had used to entertain myself until, like a disease, it had gotten out of control. When I obtained my undergraduate degree, the conflict—between philosophy and literature—really started. In the last year of my studies, I became aware of my acute inclination toward literature. I wanted to take a specialization in literature alongside philosophy, but 'Abbas Mahmud informed me that that would be impossible because it was in violation of the prevailing system. While preparing my Master's thesis, I fell prey to an acute conflict. Each night I would ask myself, philosophy or literature? It was a conflict that could have had dangerous consequences. This went on until 1936, when I resolved the quandary in favor of literature, and then I felt a profound, an unequalled, relief. But then a difficulty of a new kind presented itself.

Literature

How was I to catch up with everything I'd missed and add it to my education?

Time was limited and I had much to do. This is why, after I'd graduated and taken up my duties, I continued working at home. It was as though I were still a student, and this made my father worry about me. He used to say to me, "It's as though you hadn't graduated. I see you sitting at your desk day and night and I ask you, 'Are you going to get a doctorate?' and you tell me no. So why are you wearing yourself out?" My father was worried because I was working such long hours. I felt that time was limited, and at the same time I wanted to read, in literature, in science, in history. I wanted to listen to music, and at the same time to write, to write seriously.

In the preceding years, I'd written articles that had appeared in numerous magazines. At the same time, I was writing short stories. But I used to publish in obscure magazines—I'm referring to the stories—meaning that I'd find a small magazine, one that lived off advertisements, and I'd take the initiative in sending them a story. That's why one of the most important days of my life was when I had a story published in *al-Riwaya* magazine. I might even say it was more important than the day I won the State Award of Appreciation. It was the same the day I was published in Salama Musa's *al-Magalla al-gadida*.

I published a number of stories. I don't remember how many and I don't remember which was the first of my stories to be published; students of bibliography may be better equipped than I to make an accounting. The person who chose the collection *Whispers of Madness* was the late 'Abd al-Hamid al-Sahhar. I hadn't wanted to publish that collection; I'd already published the trio of historical novels, as well as *Cairo Modern (al-Qahira al-gadida)* and *Midaq Alley*, and he came to me and said, "Why don't you put out a collection of short stories?" I said to him, "What collection would I publish now? It's too late." I didn't write short stories for the sake of writing short stories: I wrote novels and went around to the publishers, who refused to publish them, so, because I wanted to be published, I wrote short stories. Yes, it's true: that was my motive in writing short stories. And here observe something important: I took the subjects of some of these stories from the novels. Some people have said that my short stories turned into novels but the opposite is true. Al-Sahhar insisted on issuing a short story collection. I gave him a huge number of magazines, magazines whose names I don't remember, but when he saw that I was unhappy, he said, "In that case, let's write the true date of the story. When did al-Zayyat ask you if he could publish a collection?" I said, "In 1938." Al-Sahhar said, "So think of this collection as the first of your books. We'll write '1938' on it." As a result, the reader doesn't know that *Whispers of Madness* was published for the first time after *Midaq Alley*, and not in 1938 as it appears in the list of my works that is found in every book. I was afraid that its publication would make a big stir, but al-Sahhar was the one who insisted and he was the one who made the selection and he was the one who printed it.

'Abd al-Hamid al-Sahhar was a member of the 'Abbasiya set, but a relatively recent one; he had set up the Publishing Committee for Academics and it published us. However, the first book of mine that was ever published had nothing to do with literature. I was a secondary school student when I set about translating *Ancient Egypt (Misr al-qadima)* by James Baikie, and I did so with the goal of strengthening myself in the language. Then I sent it to Salama Musa for him to publish in the form of articles, and I was taken by surprise one day to find someone knocking on the door and handing me a copy of the book in printed form. Salama Musa had printed it as a present for the readers to make up for two months when his *al-Magalla al-gadida* had stopped coming out. I never proofread the book, and that reminds me of a curious event. When it was decided to print *Khufu's Wisdom*, I was asked to proofread it. I would read and cross out the word and write the correct form above it instead of writing it in the margin, as was the convention. As a result, when the printers looked at the margins, they found them empty, so the novel was printed with its misprints. During those years, I came to know Salama Musa but I didn't form a close bond with him. I used to send him articles for publication and he asked to meet me. When I went to see him, he was taken aback because he discovered that I was a student at the university, and because of this it became harder to publish articles thereafter. It seems he had imagined I was a graduate, or an old man.

I published a lot of articles, but most of them were merely introductions to philosophical topics or summaries of some of the things we were reading at the university, which is why I refused totally to collect them in a book. My friend Dr. Muhammad Yusuf Nigm pressed me to reprint them in a book—naturally a book of that sort would sell well—but the reader wouldn't find anything new in it, especially as major writers appeared in the field of philosophy later on, and contributed to it. My philosophical article writing phase ended with my resolution of the conflict between literature and philosophy after my graduation from university, and here I'd like to talk to you in greater detail about the stage that followed that. . . .

Literary Formation and First Writings

Having resolved the philosophy–literature conflict, I found myself facing another major problem. I was twenty-five years old at the time and I had to set up a system by which I could study literature and keep up-to-date with the various aspects of general knowledge. What should I do? Should I begin with Greek literature and then go on reading? Should I pursue the modern age and just go back from time to time to the literature of the past? To review modern literature was my priority, so I started with that. I had no guide, so of course I came across difficulties. Also there was no broad translation activity, which meant that I read the world's classics in English.

It was much easier in those days to obtain the most recent English works than it is today. You could find any book you wanted, and the book that wasn't available you could order and it would reach you in a week at most. I used to make a weekly tour of the downtown bookshops and I still make the same tour every Friday, but it is noticeable how much less diverse and up-to-date are the books on offer now compared to what was on offer in the thirties and forties. I remember that during the Second World War, a certain bookshop owner offered to buy all the books I'd collected at the same price that I'd paid for them, but I refused.

A book that reviewed the history of literature up to 1930 helped me set out a curriculum for my reading. I recall that the author's name was Drinkwater. This book helped me to select my readings; because I had started late, I didn't study any particular writer from beginning to end. The book guided me to each author's particularly important works. I read Tolstoy's *War and Peace* and Dostoevsky's *Crime and Punishment*. I read some of Chekhov's and Maupassant's short stories and at the same time I read some Kafka, Proust, and Joyce. I loved Shakespeare. I loved his irony and his splendor and a warm relationship grew up between us; he was like a friend. I also loved Eugene O'Neal, Ibsen, and Strindberg. I adored *Moby Dick* by Melville and I liked Dos Passos, but I didn't like Hemingway. I was amazed at the fuss that was made over him. The one work of his that I liked was *The Old Man and the Sea*. I found Faulkner too complicated and I admired Joseph Conrad, Sholokhov, Hafiz al-Shirazi, and Tagore. You will notice that I was not influenced by any one writer; rather, all of them contributed to shaping me as a writer. And when I wrote, I did not fall under the influence of any one in particular. I was not dazzled by modern technical developments. Imagine if I'd been influenced by Joyce, and tried to follow the same stream-of-consciousness path! I read *Ulysses* in the mid-thirties. However, when I started writing, I jettisoned all that and went down the realist path.

Realism

I wrote in the realist style and at the very same time I was reading the most savage attacks on realism. Modern world literature, after having been exposed to realism via hundreds of works, retreated inward, to the stream of consciousness, the unconscious, the surrealist. As far as I was concerned, the reality to which I give expression had yet to be given a realistic treatment and it would thus be premature for me to take the lead in employing the modern literary styles about which I was then reading. How was I to dive deep below the surface of a reality whose surface had not yet been described, and whose relationships had not yet been observed? In *Khan al-Khalili*, there are live people, living and suffering, and going to cafés. Diving below the surface seems logical for the hero of Joyce because he's introverted and closed in on himself. What matters is for the writer to grasp what style is needed in order to give expression to his topic and himself. I was without a guide, without a cicerone, and I was writing in a style that was being mocked and declared dead everywhere I looked, but now I believe that my thinking was sound. What made things more difficult is that we have no tradition of novel writing in Arabic literature.

The Arabic Classics

I read contemporary Egyptian writers, but I knew that the short story and the novel were marginal to their lives. *The Return of the Spirit ('Awdat al-ruh)* pleased me as a work of literature, but I found it more like a play than a novel.

No. There was no novel-writing tradition for me to focus on.

Even the authors of novels themselves did not grant the genre recognition. Taha Hussein used to write novels in the summer, but what was Taha Hussein? He was a thinker. Al-'Aqqad wrote *Sara*, but who was al-'Aqqad? He was a thinker. In fact, al-'Aqqad despised the short story and the novel. If people such as these despised the novel, how could one be drawn to it by reading them?

I was working in semi-deserted territory and I had to explore on my own, and lay down the path too.

Another important tributary to my readings was the Arabic classics. I came to know these at an early age, when in secondary school I studied the primary sources of the Arab classical tradition such as *The Compendium (al-Kamil)* of Kamil al-Mubarrad and *The Dictations (al-Amali)* of Abu 'Ali al-Qali. Credit for this goes to my beturbaned Arabic language teachers, and the results showed in the essays I used to write. One Arabic language teacher of mine was named Shaykh 'Abd al-Hadi, and he used to read my essays and praise the old Arabic words: "See the style! See the words nobody can understand!" I read old Arabic poetry but have to confess that I have not read the Arabic classics methodically.

History

After I had resolved the literature–philosophy conflict, I thought about what I had to write. At that period, nationalist feelings were ablaze, along with the call for a return to the glories of the pharaohs. I had read Egyptian history, and at that time there were valuable books available. I decided to dedicate my life to writing the history of Egypt in novel form, and I picked out some thirty-five to forty topics. Shaykh Mustafa 'Abd al-Raziq even told me, "This is like what Jurji Zaydan used to do." That was what I'd planned. However, this desire, or this motive, died out after *Thebes at War*. The desire died out just as it did later after I'd finished writing the *Trilogy*. History was dead. What would bring it back to life? What was the cause of its death? I didn't know. I got the inspiration for *Rhadopis of Nubia* and *Khufu's Wisdom* from two legends. *Thebes at War* was a reflection of the circumstances through which Egypt was passing at the time. This is why you will find that the historical aspects of these books are weak. When they decided to give me a prize for *Rhadopis of Nubia*, Ahmad Amin spoke to me on the telephone and said to me, "I want to ask you a question. Why did you put chariots of war in *Rhadopis of Nubia*?" I said, "I know that chariots of war were introduced by the Hyksos but I wanted to use horses, and I know what I'm doing."

There was a pharaonic tide and that tide had its justifications, since the pharaonic period was the sole bright spot in the confrontation with the bitter circumstances in which we were living. *Thebes at War* was written against the British occupier and the Turkish ruler lurking in the palace. I was on fire against the British and the Turks. I had studied the history of pharaonic Egypt thoroughly, almost to the point of being a specialist in the field, and I determined to write that history in novels. Among the topics I had chosen were the pharaohs called Ramesses and those called Tutmose, and I had an important project on Akhenaton. I regularly attended the lectures of the Department of Antiquities. I studied everything connected to the pharaonic age—the daily life, the methods of war, the religion. How could I throw aside all that effort after *Thebes at War* and write *Cairo Modern*? Maybe because history had ceased to allow me to write what I wanted to. Maybe I wanted to enter directly into the treatment of social subjects. All of that may be true. Thereafter I didn't go back to history. In fact, I considered the effort I'd spent on studying history a waste of time because I never went back to it, I never benefited from it. If it has left any imprint on my formation as a writer, I may not be aware of it, but it may be real. It seems difficult now for me to go back to history, but who knows? I may go back to history one day; our present certainly often seems recalcitrant enough.

Science

I am a passionate reader of science.

I love reading books that summarize and simplify scientific theories. I would even say that reading science is more important to me sometimes than reading literature. Literature gives one pleasure and form and life experience, but general knowledge is to be found in philosophy and science. Note that reading science is not the same as believing in science. I believe in science, and the credit for that goes to the thinkers and writers who promoted science, among them Salama Musa, who alerted us to the role of science in modern civilization. It is true that we look at science differently today than we used to in the nineteenth century. There can be no doubt that it has stepped down from its high throne, if one may so describe it, while at the same time, its achievements have multiplied.

Reading Habits

I read science alongside literature and art. Thus you will find me reading more than one book at a time. I have a voracious appetite for reading that has only been constrained by diabetes, which has limited what I can do over the past year; on doctors' orders, I have been obliged to work for an hour and then take an hour off. Because I started studying literature at a relatively late age, I have never become accustomed to reading a literary work twice. The field was very wide and my appetite for the new didn't permit me to read a work twice. Though, in fact, there were some works that were very dear to me that I did read twice, such as Tolstoy's *War and Peace* and Proust's *Remembrance of Things Past*. However, as I have gotten older, my appetite for reading literature has flagged. Nowadays, if I have in front of me an intellectual book that looks into civilization or science, it's more attractive to me than a novel or a play, perhaps because the second half of the twentieth century has not seen literary giants scaling the heights of writing, in contrast to the past. I mean, when you read Thomas Mann's *Magic Mountain*, you find both artistic and intellectual pleasure. There's no one of that standard today. This year I read Garcia Marquez's *One Hundred Years of Solitude*. If you hadn't lent it to me and recommended it to me, I wouldn't have read it, meaning that if I'd found it in Madbuli's bookshop, I might never have bought it. The new work coming out of Europe is not encouraging, and one should note that Marquez is from Colombia, from Latin America. True, I follow the work of the younger generation carefully, but that's something different. In this case, there's a feeling of duty, and a desire to be aware of the new developments in our literature. This is why you'll find me reading whatever reaches me, so I can find out how the younger generation writes. I know that there's a new vision, a new development. I also read whatever contemporary non-Egyptian Arabic literature comes my way. In the past, creative work in Arabic outside Egypt was very limited; most of what was written was ideational. I've read most of what I've had the opportunity to look at. Can you believe that that was easier in the thirties? You'd find works by Iraqi writers, or Syrian or Maghrebi writers, in the commercial bookshops. That's not the case now. We don't have a common market for books, more's the pity. Most of my reading of the literature of other Arab countries has been via friends. A friend who had been away would come back and give me a book, or an author would send me his book, but there's little on the market.

Intellectualism

There's no doubt that my reading in philosophy had a great impact on me later on. I feel that personally. Some critics say that the intellectual outlook is clear in my works, that they are concerned with ideas. Of course, you know that European literature in the twentieth century was predominantly intellectual in nature. In my estimation, we have not reached that point yet, but our literature is not devoid of ideas. All the same, it is not to be compared with the literature of Sartre or Camus. Literature in the nineteenth century reflected reality in artistic form—life with all its impulses, its emotions, and its reactions, and also the pleasure of story telling, of narration. That changed in the twentieth century. There are novels that seem more like intellectual treatises, in which intellectuality takes precedence over creation.

The Absurd

No, certainly I am not an absurdist. Do you know what 'absurd' means? In brief it means life has no meaning, and for me life has meaning and a goal. My entire literary output is a form of resistance to the absurd. I may have felt the temptation of the absurd, but I resisted it, I rationalized it. I tried to analyze it and then subdue it. Some of the protagonists of *The Harafish* may appear absurd, and their lives may appear to have been lost in vain, but, within the context of the great family, they were not absurd.

No, my dear Gamal, I am not an absurdist. You will find the most perfect expression of the absurd in Beckett; that is the true absurdist vision. It is the loss of faith in anything, not just of faith in religion but faith of any kind. Sometimes feelings of the absurd creep up on us, especially in moments of despair or hardship. Life around us appears cruel, our personal lives in their specific reality appear sometimes absurd. Social absurdity, as you call it, the unreasonableness of reality. Only a triumph of a specific kind that restores our confidence in ourselves can put paid to absurdity. To this day, and from the time we acquire consciousness, we experience continual internal frustrations. We have only to breathe to find someone weighing down on our souls, stifling them and corrupting our lives, and this is terrible. This is why you will never again find that first song of triumph that existed among the generation of 1919. That same generation suffered frustrations, but it tasted victory. We started to gain consciousness as that generation began to fall to pieces—yes, fall to pieces. I began reading the press in 1926. I was fourteen years old. The Revolution had quietened down, the compromises had begun, followed by the frustrations, followed by the repression, and this continued. We were granted a breathing space in 1952, but things soon relapsed, and so it went. In any case, I confess to you that I fell into the absurd for a few minutes after the June 1967 defeat. It's true that resistance had begun, but the reality seemed absurd, terrible.

Language

I was not only a voracious reader; I also liked to acquire books, with the exception of the rare history books that were in the National Library or the university library, which was better stocked than the National Library. I read most world literature in English; I also read in French, but

English more. I couldn't read Proust in French, I read him in English. But I did read Anatole France in French. The hardest thing is to read a work of literature in its original language, because the style is polished and may sometimes be difficult. Reading a science book is easier because the style is straightforward.

The Library

My library is now divided into two sections. One section is in the old house in al-'Abbasiya, where my sister's son, Eng. Mahmud al-Kurdi lives, the other is in my house on Nile Street. The reason is lack of space. After I got married I moved the essential books to the house, and because the space is limited but I keep buying, I have ended up owning a warehouse, not a library, of books. Imagine, when I want to refer to a particular book in my library, I don't go looking for it; it's easier for me to buy a new copy. Searching has become difficult because of the way the books have piled up. I have a huge number of novels and science books, in all fields, and a rare collection of art books—the works of Herbert Read, for example. Each volume contains fifty or sixty paintings. They are priceless now.

Yes, yes. I was one of those who bought a copy of the *Encyclopaedia Britannica* when the Dar al-Ma'arif publishing corporation imported it for the first time. I acquired it because it's a reference for any field one might need. Sometimes, when it became impracticable to obtain foreign books, I would read the *Encyclopaedia*, especially when I was feeling the need for something good to read.

I used to read nonstop, three hours a day. I read after I had done writing because, if I had done the opposite, I wouldn't have been able to sleep.

My appetite for reading was great.

The limit set last year on the numbers of hours I could read came as a painful blow to me.

I am truly sad but I . . . . Praise be to God under all circumstances: I'm still capable of reading even though the time is less.

Out of the Shadows, Into the Limelight

A large number of my stories I published in the early thirties. Most of them aren't in any collection. Likewise, I've completely forgotten the magazines to which I sent my stories. In those days, the number of serious magazines in Egypt was greater than that of entertainment magazines; in fact the latter were few. There were many serious magazines that presented the classics of world literature and the modern classics, and there was no problem in keeping abreast of new developments in culture. General magazines, on the other hand, such as *al-Musawwar*, *Akhir sa'a*, and *al-Lata'if al-musawwara*, were limited in number and distribution, and these magazines only expanded after the Second World War. The number of educated people in Egypt was limited, but a large percentage of those read; if this percentage had remained stable with the rise in the number of educated people—if it had stayed the way it was—you would now have, say, two hundred thousand readers. Yes indeed—two hundred thousand readers for you, specifically. Every paper had a daily literature page and every paper had a special weekly issue, such as *al-Balagh al-usbu'i* and *al-Siyasa al-usbu'iya*, not to mention *al-Magalla al-gadida*, *al-Muqtataf*, and *al-Hadith*.

The First Pound!

I had no relationship with the owners of the magazines in which I published. I sent my stories or my articles in by mail. The only person to call me in was Salama Musa. Writing was not paid, and it seems that when he noticed that I had been writing for him for a long time he wanted to reward me morally; maybe that was the reason he invited me to see him.

I continued to write without remuneration. The first time I was paid for a story, I only received the money after I had caused a crisis. I used to write for *al-Riwaya* and *al-Risala*, for free. Then Salah Dhihni asked me to write a story for *al-Thaqafa*. I gave him a story and it was indeed published. At the end of the year, he phoned me and told me, "My good friend, you have created a problem for us." I said, "God forbid! How come?" He said, "You have one pound in remuneration that you haven't taken." I was taken aback and asked him, "But why are you giving me this pound?" He said, "It's pay for a story." I was even more taken aback. I asked him, "You mean stories get paid for?"

I discovered that while they were reviewing the general budget at the end of the year they had found this pound, which was preventing them from closing the books.

Cheap Editions

In 1943, I started publishing at the Publishing Committee for Academics, which had been founded by the late 'Abd al-Hamid al-Sahhar and his brother Sa'id al-Sahhar, God grant him long life. They printed only two thousand copies of any book. This was the situation up until *Roz al-Yusuf* issued the Golden Book series in a cheap format. They asked me to join them. I went to Sa'id al-Sahhar to let him know because I was morally committed to publishing my books with him. He agreed with a certain asperity, saying, "Look at your books. We printed only two thousand copies of each and some of them are ten years old, but we still have between four and five hundred copies in the warehouse, so what do you think is going to happen to a book that they're going to print fifteen thousand copies of. Obviously it'll never get a second printing." Anyway, we came to an agreement, and I submitted the novel

Khan al-Khalili to *Roz al-Yusuf*, where I had another surprise. For the first time in my life, a book of mine was given continuous publicity, in the form of a caricature of the author presenting his book—a new kind of publishing, and the fifteen thousand copies were sold out in a week. And not just that: the stock of my books that was held in storage at Sa'id al-Sahhar's warehouse sold out too, and then the novels were reprinted, and sold, and went into second, third, and fourth editions.

The cheap edition did not kill off the other editions; on the contrary, it gave them new life. How do you explain that? I don't know. My explanation then was that the number of readers was large and that the cheap edition got into their hands, got into the hands of readers of whose existence we'd been unaware. The Publishing Committee for Academics had extremely limited advertising, just one small advert, but *Roz al-Yusuf* undertook a large publicity campaign. The situation is the same today: there's a big difference between publishing a book with a publishing house and putting it out as part of a cheap series. If the credit for first printing my books goes to al-Sahhar, I am indebted to the Golden Book series for their becoming widely known.

Collapse over *The Cairo Trilogy*

The Cairo Trilogy dealt me a harsh blow, one that caused me great suffering.

After writing *Khufu's Wisdom*, *The Beginning and the End*, *Khan al-Khalili*, *The Mirage (al-Sarab)*, and my other early novels, and after finishing *The Cairo Trilogy*, I took the latter to Sa'id al-Sahhar. *The Cairo Trilogy* was a single novel, entitled *Palace Walk*, and how it got divided into three parts is another story, which I'll tell in a little while. Sa'id al-Sahhar looked at the novel and asked, "What's this?" I said, "A new novel, *Palace Walk*." He took hold of the book, leafed through its thousand pages, and said, "How am I supposed to print this? It's impossible."

I went home in the depths of depression. You have to understand: in my study there were sometimes three unpublished novels and that didn't upset me at all. But that night I fell apart. After all those years of labor, after all those years of exhausting effort, I wasn't going to be able to publish my longest and most precious work? I experienced days of despair. Then once I was at the Story Club and I spoke about my huge novel that had failed to find a publisher, and lo and behold, Yusuf al-Siba'i asked to see it. He said, "We'll put out a magazine." I don't remember exactly when this conversation took place, before the Revolution or after it. I finished *The Cairo Trilogy* in April 1952. Yusuf al-Siba'i took the whole of *Palace Walk* from me. It was a hand-written manuscript, meaning I didn't have another copy. I hadn't had a typewritten copy made. You're right, it could have been lost. If Yusuf al-Siba'i had lost that single copy for any reason, *The Cairo Trilogy* would have been lost forever. After the Revolution and the change in circumstances, he phoned me and said, "We're going to publish the magazine and we're going to publish the novel." Then *al-Risala al-gadida* came out and started publishing *Palace Walk*. Who acknowledged the success of the serialized version? Sa'id al-Sahhar. He told me that the novel was a success, but it would have been impossible to put it out in one volume because it was so big. He suggested that it be divided into three volumes rather than simply three periods. "What about the title?" I asked him. He said, "Give it three titles." That's how the two other titles—*Palace of Desire (Qasr al-shawq)* and *Sugar Street (al-Sukkariya)*—came into being and *Palace Walk* became *The Cairo Trilogy*.

I remember with pain the period following al-Sahhar's refusal to publish it. It was a terrible blow, indeed an insult, especially as he said, the second that he saw it, "What the hell is this?"

The Cairo Trilogy came out and quickly became well known. *Palace Walk* was the first book of mine to sell well outside of a cheap edition. Then it was repeatedly reprinted and the sales continued to the point that the book was pirated in Beirut in 1965. Between 1965 and 1970, sales fell off seriously. The books were dying on the shelves, while Sa'id al-Sahhar's friends abroad were sending him pirated copies. It wasn't only me, but lots of authors who suffered. Piracy continues, but it may have had some justification then; I am referring to the boycott because of the political situation. However, even at the height of my distress over the piracy, I found consolation of another sort, since the pirated copies took me to areas I had never reached before, such as North Africa, because we were not good at distribution. It was a literary, not a materialistic, approach to distribution. More than a million copies of my books were printed, of which I obtained payment for only one hundred and fifty to two hundred thousand. It is ironic that the pirates used to preserve the name 'Maktabat Misr and Sa'id al-Sahhar' on the covers; they were the same covers, but a little faded.

In the past, I used to imagine myself at the age when I had earned a full pension and planned to become a full-time writer, far removed from my job. But when I reached that stage of my life, I discovered that I still needed my full salary. Living costs increase all the time. Can you believe that the only salary I ever received that lasted me from the beginning of the month to the end, and from which I was even able to save, was the salary that I received when I joined the ministry of religious endowments in the thirties? I got eight pounds net, and it was during the years of the economic crisis when businesses went bankrupt and only those on fixed salaries, by whom I mean government employees, escaped its miseries. I never thought of literature as a permanent source of income. Practically speaking, that was impossible. However, there was one period when it was possible for me to live off my earnings from literature, and that was the few years during which my books were continuously being printed. That came to an end in 1965, when the pirating of my books abroad started.

Now I'm well taken care of, praise God.

The Major Novels: *The Cairo Trilogy*

To tell you the truth, the idea of *The Cairo Trilogy* came to me in fits and starts. I can pin down the first flashes: I was reading a book about the ABCs of the novel (in fact, I read numerous books about the art of the novel). The first kind of novel this book reviewed was what they call 'the generational novel,' in other words, the novel of different time periods that reviews many successive generations. I liked the form. As I read about this particular type of novel, I tried to remember if I had read a literary work of this type. I hadn't. By the way, there are things that you read and don't respond to and there are other things that you do react positively to. The thing that I felt strongly within me was my need to write a novel of this type. However, I hesitated. Novels of this sort require long practice and total absorption, meaning that if I had any other ideas for novels I should finish those first—such as *Midaq Alley* or *The Mirage*. During this period, Taha Hussein published his novel *The Tree of Misery (Shagarat al-bu's)*, which I found very similar to this type, the generational novel, though it's a bit short.

At the same time, I made a major mistake, one that I have never since repeated: at this period, I spoke a great deal about this type of novel and went to great lengths to explain my ideas and how I intended to write one one day. Then one of the writers who had heard me went and set about writing a novel of this sort, which he published six months later. This experience taught me never to say anything; that is, never to give away any details of my work in progress. Obviously, you can imagine what artistic merit the novel had, given that it was written and published in just six months.

Anyway, to go back to Taha Hussein, *The Tree of Misery* was a generational novel, but it was short. The idea took hold of me completely and I now started reading the great novels that concern themselves with the passing of generations. I read *The Forsythe Saga* by Galsworthy, *War and Peace* by Tolstoy, and *Buddenbrooks* by Thomas Mann. At a certain moment, I felt I had got the hang of the subject, but here I have to clarify one thing: I wasn't accustomed to reading any particular works before writing one of my own novels. These readings were a part of my broader cultural and literary background. My works belong to the realist school, to which countless novels belong. The sole literary work I have written that is unlike anything else I have read and that I cannot place within any particular school is *Fountain and Tomb*.

Characters Real and Created

In the years preceding the *Trilogy* details were building up, details taken from all over the place—from the times I spent sitting and talking with my friends, from discussions, from late-night gatherings. Ninety percent of the characters in the *Trilogy* have their origins in real people, some of them from my own family, some of them neighbors, some of them relatives. Naturally, the real-life model is forgotten, because the act of creation transforms them into something else. The original as it exists in reality is forgotten and is known historically only as a tablet on which you inscribe. The original is not important. I have found that this is an experience in which my own personality has no role.

The *Trilogy* is the only work to contain a large part of my own thoughts and feelings. Some people say to me, "Isn't there something of you in the character of Ahmad 'Akif?" That's completely untrue. Ahmad 'Akif was a real person. He was an official at the university, in the university administration to be precise. He read the novel after it was published and didn't recognize himself. It never occurred to him that I had taken the inspiration for the novel's hero from him. This points to another strange thing—people's vision of themselves, other people's vision of them, and how far apart the two are. The Ahmad Effendi 'Akif whom I knew was no more than a petty official in the university administration, but he thought he knew everything about Egypt. He had only an undergraduate degree, but he thought he knew all the sciences in the world. He was silly and superficial and the risk I took was that, if he discovered that I had used him in *Khan al-Khalili*, it might threaten my life: he might have assaulted me, since he was in no way normal.

While we're on the subject, I risked my life one other time because of a character I took from life—the hero of *The Mirage*: he was a real person who'd obtained a law degree and his name was Husayn Badr al-Din. He never read novels or any kind of literature. One of our friends in the 'Abbasiya set—maybe you remember him, 'Ali Muhammad 'Ali—went to him and told him mockingly, "Naguib's writing about you," at which the man pulled out his revolver and made threats against me. Naturally, I kept out of his way. He was a rich man who had lost his fortune and was reduced to begging. He used to sleep at Fishawi's and went to prison on drug charges. The problem in his life was his relationship with his mother. He always used to go around with lots of women, but he never actually had sex with them. He might have killed me, even though he hadn't read the novel: he was a violent, abnormal person. In the novel you find a different person, gentle and mild-mannered. My friend 'Ali Muhammad 'Ali almost brought about a tragedy with his love of mockery. Husayn Badr al-Din went to Kuwait, where he worked as an assistant to a friend of his father's. Then he died.

As for the real Ahmad 'Akif, though, I don't know if he's still alive or has passed away. I remember that he visited me for the last time thirty years ago. Then he disappeared. Now let's get back to the *Trilogy*.

The *Trilogy*

I wrote the *Trilogy* when I was in my prime—perseverant, full of endurance. A work like that needed perseverance, and health. If you ever saw the archives I made for the *Trilogy*, you'd understand just how true that is, how much planning went into each character. Each character had something like a file, so that I wouldn't forget their features and characteristics, especially as I only worked each year from October to April because of the allergy that affects my eyes. The planning for the novel as a whole was similar in that a lot of paper and notebooks were used up in providing a consistent structure. It took me more than four years to write it—carefully, calmly, slowly, urged on by the desire to achieve something excellent. My struggle with language had yet to begin; that went along with modern forms. I was writing in an understated style.

By the way, the greatest struggle I ever got into in my life was with the classical Arabic language, starting with the first book. In *Khufu's Wisdom* you'll find a Qur'anic style. As we have learned, style has no relation to content, and when I came to write in a realist style, it was difficult. The style didn't respond to my control, it didn't obey me. Unawares, I entered a struggle between the language and myself. If I'd realized that I was having this struggle, I might have lost my way, but the quarrel went on unconsciously. How could I subdue the language? How could I make it obey my will? How could the dialog be acceptable even though it was in the classical idiom? This is why, if you review some of the early stories, you'll find things that make you laugh. For example, you may find a character in a low-class café speaking in the most bombastic classical style. I had no model to guide me. None of the geniuses who had gone before had written of the popular neighborhoods, or, if they had written about them, they had written the dialog in colloquial. There was nothing difficult about that. The problem was how to develop the classical language so that it could become artistic and realistic, and it was the most difficult thing I found, or stumbled into, in my life as a novelist. There was no model to use as a guide. It is noteworthy that Dr. 'Abd al-Muhsin Taha Badr, in his *Naguib Mahfouz: The Vision and the Performance (Nagib Mahfuz: al-ru'ya wa-l-ada')*, did not speak about me in terms of my context; he didn't speak of the state in which I found the novel, how I developed it, and how far I got; he didn't take into account the circumstances in which I worked at the beginning. He speaks in absolute terms, as though he were describing an English writer. If he had gone back to the moment in time when I started writing and discovered the difficulties that had faced me, he would have written differently. This is why his study is abstract, a purely intellectual study.

In My Head Forever

Let's get back to the *Trilogy*. You could say that the material for it had lived with me since childhood. I had lived with the people I wrote about at different times of my life. The point is, how was it possible for me to pour all these details into one work? To tell you the truth it's difficult to say why it came out that way and not in some other form. It could have come out in the end in multiple forms. How it came to be arranged in my brain cells in that particular way, that's what I can't find a clear explanation for.

The *Trilogy* was my preoccupation throughout the years during which I worked on it, and here I'd like to make an important observation for you. If you have a particular subject in mind, don't put it off. Why? After the Revolution, I had an idea for a novel on modern Egypt. I didn't think of it as a trilogy, though I planned it out on that basis. At that period, I didn't have the patience or the endurance or the confidence that life would be long enough to complete it. While I was writing the earlier *Cairo Trilogy*, on the other hand, I had an undeniable feeling that I would finish it. Of course, one can die at any time, but I miss that feeling now. I don't think I could take the risk of such a huge work at my age now. No. I spent a year on *The Harafish*. I thought about it for about a year and I spent a year writing it. It was an outpouring of the imagination and didn't call for a great effort like that required for the *Trilogy*, the realist work, which called for observation and assembly. In terms of the timespan, *The Harafish* was compact, unlike the *Trilogy*. The characters of the *Trilogy* never left my mind, and that is what allowed me to preserve the novel's overall direction. Even during the vacation, or in the hours when I was separated from it due to my job at the ministry of religious endowments, even in the cinema, I lived with the characters and the events, and when I resumed writing after some time away from it, I didn't reread what I'd written earlier. God rest his soul, Muhammad 'Abd al-Halim 'Abd Allah told me that he was careful to read what he'd written before. I read the work after I've written it out for a second time: after the first clean draft, I wait for a while; then I reread it, and I always feel dissatisfied. I feel the difference between the initial vision and what I actually produced, between the ambition and what was realized. But this dissatisfaction doesn't lead me to erase what I've written. The only time I was obliged to erase work I'd written was after I had finished the novel *Beyond Passion (Ma wara' al-'ishq)*, which I wrote in recent years. After I'd finished it, I felt a terminal lack of satisfaction. It would be difficult for me to convey to you how exasperated I felt with it. I was happy with the first part, but the second part made me feel uncomfortable. However, it was a different kind of discomfort than that produced by the discrepancy between what you had in mind and what was actually realized. I had three unpublished novels at that time—*Wedding Song (Afrah al-qubba)*, *Arabian Nights and Days (Layali alf layla)*, and *Beyond Passion*. I sent the first two off to the publisher, but I kept *Beyond Passion* back for the following year so that I could look at it again.

How do I view the *Trilogy* now? The truth is that I no longer think about it. I haven't read it again. But one could say that the *Trilogy*, *Children of the Alley*, and *The Harafish* are the works of mine that I love most. In the *Trilogy*, as I said, there's a large part of me, embodied in the character Kamal 'Abd al-Jawad. Kamal does not find himself in the *Trilogy* by chance. Not because he's a piece of me; rather, he came out in this form because he's inseparable from the subject of the novel. The novel comes from a classic age, ends deep in a romantic age, and is headed toward an analytic age. In it, the East meets the West, but not through a journey such as those undertaken by Tawfiq al-Hakim or Yahya Hakki or al-Tayyib Salih. It represents the person who found the West while in the East, the manifestations of civilization coming to his doorstep, and who had no choice but to interpret these changes in the soul, the spirit, and the mind. Given that I had undergone this huge experience, it necessarily reflected itself in the novel. I found that I preferred someone from the in-between generation to represent it. Needless to say, it was impossible to find it in Yasin. Fahmi could have represented it, but Fahmi died. Kamal's crisis was my crisis and much of his suffering was my suffering. It is from this that my love of the *Trilogy* and my nostalgia for it come.

Great Literature Springs from the Self

As you get older, you both feel and comprehend that the place where your life started will also be your final refuge.

As though recapitulating the cycle of life, you encounter a new world that seems, at first blush, not to be your world. It is not enough to understand any given world for it to become your own private world. Feeling truly at home in that world demands something deeper than that. We are heading toward a new world, but that world is assuredly not one in which I shall feel completely at home. I am at the end of a stage, of a life, let me say. What is the total life experience that I have undergone? You will find it incarnated in the old, by which I do not mean a return to the latter's values, or a rejection of the new. I mean it in the sense of its being your own private refuge, because you have been at home in it and have understood it. As for the new, that which is still to come, you wish it well and nothing more, because you will never participate in it yourself. As an illustration, I have children now. I understand very well that they will live a completely different life and that I shall never participate in it. In the face of this unsettledness, in the face of this new world, you turn to your childhood, to the age of past security.

This may be an answer to your question about my nostalgia for the *hara* and the sources from which the novel *The Harafish* was drawn, and the ability to recall a reality that has disappeared. It seems to me that the older you get, the more you remember your childhood, recalling details that you thought had gone for ever. Why? Because you lived that period as a whole, spontaneous life. It was my experience that all my first experiments with the novel were the result of a life lived without planning, in which human relationships predominated, in which you knew a person as a person and no more, in which there was affection, revulsion, love—all of it natural.

As life progresses, you start to observe people and transform them into things and objects, at which point they lose a major dimension. I can imagine you, for instance, playing in the neighborhood, knowing people in a perfectly natural way, with all that is good and bad in them. Today, however, you have in all likelihood lost that past spontaneity. On the contrary, you have your developed philosophy of life and your way of looking at things. It may be that you look at people from a class perspective, in which case humanity has lost one of its dimensions. When I was young, I would see one of the poor and pity them and mourn for them. Or I would see someone wealthy and be repulsed by something in him, or the reverse. When I grew older, I started to put the one in one niche and the other in another. This one is with me, this against me. This way of looking at things lacks dimensionality.

The first part of life consists of spontaneity and naturalness and connects you to man in all his aspects; and it cannot be replaced. The older you get and the more you acquire a philosophy and a vision, the more these aspects change. You acquire a perspective that allows you to see things more clearly than another person, and there are things that that other is blind to and cannot see. This is why, when I made my first experiments, when I started to write, I absolutely could not imagine that I would reach a given point, or find therein something to write about. Why? Because everything I saw was worth writing about, and that seemed impossible. When I grew older, however, and gained a vision and experience, these appeared in the choice of topics, which corresponded to my vision. This is why you can go years without finding something to write about.

I read about lots of events in the press and they had no effect on me; then one day, I read about the incident with Mahmud Amin Sulayman and from this was born *The Thief and the Dogs*. I got into a real state over the man. I felt that he represented an opportunity to embody the reactions and thoughts that I was thinking but could not express—the relation between the individual, authority, and society. Of course, after writing about him, I hadn't written the story of Mahmud Amin Sulayman. The actual character became Sa'id Mahran. At an early stage, before that, every incident seemed to deserve to be written about. Nowadays, how many events pass before me without being, from my perspective, worth writing about! The real mine is in the distant past. There you will find you love everyone you knew and want to write about them. As for the present, it's the opposite.

Form and Content

My nostalgia for the *hara* is part of my nostalgia for what is authentic. When I started writing novels, I used to believe that there was a right form and a wrong form; I thought the European novel form was sacred. As you get older, you find that your vision changes and that you want to move away from everything that has been imposed upon you, but in a spontaneous and natural way, not just for the sake of getting out of or deliberately breaking the form. You find yourself searching for a melody that you extract from the depths of your being, whatever melody that may be, whether it takes you back to the past or leads you toward modernism, or even takes you back to the folktale. In other words, it's as though you were saying, are not the forms in which others have written paths that they themselves created? Why should I not create my own personal form that I feel comfortable with?

As far as I am concerned, my revolt against everything both European and traditional has increased over the last fifteen years. I have gained more confidence in myself. I have started to search more for the melody within myself with which I can write. My movement toward the folktale is one sign of this phase. I would single out for mention *The Harafish*. After *The Harafish* I tried to find the inspiration for a work set in the past, namely *Arabian Nights and Days*, which is an as yet unpublished novel. But I have to make something important clear to you: imitating the past is like imitating the present: both are a form of captivity. What matters is to look for what is in harmony with your identity.

Of course, the European writer who started writing at the same time I did has been looking for his identity from day one; he doesn't suffer from complexes because he doesn't get his culture from the outside. As far as we writers who belong to the world that is called 'developing' or 'backward' are concerned, however, we once used to believe that the realization of a genuine identity could be achieved only at the expense of the elimination of our own identities, meaning that the European novel form was sacred and to abandon it blasphemy. This led me to imagine, at a certain moment, that the role of our generation was to write 'proper' novels, because I used to imagine that there was a correct novel and an incorrect novel. Now, the theory has changed. The real novel is the one that springs from the inner melody. It follows that I neither imitate the *maqama* form nor imitate Joyce. In other words, the only thing that annoys me now is imitation itself, even imitation of the old. And what I genuinely hope for from the generation that follows ours, and which has brought us into the global mainstream, is that it be more loyal as far as this point is concerned, more loyal, that is, to identity, because there is no reason why only the topic should be local: the form should be too. The day we achieve this, we will be able to say that we have presented the world with a truly Arab literature.

Adrift on the Nile and *The Thief and the Dogs* may have been an attempt to break out of the novel's traditional form, as you say, but note that that still took place within the framework of the European novel. The fact is that we contain a measure of authenticity no matter how much we try to imitate. This is why the stream of consciousness is no longer, in our hands, the same stream of consciousness as over there. Similarly, the irrational has become, at the hands of our writers, a different irrationality: our irrationality leads to the rational. The matter was never one of simple mimicry, but of the creation of something different.

Every writer has a certain cast of characters with whom he prefers to deal, but this doesn't come about as a result of planning. The topic brings the right character along with it. Sometimes one may have known characters and then forgotten them; then, at a certain period, they return in force, after one has discovered his course, as a writer for the theater or a novelist. Generally, the writer, when he is in his twenties, has an infinite stock of experiences. These have their impact on his feelings and accumulate. The problem then becomes, where should you start? This is why the moments of inspiration pass quickly. It's the opposite when you get older. At this stage, you will have been liberated from the pressure of the multiple emotional states from which you have fashioned your works. With advancing age, the choice becomes more difficult. At the beginning, it's almost as though you have a big stock of ready goods. Then you finish them up. After that comes the selectivity.

It makes me laugh when people say, "That writer's said all he has to say." We're not in the presence of a philosopher here, or an intellectual, who might write one or two books and then it's all over. As far as the writer is concerned, it's something like the libido—so long as he's alive, it needs to find expression. It's the foundation. If that capacity goes, it's all over, even if the whole world is made of topics. That's the foundation. It's not about people saying to you, "That guy has something he wants to say. What is it he's trying to say?" This is why, when you ask of any writer, "What's he trying to say?" it's hard to answer. However, it's easy to answer a question like that for Schopenhauer or Nietzsche. One of the strangest questions I hear is when someone asks, "What are you trying to say in this story?" I mean, if I wanted to say something specific, I'd say it in a sentence or an article, and that would be that.

Politics and the Revolution: "I am not opposed to the July Revolution."

Politics entered my life in childhood, when I used to see the demonstrations in Bayt al-Qadi Square. At home, my father and mother were sympathetic to the Wafd, and when Sa'd Zaghlul was mentioned it was respectfully and devoutly. When I started to read the newspapers, I would run my eye over the page until I came across the name of the Leader and would linger there. However, the ones who sowed the seed of patriotism in our souls and taught us its principles were our teachers, especially the beturbaned professors of Arabic. During class, they'd stop delivering the lesson and instead deliver discourses on patriotism. They would rebuke the students who did not take part in the demonstrations or who dodged them. The woman with a pot lid, a pestle, or a stick in her hand, the veiled women who marched sedately and in good order were, it's true, much to be praised. But the real demonstrations were in the popular neighborhoods.

The disturbances would start right after morning assembly. The clapping would get louder. Then we'd throw spoons (the schools used to provide us with lunch) and the teachers would encourage us to go out and join the demonstrations. What I still remember and what still moves me to this day is the women's demonstrations in Bayt al-Qadi Square and the streets of al-Gamaliya. The history books will tell you about the demonstrations by veiled society ladies and how the students of Saniya College went out onto the streets, but they will not mention the demonstrations by the women of the lanes and alleys. I saw them with my own eyes. They were like nothing else. In the photos of the demonstrations you see the veiled women who were the wives of the pashas and they tell you, "The Egyptian Woman." What Egyptian Woman? I saw thousands of women in al-Gamaliya riding on donkey carts, women of the backstreets.

Author's Note: This brings to our mind the chapter on Shaykh Haggar al-Minyawi in the novel Mirrors:[4]

> Shaykh Haggar al-Minyawi was the Arabic teacher at our primary school and moved up with us to secondary school. He was from Upper Egypt and spoke its dialect. He was strongly built, tall, and dark-skinned, and he gave little care to his appearance—a turban too small and ill-matching colors in his jubbah and caftan. But he forced respect with a strong personality, command of his subject, and tremendous courage. He was not narrow-minded and loved a joke, and he recited beautiful poetry to us. Once he had a quarterstaff-fencing contest with the sports teacher in the schoolyard; swinging dexterously, he beat his opponent amid loud applause.
>
> Gaafar Khalil came late to class after we had taken our seats. As he loved to joke, imitating our teacher, he said 'Good morning' to him in classical Arabic: "*'Im sabahan.*"
>
> The class laughed, Gaafar was pleased with himself.
>
> The shaykh waited until he sat down, then called. "Gaafar Khalil."
>
> He stood up.
>
> "Conjugate *'im sabahan*."
>
> Gaafar failed, and the shaykh opened his grade-book and gave him a zero.
>
> "But it's difficult!" Gaafar protested.
>
> "Then why do you use what you don't understand?" the shaykh asked quietly.

In primary school—age of the revolution—he taught Arabic and nationalism. He seized any opportunity to talk nationalism, recall glorious memories, and eulogize the heroes; we followed with tears in our eyes. He talked of Saad Zaghloul as a saint or thaumaturge, considering his leadership a heavenly mission, a miracle of history. We learned about Saad's upbringing, his skill as a lawyer, his positions as Minister of Education and Minister of Justice, his leadership, his challenge of British might, his magic and eloquence, and what he held for the country's future.

"His eloquence stirred emotions, and in his name the revolution started," he told us.

He defined the perfect student. "He who acquires knowledge and revolts against tyrants."

We loved him as much as we respected him, receiving from him nationalism and a purity of identity. Because of him we loved Arabic and adored its poetry.

In secondary school, the flavor of struggle changed. English faces receded, and those of their Egyptian allies appeared. Partisan politics occupied first place in the struggle, and the shaykh fought the new battle with the same force and steadfastness.

"The battle is the same, but the enemies have increased: we must double our efforts."

The day of our strike during Muhammad Mahmoud's regime, the day Badr al-Ziyadi was killed, the headmaster demanded he ask the students to return to their classrooms. He was irascible by nature, flaring when challenged in blind fury; he mounted the dais in front of the headmaster's office and cried in a terrible voice, "Learning demands order, the homeland demands struggle. You only have your conscience, so use it . . ."

The headmaster sent a report to the Minister of Education, and he was soon fired. The day he was absent from school and the word spread, students stormed the headmaster's office; he was forced to flee the school, and the Ministry transferred him for fear of his life. The shaykh returned to the school during the Wafd government, but was fired again in Sidqi's regime and moved to Bayn al-Ganayin, to a private school owned by a known Wafdist. During the treaty government, he was appointed inspector in the Ministry of Education, and received a just settlement. In the 1942 elections, he ran on the Wafd platform and won, and again in 1950. I met him several times at Reda Hamada's house, and met some of his sons. When political parties were dissolved after the July revolution, he returned to his village in Upper Egypt and never left it again. I don't know if he's still alive or if he has passed on.

In September of either 1952 or 1953, walking in front of the old army club in Shatbi, I saw members of the Wafd in the club yard ringed by soldiers. I gathered from passers-by that they had been arrested and were being taken to Cairo. I spotted, among the officers supervising the operation, Muhammad Haggar, son of our old shaykh Haggar al-Minyawi. I contemplated the situation, looked long at the son, remembered the father, then imagined I was hearing the roaring of time, carrying its conflicting contradictions.

I Almost Lost My Life

I took part in all the demonstrations. I remember that once I was walking with a number of friends on Muhammad 'Ali Street when suddenly we saw an Egyptian pick up a large rock, strike the head of an English policeman on a motorcycle, and bring him to the ground. At the same instant, we saw soldiers on horseback coming from the direction of al-'Ataba al-Khadra'. We looked behind us as we made to turn and run away and were surprised to find our way blocked by the army. We were surrounded, there was no one but us on the street, and the body of the dead Englishman lay in front of us. The Egyptian had fled. As you know, some of the backstreets off Muhammad 'Ali slope downward, and to get to them you have to go down some steps. One of us yelled, "Run! Run!"

We ran. I ran as fast as I knew how, from *hara* to *hara*, until we were taken unawares by a dead end that gave onto no further point of escape. We felt a devastating despair, but suddenly a woman looked out from a balcony and pointed to the door of the house. We entered, closing the door behind us, and she looked at us from the top of the stairs.

"Come on up."

We went up to the roof, crossed it to another neighboring roof, descended by the stairway, and waited for about half an hour, during which a terrible silence reigned. Then we went out and walked to 'Abd al-'Aziz Street, and from there to al-'Ataba al-Khadra'.

The demonstration in which Fahmi 'Abd al-Jawad dies in the *Trilogy* was a real demonstration, historically speaking. I didn't make up this incident in the *Trilogy*. Fahmi's demonstration took place in the Azbakiya Garden. It was a licensed demonstration and there were students, workers, and judges, and suddenly the British opened fire and killed a number of people. I don't know why I chose that demonstration specifically for Fahmi to die in. This is a point I can't explain.

Blasphemy

There was no debate that the Wafd was the party of the nation, and anyone who said he wasn't a Wafdist seemed to our eyes to be committing blasphemy. The Wafd gave expression to the national and social cause. The first coup against the constitution was a disaster. Afterward, I used to walk and talk to myself out of frustration and grief. Then the social problem started to attract attention, and added to that was the influence on me of Salama Musa. For all these reasons, I decided that the most suitable place for me was the left wing of the Wafd. Thus, when the July Revolution came and proclaimed its principles, I thought that they were the very principles the Wafdist left wing would have applied if they had been in power, and that is why I truly welcomed the Revolution. Indeed, the Revolution went beyond the Wafdist left wing in changing the property laws, which is something the Wafdist left would not have brought about. I truly welcomed the Revolution. Of course, we would have preferred the Revolution to have taken the Wafd as its foundation, given that it was the old popular base. But what happened was precisely the opposite of that, because the Revolution had its own popular base, and later on this was threatened.

Unfortunately, the Revolution saw the Wafd as an enemy, and because it represented a popular base this led to the beginning of the attack on democracy. In my opinion, the democratic course could have continued if the Revolution had relied on its achievements, such as the attack on feudalism and the ending of the occupation. The best of those in the political parties would have joined the Revolution. However, it lost the opportunity and thus fell into the format of military rule. It's true that it achieved important things, but the absence of democracy threatened the reforms, and if you look now at what took place, you will find that it was all compromised by the lack of consultation and democracy. Most of the mistakes that occurred were the result of one person's having unique freedom of opinion and decision. Individual rule ends up acting like fate and destiny, and how you do depends on luck.

The Leader

I didn't see Sa'd Zaghlul with my own eyes. The day I went to 'Abdin to see him, he came in his automobile to meet the king, but there were too many people in the way for me to see him. I didn't catch a glimpse of him. I went to the House of the Nation, Sa'd Zaghlul's home, in al-Nahhas's day. Among the scenes that I remember is Sa'd Zaghlul's funeral. Of course, it's difficult to compare it to Gamal Abd al-Nasser's because Cairo in the early years was only a million people, but for sure the two scenes were among the most impressive Cairo witnessed this century. Sa'd was loved to an amazing degree. I have a Coptic friend. A year or two ago—I don't remember exactly—he showed me the invitation to his sister's wedding. As you know, a wedding invitation has to be joyful. This one, however, had a black border and on it was written "So and so invite you to such and such a church to attend the wedding of . . . and condolences on the death of the Leader of the Nation." Naturally, under normal circumstances this would have been regarded as an evil portent. Have you ever seen or heard of a wedding invitation of that type?

It was an indescribable period. Even the historian who writes about it differs in his description from those who lived through it.

Some people see this love for Sa'd as excessive, but that love was a school for patriotism. Egypt boycotted foreign goods at the slightest provocation. You would find the big foreign stores completely emptied of customers while the companies selling Egyptian manufactured goods were unbearably crowded. Anything Egyptian, no matter how badly made, was a source of pride.

I Am Not Hostile to the Revolution

You will find politics in everything I write. You may find a story that is devoid of love, or anything else, but not of politics, because that is the axis of all our thought. The political conflict is always there. Even in *Children of the Alley*, which might be described as a metaphysical novel, you will find the struggle over the religious endowment. After the revolution of July 1952, I dealt with very sensitive topics, as in *Miramar* or *Adrift on the Nile*. In fact, you said something very true two weeks ago. You said, "Naguib Mahfouz, when he writes, doesn't give a damn about anything and he forgets everything." That is very true.

Sometimes, when I heard the reactions, I used to expect terrible things, especially after a story like "Fear" *(al-Khawf)*. Once someone asked me in the street what it meant. It may have been an innocent question, but I got scared. But I want to make it clear that I criticized the way things were as one who was part of them. I never rejected the July Revolution, and I wrote nothing against it. As you know, there are anti-revolution novels. I used to pay careful attention to anything negative that might harm the reputation of the Revolution. You won't find a word, either direct or implied, against the agricultural reform or the gains of the workers and peasants. In *Miramar* there's the opportunism of the Arab Socialist Union. That was a fact, which may have been a reason for my not getting smacked down. It's also true that your feeling of innocence gives you courage, meaning that I wasn't a member of a secret organization or connected to some embassy or other. It would have made no sense for me to be against the Revolution and then write for *al-Ahram* and be given all the opportunities that I was granted.

My Daughter Asks, "Who Was Sa'd Zaghlul?"

I didn't know any of the Wafd leaders personally. All the Wafdists I loved, I became acquainted with at Tawfiq al-Hakim's symposium during recent years. Do you remember Mahmud Ghanim? I met him at Tawfiq al-Hakim's and he told me he'd seen me on television and heard me say that the leader I loved most was Sa'd Zaghlul, and he'd jumped out of his chair in fright. He told me, "I thought they'd arrest me, not you, and I went and asked, 'Who is that?'" After the *Trilogy* came out, many Wafdists found in it the good things to be said about the Wafd. Even those who'd left the Wafd before the Revolution read it and recognized themselves in it. Ibrahim 'Abd al-Hadi, for example, used to read it and urge others to read it. Many of those from the period that the *Trilogy* deals with had died. The name of Sa'd Zaghlul wasn't mentioned in the schools. After the appearance of the New Wafd three years ago, they wanted to revive the memory of Sa'd and of al-Nahhas. My youngest daughter, hearing a new name, asked me about Sa'd Zaghlul—if he was still alive and where he was from. Naturally, it gave me a big shock.

'Young Egypt' and 'The Brotherhood'

I knew about the Muslim Brotherhood and Young Egypt and I followed their news. Young Egypt started as a youth activity, along with the 'piaster project' for building a factory to make tarbooshes, but it concealed a political goal. Its leader was an opportunist: he announced his support for Muhammad Mahmud. How can you support a moderate trend when you yourself are proclaiming extremism? Suddenly we found they'd become Fascists. We thought of them as enemies and I had no sympathy for them. But the ones I hated from the beginning were the Muslim Brotherhood. At the start, the Brothers were a religious society that brought together Wafdists and non-Wafdists, but when we came across them they had started to compete with the Wafd and regard them as enemies. We believed any competitor to the Wafd undermined its striking power. In the elections, the Wafd would always nominate Coptic candidates to oppose the Brothers', and the Wafd's candidates always swept the board.

With very few exceptions, such as 'Abd al-Hamid al-Sahhar, who leaned toward the Brothers, I didn't have any friends from other political tendencies. He used to tell me, "Come and meet Shaykh al-Banna and then make up your mind," but I couldn't stomach that way of life under any circumstances.

'Abd al-Nasser

I never met with Nasser privately, but I did see him three times. When I won the Order of Merit, First Class, I went up to the stage and shook his hand and then returned to my seat. The second time was in 1957; he met with a number of Arab writers and I was one of those who went to the meeting. The third time was at *al-Ahram* when he visited it in 1969, if my memory serves me correctly. He spoke to everyone and to me he said, "How are those people of yours from al-Husayn? It's been a long time since we read a story of yours."

Haykal said to him, "Don't worry. He's got a story coming out tomorrow."

It was a Thursday. Haykal said, "What can we do? Those stories of his could get him sent to prison!"

"No," Nasser told him. "They could get the editor-in-chief sent to prison!"

Needless to say, Nasser and Sa'd Zaghlul were altogether different kettles of fish. Nasser achieved many notable things for the country that cannot be ignored, and it's difficult to compare them. Sa'd Zaghlul was the first spark. He wanted independence. Nasser came to the country when it was already semi-independent. He carried out a true social revolution, but unfortunately the Revolution took a stand hostile to Sa'd Zaghlul. His name was even banned from books and movies and so on. Now things have changed again as they always do. A few days ago, I saw a movie about the death of Tito; all the world leaders who knew Tito were shown—with the exception of Nasser, and you know how close he was to Tito!

History and Tragedy

I was averse to forming any relationships with politicians or people in official positions. I didn't make an effort to meet anyone. Unfortunately, our recent history is all revolutions and reversals. If things had gone properly since the time of Muhammad 'Ali, we'd be like Japan by now. The politician of genius is the one who understands the circumstances, then takes the appropriate decision—how far to take on the foreign powers, and when? What if . . . ? But history doesn't have a place for 'What if?' and people don't remember history until things have turned to tragedy.

The Gang Leaders and the Cafés

My memories of the gang leaders, or *futuwwat*, go back to the district of al-Husayn. It was the normal thing when I was young for every neighborhood, or quarter, to have its gang leader. I saw them on two types of occasion.

The first was the wedding procession, which would start after midnight. I'd wake up to the sound of someone singing and his hashish-smoking fellow song enthusiasts picking up the refrain, and there would be men carrying lanterns. They would pass in front of the police station in Bayt al-Qadi Square, emerging from any of the neighborhoods. Usually the gangs would confront a wedding procession, since this was the best opportunity to take revenge if there were any old feuds. The wedding would then turn to woe. I saw a procession turn into a bloody battle in front of the police station.

The second occasion would be when rival gang leaders decided to go out to an open space to settle a quarrel—the *futuwwat* of al-'Utuf, for example, with the *futuwwat* of Qasr al-Shawq. Each gang boss had his men. These would shoulder panniers full of bricks and bottles and they'd all set off. There was an open space called Ard al-Mamalik. After they'd all smashed one another up, I'd see the results—cars carrying them to the Gamaliya police station, where police reports would be written up on them; then the ambulances would come and take away the wounded.

I also saw a third sight: a man of amazing size, a blind giant, though you couldn't really call him a gang boss. He usually went about minding his own business, but if he was provoked, he would turn into a terrifying force. With my own eyes, I saw him defeat an entire police platoon. Any order to arrest him was considered a near impossible mission. In fact, about fifteen years ago, I read an article about him in either *Akhir sa'a* or *al-Musawwar*. There were no pictures, just memories that seem to have been written by someone from the neighborhood.

Author's Note: This brings to our mind Story No. 41 from Fountain and Tomb:[5]

> The most gargantuan form I've ever seen belongs to Ibrahim the Ape. I can't imagine a taller or broader man existing in any time, any place. A minaret, he picks his way around by poking with a dreadful great staff, his feet shuffling along like immense turtles beneath him. Our alley believes his blindness is really a sign of God's mercy.
>
> When he turned his hand to begging, all other beggars quit the vicinity because none of them dared repeat the formula, "For the love of God, good people, for Allah," when he was around.
>
> Propped up against his staff, he sits cross-legged just outside the vaulted archway, silent for hours at a stretch. Then he'll suddenly thunder, "Generous patrons!" That, and no more. His meals arrive on a fixed schedule, millièmes pile up in his pocket, and he exchanges pleasantries with passersby.
>
> The contrast between his mighty strength and his puny profession does make people chuckle a bit, though not—since he's a native to our alley and never throws his weight around—with resentment or malice.
>
> I happen to be there the day of his great battle.
>
> It's grave-visiting season again, and Zalooma, another blind beggar, comes into our alley through the archway to the cemetery. He's had a good day, but tiring as well, so, weary with the weight of dates and pastry, he decides to rest a while on a spot near the Ape. There they sit, two blind beggars, sentinels on each side of the arch. The Ape's sharp ears pick

up the soft smack and munch of Zalooma's lips, his nose drinks in the seductive smell from Zalooma's huge package of food, and he turns his head toward the source with intent curiosity and anticipation.

But Zalooma chooses that very moment to shout one of his favorite formulas: "O Hussein, beloved of the Prophet, master of martyrs, succor!"

Ibrahim the Ape, gruff and frowning, asks, "Who's there?"

"Nobody but one asking for a bit of generosity," Zalooma answers in all innocence.

"Who brought you here, you son of a bitch?"

"So Allah's earth is yours?" Zalooma retorts.

"Can't you see me?"

"I see only the light of my heart."

Ibrahim the Ape mutters, "Wonderful," gets up, spreads his hands, and goes toward Zalooma as straight as if he were able to see him. He grabs Zalooma's arms and, though he can't see what he does to him, I do see the poor man thrashing around, twisting and screaming for help.

A crowd gathers and pulls them apart, no easy task. Some in the crowd make angry remarks.

"Unfair."

"Tyrannical."

"Monster."

"Where's your fear of God?"

Ibrahim the Ape yells, "Damn all of you!"

Someone loses his temper and throws a broken basket at him.

At that, the Ape rebels. His revolt is more impressive than most mass demonstrations, an exploding ball. He gets madder and madder, spews the ugliest insults he can think of, then extends his staff and spins around, clobbering everything and everybody inside an ever-growing circle of terror. The crowd scatters. Running in low circles, men crash into each other, fall, scream, and shout for help. Soon the Ape is a blind destructive force that engulfs the whole alley. People hurry to shut up shops and dive down small lanes out of sight. Chairs and wares are scattered, baskets toppled right and left.

The police burst into the alley. Astonished to learn the troublemaker is merely a blind beggar, the chief officer blithely orders his arrest.

The battle is rejoined, now between Ape and police, who, as ordered, use no weapons. They therefore go sailing through the air like so many toys. The Ape is invincible.

Young boys gather at the fringes of the fray to egg the Ape on with inspiring cheers. I've never seen a government force reduced to such a mess before. Out of the white uniform with red ribbon comes the shout of the chief, "Hey, Ape! Give up right now or you'll be shot!"

Drunk with victory, the Ape doesn't even slow down. Mercifully, the officer doesn't order his men to open fire or even use truncheons but instead calls out the fire department.

Water gushes out of the hose, an inescapable cascade. The Ape is confused. He stumbles, spins around in staggers, and finally—defeated, bitter, and still hurling filthy insults—falls flat on the ground, helpless. The cops pounce on him with handcuffs.

For quite a while the Ape steers clear of our neighborhood, but one day he comes back with all his mass and height in full, proud display. Cordial greetings and warm welcomes hail his return. He takes up his old life, parking his enormous frame at the archway like a myth.

'Urabi and Sa'd

I moved to al-'Abbasiya. The image of the gang leader became mixed up in my mind with that of the heroes of the Westerns I saw at the movies. I used to watch such movies at the cinema of the Egyptian Club when I was four years old. The Club's movie theater is probably the oldest cinema in Cairo. In al-'Abbasiya we lived in a middle-class district, but it was situated between two popular areas—al-Husayniya, which had its gang leader, and al-Wayli, which also had its own gang leader. The socially elevated quarters, where it was unthinkable that such a person should appear, were considered to belong to the nearest popular quarter, meaning that al-ʻAbbasiya for example belonged to ʻUrabi, the gang leader of al-Husayniya, and Misr al-Gadida fell under the aegis of al-Wayli's gang leader. We started hearing the legends about ʻUrabi. Around this time I saw two of his assistants—you could hire such people to beat somebody up and things of that sort. We used to hear about their adventures and their impact would be felt on election days. Of course, their impact on the 1919 Revolution was well known—they led the resistance to the British—and in the elections they had a similar influence. It was ʻUrabi who cost Salim Bey, the father of Kamal Salim the movie director, his chance of success, even though both ʻUrabi and Salim Bey were Wafdists. ʻUrabi toppled him, however, to help another Wafdist, ʻAbd al-Hamid al-Bannan, who was a native of al-Husayniya and had a palace in al-Husayniya itself. Salim Bey was the candidate of the Wafd, while al-Bannan nominated himself, "on the principles of the Wafd." Salim Bey complained to the district committees of al-Husayniya and al-Gamaliya because of their bias in favor of al-Bannan. We heard that Saʻd Zaghlul had decided to go himself to Salim Bey's marquee to lend him his support. Saʻd Zaghlul's motorcade arrived and entered al-Husayniya; it was a day unlike any other. At the corner of al-Husayniya were ʻUrabi and his gang, waiting for Saʻd Zaghlul's motorcade. The moment it appeared, their shouts rang out—Long live Saʻd! Long live Saʻd!—and, in an exaggerated gesture of respect, they lifted the automobile off the ground and took it into al-Bannan's marquee. Word spread through al-ʻAbbasiya like fire: Saʻd's in al-Bannan's tent! Salim Bey lost his deposit and was never heard of again.

The Bus

In the twenties, the bus company started to run a route through al-Husayniya. Soon, however, there were problems, as ʻUrabi's boys would abuse the passengers. You might be sitting in the bus and suddenly one of them would slap you on the back of your neck. The company was at its wits' end. What to do? In the end, they went cap in hand to ʻUrabi and a number of the boys were appointed conductors at the company, or workers, wearing a yellow uniform and carrying whistles. They would stand in the road to ensure the safety of the buses and passengers.

The end of the gang leaders came about as a result of an incident in 1930; we heard about it when we were on vacation in Alexandria. It happened that 'Urabi struck a British officer and stripped him of all his clothes, and the officer went as naked as the day he was born to the interior ministry. A force was soon dispatched to seize 'Urabi, and they beat him up terribly in the police station. The man was broken and his rule came to an end. 'Urabi was transformed from the man who used to protect the Zahir police chief into one who could be detained at any moment if anyone complained; even the smallest complaint was enough. 'Urabi spent the rest of his life under surveillance. Do you remember the café where we used to meet every Thursday evening? It was called Ahmad 'Atiya's even though 'Urabi was its real owner because 'Urabi couldn't put his name on anything. Sometimes the arrogance would return and he'd fly in the faces of the customers, but soon he'd come to them and ask to be reconciled. I saw him in those days, when his spirit was broken. You didn't see him because you started visiting me after he died. He was impressive in appearance. He looked like the leader of a political party or a great general. What a personality! He was very chivalrous and his personality was attractive, that of a knight.

On the literary level, I wrote one short story about the gang leaders as they were in reality, but I didn't include it in any of my collections. It was published in the thirties. My use of the gang leader thereafter was like my use of the *hara*. For example, in *Children of the Alley*, the gang leaders were a symbol of brute force; in *The Harafish*, they were like the rulers, just and unjust—it was a symbolic usage. In the story "The Second Man" *(al-Ragul al-thani)*, the gang leader resembles Fate. In the *hara*, you find traditional characters who have a special significance—the gang leader, the muezzin, the shaykh who oversees the *hara*. And, just as I knew male gang leaders, so I also knew women gang leaders. I saw one such *futuwwaya*, and I was the first person to present such a character in the Egyptian cinema. She was a chicken vendor in al-Husayniya. The woman I saw was incredibly strong. She could knock a strong man to the ground with one arm. I had seen women quarreling. I remember a fight among women that broke out at the Raml streetcar station in Alexandria. They tied their wraps around their waists and weighed in, punches flying; every one in the square was agog. However, that kind of thing isn't a mark of being a *futuwwaya*: the other one was a woman any man would quake before. The *mi'allima*, or female 'market boss,' was considered to be a rung lower—it might be that life had forced her to work in the market. But the true *futuwwaya* whom I remember was something amazing.

The Café

The café plays a big role in my novels and, more importantly, in all of our lives. There were no clubs, and the café was the axis around which friendships revolved. The houses did not allow for uproariousness. In the beginning, the streets gave us space enough; then we ventured into the cafés. I became acquainted with cafés at an early age, from the first years of secondary school, thanks to Sayyid al-Shamma', our friend in al-Ghuriya. We had a café in al-Darrasa, and others here, there, and everywhere, but the best-known cafés we went to were al-Fishawi's, then 'Urabi's and the café in Midaq Alley, and al-Firdaws, Rex, and Luna Park. We inaugurated Luna Park: we were the first people to go in during the opening. It served a good waterpipe and we would smoke, sip a few glasses of whisky, and listen to Umm Kulthum. Ah yes Ahmad 'Abduh's café that I mentioned in the *Trilogy*, where Kamal would meet his friend Fu'ad al-Hamzawi. I used to love that café. It was underground. You went down some stairs and you found a circle with a fountain in the middle surrounded by a little balustrade. It was famous for its tea, the best tea. I call it Ahmad 'Abduh's café but in fact I don't remember its real name. Didn't anyone from al-Husayn mention it to you? Ah yes . . . . So people have forgotten it, then. It was demolished years ago. It was a beautiful café and the one I loved best.

Sitting at al-Fishawi's café inspired me to thought; every puff on the waterpipe brought with it another scene. My imagination would become very active while I was smoking the waterpipe. On my days off, I would spend most of my time at al-Fishawi's. The café is a world of conviviality, where friends meet.

The Opera café symposium began in 1943, with the formation of the Committee for Writing, Translation, and Publishing. At first we used to go to 'Urabi's, but my new set of literary friends didn't feel comfortable with the 'Urabi set of friends from al-'Abbasiya, so we transferred to Casino Opera where we stayed until the police kicked us out at the beginning of the sixties—in 1961 or 1962 I think, the date has vanished from my memory. It was there that I become acquainted with a large number of writers. Salama Musa used to come, and Luwis 'Awad. He came and presented the idea of setting up a magazine. He had the conviction that al-Sahhar had the means to fund the magazine. And Shukri 'Ayyad came to us, and Badr al-Dib and Fathy Ghanem—most of the generation of writers after ours. It the end, it became a place of work: we would read literary works, and when I decided to bring it to a close, the police said to me, "I beg you, keep the symposium going; it's useful to us." Of course, they used to write reports on it. Anyway, the symposium was discovered by accident. One day there was a march in support of Abd al-Nasser passing in the street. The security men noticed that a number of people were going up to the café. One of them went up. He took a look and was amazed at how many we were. He came back and held a quick investigation. Who are you? Why do you meet here? Then he said, "This is an assembly" and asked us to get permission from the police each week, and a policeman started attending the symposium. He followed the literary discussion with astonishment, hearing names such as Kafka and Proust and terms such as realism, modernism, and so on. He asked me to help him write a précis of what was going on or, in plain Arabic, wanted me to write the police report on the session. That, however, was an order that could not be tolerated, and the symposium came to an end. After that we transferred to the Sphinx café, in front of the Cinéma Radio. At the beginning we were three or four friends, then writers started coming in droves. It was in this café that I got to know the sixties generation. For me, cafés are an endless source of memories, all of them dear to me, for they are linked to friends, and youth, and the best days of my life.

> Alexandria. At last. Alexandia, Lady of the Dew. Bloom of white nimbus. Bosom of radiance, wet with sky water. Core of nostalgia steeped in honey and tears.
>
> —*Miramar*.[6]

Alexandria and Tawfiq al-Hakim

Alexandria is the only place I go regularly outside of Cairo. My relationship with Alexandria began when we moved to al-'Abbasiya. I went for the first time with my brother one summer, and when I was in secondary school I used to go to Alexandria in the summer holidays. Whenever I passed an exam, my father would reward me by giving me ten pounds, which was enough to cover my expenses for an entire month, plus the cost of taking the second class train there and back. My uncle on my father's side used to tell my father, "You're spoiling him, because when Naguib gets a government job, he'll never see ten pounds again."

Among my memories is this: we would have lunch—by the way, my companion on the journey was my friend Ibrahim Fahmi, from the 'Abbasiya set, who later became one of the Free Officers, then head of a company—we woud have our lunch at Hamidu's. In those days the Corniche hadn't yet been built and there were only two beaches, al-Shatbi and al-Anfushi. Hamidu used to think of the summer holidaymakers who came to him regularly as his special customers. We'd order, for example, vegetables with rice, or fish, and because we were regular customers he'd present us with an additional dish, compliments of the establishment. Do you know what it would be? It would be two large mullet. I remember going into a German restaurant in Alexandria, a very grand restaurant. It was spacious and had two floors; it was where the Omar Effendi department store is now. The restaurant had waiters dressed in imposing uniforms. I sat down and was amazed to find four of them, one putting the plate in front of me, the second the napkin, the third offering me the menu, and the fourth inding all this hullabaloo, I took the opportunity of a moment when they weren't near me to withdraw and made a rapid exit to the street. The meal would have cost me a pound, at a time when I used to pass a whole month with ten, and that's why I ran.

Petro's

From that time on I never stopped going to Alexandria, except during the Second World War, when no one would run the risk of going there. A branch of our family lived in one of the districts of Alexandria and when the district was bombed, every member of the family died; in other words, that branch of the family was wiped out. I went back to Alexandria the first year after the war. 'Adil Kamil and Muhammad 'Afifi were with me. During the war years, I spent my vacations in the cafés of Cairo.

You were asking me about Petro's, the lovely café that I used to go to in Alexandria. It's been knocked down now, unfortunately. It was got rid of the year before last. I got to know Tawfiq al-Hakim in 1947, after *Midaq Alley* came out. Muhammad Mutawalli, who was a director of the Opera, told me that Tawfiq al-Hakim wanted to meet me and that he used to sit in the café opposite the National Bank. It may have been 1948. I went and met him. He asked me, "Do you go to Alexandria?" I said yes. He told me that he went to a café in Sidi Bishr. This was the period when my eye allergy had gotten bad. My friends would go into the sea and I would stay on the beach. When I was on my way to see Tawfiq al-Hakim, I saw Petro's café. It was the last café to open directly onto the sidewalk and thus was not exposed to disturbance from passersby. I told him, "I saw a quiet, isolated café where you and your friends could be by yourselves, and it's not far away." From that time on, we started to have our meetings at Petro's. I was the one who discovered it, and after the Revolution took place, the pashas appeared in the café and I witnessed the terrible state of fear that had seized them.

There was one pasha there, al-Margushi, who'd been a merchant all his life. A few months before the Revolution, he had liquidated his business, declaring that he'd had enough of trade, that his children had all graduated from universities, and that he loved the countryside. He sold everything and bought a 500-feddan farm. Then the Revolution came and the farm was nationalized when the amount of land one could own was restricted. Of course, you're aware that the Revolution didn't touch the merchants. Just luck. Al-Margushi wasn't an agriculturalist or a peasant. All his life he'd been a merchant, but this was fate's little joke. This is how my relationship with Tawfiq al-Hakim started. Of course, his talk was very entertaining and I used to listen to him often.

Abroad

With the exception of Alexandria, which I used to travel to regularly, I only traveled twice, once to Yugoslavia and once to Yemen. I have a spontaneous hatred of travel, but I enjoyed both journeys and to this day I think fondly of the scenes I saw, whether in Yugoslavia or Yemen. I wasn't depressed there. On the contrary, I had a good time.

My relationship with traveling is strange. If you tell me, "Travel!" everything becomes disturbed, as though you'd brought the whole world down on my head. But when I travel, I really enjoy it. I didn't feel any repugnance toward travel when I was in the prime of my youth, and the proof is that I was nominated for two student overseas study opportunities, one to study philosophy and the other to study language. You could say that the philosophy opportunity might have changed my life, but the language opportunity would also have been useful for me without a doubt. I was going to study French intensively and come back as a teacher at the university instead of a bureaucrat, and I would have taken advantage of my being in Paris to study literature and art. I didn't hate travel then. Maybe my hatred of it now comes from a lack of flexibility resulting from the routine I took on when I became free to write full time. Travel breaks that routine.

I would have liked to have seen the world. You know, of course, why I was denied the two study opportunities. The first- and third-prize winners were Copts and I was in second place. They thought I was a Copt too because of my name, Naguib *Mahfouz*, and the committee thought it was too much to send three Copts—and so I was denied a chance to see the world. In Alexandria, we used to stay up late with the gang and in the morning my friends would go to the sea and I'd walk on the shore. I'd start my journey by walking as far as al-Shatbi on foot and then the second day I'd start from al-Shatbi and go to al-Ibrahimiya, and on the third I'd walk from al-Ibrahimiya to Cleopatra, and so on. This went on until I met Tawfiq al-Hakim.

Author's Note: The events of most of Naguib Mahfouz's novels take place in Cairo and the scene of the action rarely extents beyond there. There is, however, one other place that has an equally strong presence, which is Alexandria, especially in Miramar, Autumn Quail (al-Summan wa-l-Kharif), *and some of the short stories. There is also one short story whose events take place outside Egypt, which Mahfouz wrote after his return from Yemen.*

Rawd al-Farag and Umm Kulthum

You're right. Rawd al-Farag, as a place with its own special features, appears in a large number of my works. I remember that my father took me with him there. It had a lot of theaters where the whole season was repeated, meaning that you could find a theater imitating al-Kassar and another imitating al-Rihani. It was all mimics. We saw all the old works of al-Rihani done by other people. Of course, there were dance theaters there and troupes belonging to singers. Umm Kulthum, on the other hand, I didn't hear there first. We heard her on records in 1926.

Author's Note: Naguib Mahfouz wrote an article about Umm Kulthum in the al-Ayyam *newspaper on 21 December 1943 in which he said:*

> What could be more insensitive than to compare any of Egypt's various voices with this sublime one? Say what you like about the singing of Asmahan, Layla Murad, and Nur al-Huda but to compare any of these with the voice of Umm Kulthum is to do harm to what you would help, to slight what you would honor, and to rub in the dust what you would raise to the skies.

Talking of Umm Kulthum, I have a preference for oriental music. I was raised on it. We had a gramophone in our house in al-Gamaliya. When I was little, in Bayt al-Qadi Square, I learned the songs of Sayyid Darwish by heart from the street. There was no radio there or records, but I learned them without knowing who they were by until I got older and heard them on the radio. It came as a surprise to me—"Fancy that! I used to sing those things." I studied classical music from books and would go to concerts given by visiting orchestras. The zither is the instrument I love best. In the old days, the Arabic music ensemble was very limited in the number of its instruments: there was an oud player, a violinist, someone playing the tambourine, and a zither. I preferred these instruments and I joined the Music Institute, where I studied for a year. I was at the university and there were no exams between the third and fourth years. It was during that year that I joined the Music Institute. I was studying aesthetics, and I thought that this institute would teach the aesthetics of music. I knew figurative art from books, but how was I to learn the aesthetic side of it? I thought, I'll find it here, at the institute. Of course I didn't.

The Cinema: Flourishing in the Years of Literary Despair

The cinema came into my life from the outside. I knew nothing about it. True, I used to like to watch movies, but how was the movie made? I had no idea. All I knew was that this movie was by Rudolph Valentino, that by Mary Pickford, and so on. I didn't know that there was a screenplay writer or anyone else. In 1947 my friend Fu'ad Nuwayra told me that Salah Abu Sayf, the director, wanted to meet me. By that time I had had a number of novels published, of which the latest was *Midaq Alley*. I went with Fu'ad Nuwayra. It was summer. We met Salah Abu Sayf at the Talahmi Cinema Company. He told me, "The fact is, I read your *Khufu's Wisdom* and it became clear to me from that that you could be a good screenplay writer." He went on to say that he had in hand the story of 'Antara and 'Abla. I told him I had no idea what it was about and he said, "Never mind. You'll pick up how to write the screenplay." Fu'ad urged me to accept the offer. Abu Sayf started asking me to do things, one by one. For example, he'd say to me, "The subject of 'Antara and 'Abla is thus and so. Write it down for us in ten pages, write the story." I'd go and hand it in and think my job was finished. He'd read it, we'd agree, and then, out of the blue, I'd find him saying, "We haven't started yet. This is the *idea* of the story. We need to turn it into a screenplay. Imagine the movie. What point should we start at?" and he'd start explaining the subject to me and I'd apply it practically. After the treatment, he taught me how to divide up the scenes, and after he'd read the results of my work, he'd give me books on the art of the cinema, and I bought a few more. I learned how to write screenplays at the hands of Salah Abu Sayf.

Anyway, he asked me to work with him on a permanent basis, but I excused myself because I was a full-time writer. He told me that he worked only in the summer and said, "If your eye allergy makes things difficult for you, you can dictate to Kamal 'Atiya." I started writing screenplays. As to the question of whether I wrote stories and screenplays together, or whether I would make screenplays out of stories, I want to tell you that I only wrote screenplays in the period when I was not writing literature, and if doing so had held me back for one instant, I would have given it up without hesitation. Other directors frequently asked me to work with them, but I refused. Salah Abu Sayf was not well off; he only made one film a year. He went easy on me. I only worked in a totally absorbed manner during the years of literary despair that followed the writing of the *Trilogy*. I went then and registered myself in the syndicate and would work with any director. I also gave up writing screenplays one other time, when I was appointed director of censorship, at which time I had contracts for seven screenplays. That was in 1959. The fact is I wasn't happy writing screenplays. As a writer, one is the master of one's work, but that kind of collective creation—you say 'right,' you find someone else telling you 'left' is better, some of these points of view being well conceived technically, some commercially conceived, yet others because the person likes a particular actress—I wasn't happy with that way of working. Abandoning screenplay writing after having succeeded at it was a sacrifice like no other—a material sacrifice, I mean, of course. The total number of movies I wrote was about thirty.

The Cinema and Concision

The strange thing is that I wrote all those movies, but couldn't find anyone to produce my own stories. I'd find people telling me they were 'difficult.' Then Ahmad 'Abbas Salih produced the novel *The Beginning and the End* for the Voice of the Arabs radio station and the cinema people took notice and said, "Give us that novel. Good lord! The novel's been there all along!" Then all the novels were made into movies and were successful. The first movie made from a novel of mine was *The Beginning and the End*.

Yes, I agree with you: television series today do indeed constitute a big temptation for the writer. A series equals getting rich. Likewise screenplays in the fifties represented a huge temptation, but I never wrote a screenplay except during the times when I was not busy with literature, or during the period of despair that I spoke of. I frequently turned down tempting offers, and if the circumstances of my work with Salah Abu Sayf hadn't suited me, I would never have got into the field. Another thing that's beyond any doubt whatsoever is that I never wrote anything in my life with an eye to the cinema. That never ever happened. Literature is literature, and the proof is that the novels that were made into movies were only done so with great difficulty and by a miracle. Could a writer write *Adrift on the Nile* with his eye on the cinema? Absolutely not.

But the cinema does have another form of impact—the quick tempo, the concision—and that is a general impact of the cinema on literature. Why did I turn to concision after expansiveness? There are a number of reasons, but the primary one is time and its tempo. I mean, if I were of a suitable age, I wouldn't now be able to write the *Trilogy* with this new tempo and all the circumstances that surround us now. Add to that the impact of cinema and television and their characteristic concision. This has its impact on people's tastes, and consequently reading is affected too. The sentence that doesn't need a whole page is what is preferred now. Over and above this, my writing was naturalistic and has now become intellectual, and ideas don't need one to go on at great length. All these factors led to concision. The cinema was useful to me in learning to focus. Some people say that literature took montage from the cinema, but that is not true. It existed in literature before it appeared in the cinema; the same goes for the flashback. However that may be, the different arts feed into one another.

The cinema never ever represented a material temptation. And I'll tell you something else: Mustafa Amin gave me a copy of his last book, which was published with a dedication that said, "To the writer whom I once asked to write for *Akhbar al-yawm* and who refused." There's a story behind this dedication. In 1944 I was an official in the ministry of religious endowments. My salary was eight pounds. Mustafa Amin contacted me via a relative of mine who worked for *Akhbar al-yawm* and asked me to write two stories a month for fifteen pounds. It was the most difficult period of my life financially—my salary was tiny and I was responsible for my family after my father's death. It was a strong material temptation, especially as they weren't asking for a short story of any particular specifications. I refused. Why? Because I didn't write short stories for their own sake until the sixties, until after *Children of the Alley*; during this period I was taken up with writing novels. Mustafa Amin couldn't believe that I had refused the offer because I wanted to be free to work on my novel, so he interpreted it to mean that I was a Wafdist, and *Akhbar al-yawm* at that time was attacking al-Nahhas. I only learned of this interpretation a month ago, from my friend Muhammad 'Afifi.

Author's Note: The curious thing is that I asked Mustafa Amin about this incident, and he said that he had started reading Naguib Mahfouz in 1943 and that the novels had caught his attention, so he contacted Mahfouz via a relative of his who worked at Akhbar al-yawm *asking him to write two stories a month. Mahfouz was to write alternately with Tawfiq al-Hakim, who had a big reputation in those days and earned forty pounds in a single week. He proposed compensation of twenty pounds per story for Naguib Mahfouz because Mahfouz wasn't as well known as Tawfiq al-Hakim. According to this, the amount offered to Naguib Mahfouz would be forty pounds, not fifteen. Which of them has forgotten? Has Naguib Mahfouz forgotten the figure with the passing of time? Or did the go-between not communicate the correct figure to Naguib Mahfouz?*

I refused because it would have kept me from the novel. As for the short stories that I published before that, most of them were basically summaries of old novels that hadn't been published. It wasn't until the sixties that I started writing short stories out of a real desire to do so. I would sacrifice anything that kept me from literature. That is why the cinema never carried me far away from literature and I never stopped writing a literary work in order to write a screenplay or anything else. Nothing could keep me from literature, from writing.

Stopping

It happened to me twice in my life that I stopped writing. The first time was in 1952, after the *Trilogy*. I had subjects that only needed to be written, but my desire died. The second time was after 5 June 1967. I had great desire and extreme excitement, but there were no subjects, so I would have to start from zero without having any idea where I would end up.

Why did my desire to write die on these two occasions?

My explanation to anyone who asked me about the first period was that the Revolution had realized its goals and that society no longer manifested the issues that provoked me. It was an explanation that kept suspicion away from me, especially given that the question about why I had stopped writing had a political side to it. It seemed to me that this explanation of mine was reasonable; but was it true? It was simply an interpretation of the truth. I stopped writing for four or five years. What were the reasons? I cannot in all conscience say what the reasons were. I cannot explain it.

I stopped another time for a year, after October 1973, but then I resumed work. The first time I stopped, I didn't write any literature—not even a short story—and when I started writing again I did so with *Children of the Alley*. But I ask again: Why did I stop? The *Trilogy* may have been the reason, since you could say that in writing it I exhausted my vision. However, I cannot be absolutely certain of this, especially when I had seven topics in front of me. I remember that I went over them once with 'Abd al-Rahman al-Sharqawi when I was working as an official at the Arts Department, and he liked a topic that concerned the district of al-'Ataba al-Khadra'.

I thought at that time that I was finished, especially given that every writer has a set term as an artist. Rimbaud stopped when he was twenty-two years old. Screenplay writing was a limited consolation and a way of passing the time with the cinema people, but none of that could make up for my loss of literature. I was in the worst condition I had ever been in, to the point that I wanted to die.

The First Short Stories I Wrote for Their Own Sake

God's World (Dunya Allah) contains the first short stories that I ever wrote for their own sake, out of a desire to write short stories. Many of them were about death. The fact is that I only triumphed over the idea of death after I had written about it. Only writing about it will liberate you from something that has power over you. I also agree with you that when a person thinks a lot about death, there's some other subject that has taken control of him and he is passing through a major crisis.

Criticism

The first critics to write about me were Sayyid Qutb and Anwar al-Mu'addawi. The former was the first to write about me, in 1948 or 1949, although I had started writing in 1929. After that I was subjected to organized attack in the newspaper *al-Gumhuriya*. To tell you the truth, I don't know why. Then opinions changed. I became a 'socialist writer'; bourgeois literature became 'socialist.' And after *Karnak Café*, my works became 'reactionary.' In any case, I have an opinion on criticism: just as the writer is free, so the critic too is free. The critic writes according to his point of view, and a book hasn't been properly studied until all opinions on it have been reflected, though there is a foundation, which is arts criticism. It's as though I were to tell you, for example, "This watch is gold" and you were to reply, "Then religion forbids us to wear it." You may be right, but before that, how many carats is it? There came a time when politics dominated everything and the politically minded were forbidden to express their political opinions. Thus what couldn't be said directly was said via literary criticism. At the same time, such criticism is hard; it needs study, taste, and effort, and not every writer is capable of it. Criticism that is essentially politics, on the other hand, is easy.

My excitement over the first article written about me was great. It came after a long silence. I remember that it was by Sayyid Qutb. Silence, of course, is hurtful, but if you wrap yourself in a love of the work, there is great consolation to be found there. One could say that criticism was useful to me, but it was disconcerting at the beginning. For example, I wrote *Midaq Alley* in all innocence. Then along came a critic and said that Hamida stands for Egypt. I was flabbergasted. Sometimes criticism opens wide new horizons, but I only ever cared at the beginning. Today I might find an article in a magazine and read it quickly. In the beginning, criticism could be useful, but now, would you expect that criticism might change me? I think you'll find out for yourself soon enough.

What Remains

Now my literary works have become independent of me. I don't read a novel twice. What do I feel about the first novels? I don't know. The new editions are proofread at the printer's and I only know that they've come out at the end of the year. But if I think about my works now, the ones that leap to my mind are, as I told you, the *Trilogy*, *The Harafish*, *Children of the Alley*, and *Fountain and Tomb*. Yes—*Fountain and Tomb*. I know that you say it's because it's linked to my childhood, and that may be true, but most of it is pure imagination. There are things I started out on in life as though there was nothing to them and they then escaped me. I agree with you, it may have been a preparation for *The Harafish*.

I started on *Mirrors* several times. It occurred to me to write about the people who had passed through my life but hadn't inspired me artistically. Then another idea came, that I should write something nonfictional about the people I had known. Neither project came to pass. When I stuck to the truth, I found that the yield was very limited. I switched to a novel during the writing even though I'd started with the idea of writing about a limited number of characters from a nonfictional point of view. Sometimes you think that you know everything about a person, but when you come to write about them you discover that you know nothing. When it's a matter of the imagination, however, diverse brand new characters present themselves!

Working for the Government

I started my job with the government in 1934. I found that there was a sharp division in my life: the job was one thing, literature another. I liked my job. I had intended to retire as soon as I reached the age eligible for a full pension, but when the day came the material demands had grown, so I remained in the job until I reached the mandatory retirement age. From 1955 to 1965, literature could have provided for all my material needs, but with the pirating of my books abroad that became impossible. I always refused to devote myself full time to journalism out of fear of losing my way because it was an unfamiliar field for me and I hadn't prepared myself for it.

My government job wasn't boring, and I dealt on a daily basis with numerous people and an infinite range of types. One of the most fruitful periods of my government service was when I worked in the ministry of religious endowments. This ministry is like a number of different ministries in one—health, agriculture, religion. One used to see the beneficiaries, and many different types, from the grandson of Sultan 'Abd al-Hamid down to the poor peasant who had a right to a portion of an endowment. Amazing things took place there. I saw government service go through a number of changes. There were no laws protecting the government employee. The first law was introduced by Amin 'Uthman during al-Nahhas's government in 1942. Before this, the only people to advance in the government were its worst elements. There were people who would sell their honor. We knew that the *chef de cabinet* of one of the ministers had prepared a private apartment for the minister. In addition, there was the widespread presence of homosexuals, which is to say that types such as 'Abd al-Da'im Mahgub and Radwan, the son of Yasin, in the *Trilogy* were very common.

It was a time reminiscent of that of the Mamluks, with a corrupt administrative apparatus. However, as far as bribes were concerned, things were better than now. There was discipline and a strong administration. For example, in the university administration, there was one employee who took bribes, and it was well known. Of course, the occasion for the bribes was the need to shorten formalities. The same procedures can take a month or a day depending on the way formulae such as "Inform us as to such and such," and so on are used in the memoranda.

The turnover in governments eventually started to have an effect on the ministries. The big fish departed while the ordinary officials looked on. There was always a big welcome for the Wafdist governments because it had become a custom that lower level officials should receive rewards on these occasions. When I was transferred to the Ghuri office, it was because of a change of government. I had had a connection to one of the ministers. It wasn't a strong connection, but when the change in government occurred they asked me to select another place. I chose to transfer to the Ghuri Mausoleum. They thought I was protesting, but I told them I was going to be very happy. Of course, as you know, the Mausoleum contains a huge library. It was during that period that I read Marcel Proust. I also worked for a period in the Good Loan project. It was an enjoyable period. The women would come to pledge their jewelry and gold. All day long I'd talk and chat with the women coming from the popular neighborhoods.

Author's Note: See the chapters on Thuraya Ra'fat, Sharara al-Nahhal, Sabri Gad, Saqr al-Minufi, Tantawi Isma'il, 'Abbas Fawzi, 'Adli the Muezzin, 'Abd al-Rahman Sha'ban, 'Abduh Sulayman, Fathi Anis, Kamilya Zahran, and Widad Rushdi, in Mirrors.

The First, and Greatest, Love

"Ayda, my destiny and my fate!
Had I not known Ayda, I would have been a different man,
the universe a different universe."
Kamal 'Abd al-Jawad, *Palace of Desire*

My first love died out long ago. I can't keep up with her news now because she is the daughter of a family that ceased to exist many years ago. Their palace has been turned into an apartment block. It was on a street in al-'Abbasiya called Hasan 'Id that runs from al-'Abbasiya Street to Queen Nazli Street. On the site of the palace there are now two modern apartment blocks. I don't know what became of her or where she is now—in Egypt, outside of Egypt. I've even lost track of her brothers. There are strange things. Sometimes they say that the world spins and turns and then you see, but that woman I have lost track of completely. The strange thing is that the little house where I stay in Alexandria is the home of a female relative of hers, who is on the floor under mine. Her nephew, a doctor, ran into me and recognized me, but it would have been unthinkable for me to ask about her. It's very likely that she's died, very likely indeed. If she's still alive, she'd be more than eighty. I believe she married an engineer. That's what they said a long time ago. I don't remember. I only saw her once after she married, in Isma'iliya Square, which is now called al-Tahrir Square. That love held great sway over me in my youth. The strange thing is that you sometimes find some face or other and you think that you are destined to meet it. Why that face in particular? I don't know. Why should precisely that form in that shape have that effect on you. Again, I don't know. It's something mysterious for which I have no explanation.

Author's Note: Here we recall the chapter on Safaa al-Katib from Mirrors:[7]

> The al-Katib residence was one of the noblest houses in old Abbasiya. It stood in the eastern quarter, an imposing structure with a sprawling garden that extended beween two tram stops. We often walked along its wall on our way to the desert to play ball. I never saw more than tree tops, jasmine bushes, and drawn curtains. One day, on my way to the desert, a carriage pulled out of the east drive toward the main street with an old woman, her face showing a pair of sleepy eyes above the rim of her veil, and a girl glowing with youthful light. As my eyes fell on the girl's face, they embraced one of life's explosive secrets. The gates of heaven opened and showered me with a deluge of love's blessings.
>
> "It's Safaa, daughter of the master of the palace," said Shaarawi al-Fahham, our most knowledgeable about the eastern quarter.
>
> "She's twenty," added Khalil Zaki. Whenever he got the chance, he burglarized the gardens of the eastern quarter for a bunch of grapes or a mango.
>
> "And you're only fifteen!" whispered Gaafar Khalil in my ear, noticing my change.
>
> Her image, despite the passion she had created, vanished completely into a mist of the past; never in focus even while I was a prey to her magic. I don't know the color of her hair or its style, or the color of her eyes, her height, or her shapeliness—that dissolved in a magical potion. When I

remembered—or imagined I did—it came indirectly, an inspiration, like the scent of rose that surprises you from behind a wall as you pass by—nothing moved my heart unless it mysteriously led to her. I became infatuated at relatively late stages with features, looks, characteristics, and glances I imagined reminded me of what I had missed of her. I never loved a feature in a human face that she did not loom behind, in truth or imagination. Because of this fleeting love, my emotional life suffered continuous, complicated crises, as though she were black magic. It was a love without places, incidents, or a history. I saw her in the carriage for an instant, lost my will, and was thrown into a new world. My love for Hanan Mustafa had been recent—I realized my error and was convinced I was in love for the first time. I understood how one can be absent while present, to be awake while asleep, to vanish in a crowd from loneliness, to befriend pain and penetrate to the roots of plants and waves of light.

I hovered around the palace—locked windows, drawn curtains, and no souls except the doorman, the gardener, and some servants. Once I heard a soft voice calling the doorman, my heart trembled, immediately assumed it was her voice, then believed it. I saw her the second time on a sad occasion, in the window of an ancient house on Muhammad Ali Street where a group of women crowded to watch Saad Zaghloul's funeral procession. I noticed her only after the coffin had passed. Through my tears I glimpsed her shining face as she wiped her eyes, stretching her neck toward the blessed coffin. My heart gave a sudden leap, but I wasn't rewarded with a vision, and lost the thrill in a sad, broken heart. I was overwhelmed by conflicting emotions and the wave of weeping people. I only saw her again as she descended the steps of the salamlek in her bridal gown to mount the car that carried her to the bridegroom's house. I was in the crowd of onlookers on the opposite sidewalk.

The period lasted almost a year, the most incredible year of my life.

My affair was discovered by my friends. The jokers ridiculed me and called me Magnun Safaa, others warned me of persisting in a useless passion. We were young, our naive ideas borrowed from novels and what we had learned of Arabic literary history.

"Don't give up, or you'll go mad like Magnun Layla," Surour Abd al-Baqi told me.

"Your love shows that you loved her in an ancient time, maybe during the time of the pharaohs, like Rider Haggard says," said Reda Hamada.

This love, a powerful, consuming force, sought nothing less than devouring body and soul, tossing me into a painful purgatory. I smelted me into a new metal that craved existence, attracted to all that was beautiful and true. The love remained—after its creator had vanished—no less than ten years, burning like an incurable madness. Thereafter, it resided dormant in my depth; roused by a tune, a view, or a memory, it would pulsate with momentary life, proving it had not yet been annihilated.

I'm bewildered when I recall those days, at the secret of the life I led. Was I touched by madness? I regret my love did not experience reality, that in its violent vortex heaven and earth did not meet, that I could not test my true abilities in endurance, in confronting its secrets under the cruel, coarse light of reality.

How wise Reda Hamada was when he told me one day after we'd reached some maturity, "Safaa was thrown into your life as a stimulant, she was a code that pointed to something. You had to discover her symbols to reach it."

"Our life has dissolved into ironies, but I hate to recall those days with scorn," I replied.

"Scorn?! How can one scorn the best days of his life?"

I walked by the Katib palace in the sixties and found it had been torn down and its rubble removed, the open space was being dredged for four apartment blocks. I smiled as I surveyed the lot, and sadness fleeted by. I remembered Safaa, whom I had not seen since she descended in her bridal gown. I knew nothing about her: alive or dead, happy or miserable? How had she aged now that she was sixty? What had happened to her, what did others think of her? Did she not deserve to know that she had been worshipped as a deity, that she had exploded into a heart life that still pulsated, now and then, with her memory?

I wrote many of my works under the influence of love—not necessarily while actually living the experience, but after it had gone—and I believe that the writer does his best work when he is in love. Given that love for a woman wasn't always forthcoming, love for anything else could take its place. To give expression to an experience of love after it has finished is to reveal all its dimensions stripped of special pleading and helps in the creation of new work.

It's true that in my stories I do refer to many forms of deviant behavior. Some people find that unpleasant, but reality is much more appalling. I think of my novels as being decorous compared to reality. I have learned terrible facts from the statistics. What I have actually witnessed is not much, because direct observation doesn't lead one to the truth exactly. One day, I was introduced to an officer with the morals police. He was the brother of a movie distributor. He came to see me at Café Riche and started talking about things he'd seen, terrible things. The underbelly of social life is terrifying. Why do we ignore it? The cause of most cases of deviant behavior is want. Most of these women went wrong as a result of crushing circumstances. The deviant life is hateful. Only if a woman is afflicted with deviancy in her mind will she accept such a life. When you place the fallen woman in *Cairo Modern* next to the high official, the minister, clearly the responsibility falls on the shoulders of the minister.

I got to know the women of the popular quarters by living right next to them. It is enough that I used to sit in front of our house in al-Gamaliya. They would come to my mother, one to sell chickens, another to tell her fortune, others selling clothes from door to door. Some of them continued to visit us regularly in al-'Abbasiya. I would listen to their conversations with my mother as they told her the news and I came to know numerous further examples in my novels later on.

As far as making my wife a reader of my works is concerned, the principle is broader than that. There are some writers who are accustomed to make others their partners in the creative process, meaning that a writer will show his work to his wife, his brother, or a friend, and if this is an established principle of his, then the wife has priority, of course, especially if she has literary interests. There is another kind of writer who considers his work a secret until it sees the light. I belong to this latter type, since, in my opinion, no two people exist who can agree in their view of a literary or artistic work.

Sometimes I watch my daughter in amazement. Umm Kulthum has a talent for figurative art; I thought she would study painting, but that didn't happen. Why didn't she take her only hobby as a specialization? Instead, she joined the American University. Umm Kulthum looks like a modern girl, and she's religious. Before she goes to sleep, she reads from the Qur'an. I discovered by accident that she prays. At the same time, she likes Western songs. Once, after she'd received her secondary school certificate, my daughter paid with two years of her life as a result of my interference. I wanted her to study Humanities at Cairo University, in the English Department. She wanted to go to the American University in Cairo. I insisted on Humanities, but she couldn't continue after she'd really been there for a year. She applied to the American University. The criteria for entry had become harder, and they also required her to do a year of language.

My younger daughter studies how to be a secretary at the American University too. Of course, they have different tastes from me. They like Western music, I like oriental music. The strange thing is that until quite recently they were not at all outgoing, just moving between the house and the school, and they were always with us. They ought to have become imbued with my spirit, but they're my opposites in many things. I ask myself where these influences can have come from despite their lack of outside contacts and their not mixing with the outside world for such a long period. They have all the characteristics of their generation, the taste in music, the interest in the outside world and not in the local scene. Quickly, however, I remember that I grew up in a house where nobody read and yet I read and fell in love with literature. They have a huge library at their disposal and countless records of Umm Kulthum, but neither the library nor Umm Kulthum interests them. Truly, times have changed and this is a different age—one that isn't ours!

Marriage and Family

The truth is that the woman is one and the same in my life and in my writings. Women have played a major role in my life, perhaps even greater than that played by politics. First there was my mother's impact on my education and the type of culture that she bestowed on me, even though she was not well educated. Then came the experience of my first love that dominated my life to such a degree, and later on other experiences of love—experiences one might call 'love on the run,' but which had their own large impact on me in the sense of acquainting me with a large number of women and girls, wonderful, strange specimens who later appeared in all my works. And then there was the strange story of my marriage, which is, that I married without planning anything and after a period of conflict (Shall I marry? Shan't I marry?), just like the crisis I passed through in the thirties (Philosophy? Or Literature?). I resolved the conflict by deciding not to get married. My mother was always urging me to get married. She set me up with numerous offers, reasonable and quite acceptable unions, and I would refuse. So how did I get married? I had a friend whom I knew as well as I know you, and one day he introduced me to his wife and his wife's sister and I found myself marrying his wife's sister, just like that! That's how the marriage came about, despite the fact that there were a lot of complications within the family, so much so that only a few of the family even knew of my marriage. I felt sorry for my mother because she was getting a special arrangement ready for me. My brother and my sister knew about my marriage and advised me to keep it a secret. I revealed the news to my mother bit by bit so as not to give her a shock. And there's another thing that was very strange.

The Time of Despair

I got married in 1954, during the period when I had stopped writing novels, during the period of literary despair. I got married when I was writing screenplays for the cinema. It may be that the emptiness I was suffering played a large role in pushing me into marriage. Otherwise, what was it that had scared me away from marriage before? I had thought it was literature, but that was a wrongheaded notion; the details are written in my diaries, which I used to write in every day but then stopped, and where, when I read them now, I find things that amaze me. That notion of mine was incorrect. I would discuss things with myself in my diaries (Should I get married or not?), tell myself that marriage would ruin my literary life, and end up deciding not to get married. I think that later on, after I had recovered my literary life and resumed writing, being married helped me, not the opposite.

Social Obligations

It is well known that marriage imposes certain social obligations that come to take up all your time, but my marriage had special circumstances. My wife's family was small; even her sister and her husband had gone to Libya. She had an aged uncle on her father's side who still lived in the village and rarely came to Cairo. This was unlike any of the other possible marriages that had been prepared for me, which were situated in a mare's nest of interlocking social relations which would have obliged me, had I accepted any of them, to waste my time on reciprocal gestures of esteem and visits or else become the object of disparaging remarks, as when people say for example, "He's one of those husbands who doesn't visit people and doesn't like to be visited," etc., etc. When I used to visit my brothers Ibrahim or Muhammad, I would see just how much married life was a social life; you couldn't ask after one of them on any given day without finding that he was at a tea party here, or a birthday party there, and these examples scared me off marriage. Naturally, a change entered my life after marriage as far as my work was concerned. I set Friday morning in its entirety aside for the family; we would go out to the parks, and in the summer holidays we would spend most of our time together. When my children were very young, they took up very little of my time: my wife shouldered the major part of the burden. With time, I discovered how I liked things to be and how I wanted to organize my life, and she was always understanding and cooperative. Probably any other wife would have gotten sick of me, but that didn't happen; from this side of things, the experience was a success, as it also was from the social relations side of things. So much so that when her sister used to come to Egypt, I would only rarely go to see her. And not just that, but when my own brothers came to see me, I wouldn't sit with them most of the time. They'd come and shake my hand and then they'd go out with their wives and visit with the family. My brothers were used to this; they knew me. I remember that whenever my brother Muhammad, God rest his soul, came to visit us, I'd sit with him a little after lunch but he'd tell me, "Go and work. I know you. I only came to spend time with your children." I confess that I wasn't a success in my social life—the relations and the visits and all that—but I was very careful never to waste my time.

Alternatives

How would my life have turned out if I had entered one of the unions that my mother tried to set up for me? The question may appear hard, but what helps me to answer it is that I followed the news of some of the women I might have become joined to. Of course I followed the course of events. My mother had her eyes on a relative of mine. She was wealthy and my mother believed she would make me happy. My relative's mother welcomed the idea for a very strange reason. The girl was ordinary looking, not ugly and not very beautiful, but the mother thought that whoever married her would steal her wealth, wealth that was estimated at a quarter of a million pounds (can you imagine, in the days when everything was cheap?). Her father was a man who had made his money by various means. He was famous for his lack of conscience. He died and left his family in this situation—his daughter, a son who was a lawyer, and another who was a pilot. The children were people of very high moral standards, but their father was a big thief and of course very well respected in society. I saw him at some funerals, as everyone would stand up when he came in. If he were held to account for his deeds, spitting on him would have been too little, but everyone turns into a weakling in the face of money and wealth. I won't tell you that I refused the girl because of her father. Her mother was a very upright lady and very solicitous of me because she felt I was the only one who wouldn't put his hands on her daughter's fortune, wouldn't steal it. In other words, I was nothing but a minor official at the ministry of religious endowments and if she had wanted to marry her daughter to the minister she could have done so, but she wanted a husband who didn't have his eyes set on her daughter's money, and she had found in me exactly what she was looking for. Her husband had left her with a bad impression of men and that had been transformed into fear for her daughter. I didn't marry the daughter, and later on she married an upstanding young man. I knew him. He used to come to the Story Club and was always complaining because his salary was low and her mother expected him to pay all the household expenses. See the anxiety over the money! He used to say to me, "Does it make you happy to see me this way? My salary isn't enough and my wife has all that money." What he said was not unreasonable, but the money complex is a terrible thing. I sent a relative of mine to talk to the mother: "It's not reasonable for your daughter to have all that money and live in poverty. For shame! Your daughter deserves better than a salary of forty-five pounds a month!"

My Mother and Father

I agree with you that Amina has many of the features of the Egyptian mother, but Amina, the mother in the *Trilogy*, is not my mother. There is little of my mother in Amina. My mother, despite her generation, was liberated. I mean, can you imagine that she was capable of leaving the area of al-Husayn to visit the Pyramids, the Egyptian Museum, and the mummies section? Even now I don't know how she did it, and I wasn't of an age that would have allowed me to ask her questions. I used to walk along holding her hand and that was all. My mother, God rest her soul, was somewhat quick-tempered. My father was 'old school,' but kind and lovable. He spent most of his time in the house. He spent only one evening a week out, both when he was a government official and when he became a merchant. Yes indeed. My father worked for the government, and when he completed the period of service needed for a full pension, he took early retirement. He had a friend, the owner of a large store and a factory, who was always going to Port Said. His friend said to him, "Why don't you come and work with me? I need someone I can trust. You can add the salary to your pension and I will have the assurance that my business is in friendly hands and be able to travel and devote myself entirely to my work." My father thought it over. He was a bookkeeper, and the work with his friend would be less complicated. He accepted. There is no resemblance between my mother and Amina in the *Trilogy* and none between Ahmad 'Abd al-Jawad and my father. God rest both their souls!

Well-Loved Places: Cairo and Alexandria

In the seventies—in 1978 to be precise—I accompanied Mahfouz on a trip during which we explored together the places he loved best in historic Cairo. It was one of the few occasions on which he undertook an extensive tour of this sort at such an advanced age. Following the 1994 attack he never again set foot in al-Gamaliya and the haunts of his childhood.

Place

I never beheld a person so tied to the place where he was first raised as Naguib Mahfouz. He lived the first twelve years of his life in al-Gamaliya. He then moved to al-'Abbasiya, but continued to be attracted to the old neighborhoods, alleyways, and passageways—to al-Husayn and al-Gamaliya and the people whom he knew and who knew him. Later, this place became the axis around which many of his greatest and most important works revolved. At the start of the summer and because of an allergy that affects his eyes, Naguib Mahfouz gives up writing for the entire vacation period, starting again in the fall. In the first week of that summer, he went to al-Husayn and al-Gamaliya and I was with him. I had accompanied him often to al-Husayn, observing his reactions there and roaming the neighborhoods and streets in which I too had lived for thirty years.

We started from al-Ḥusayn Square. In the middle of the square we stopped for a few moments. Mahfouz's face seemed calm, submissive to the impact of the successive memories that flooded his mind. He looked at the Azhar Administrative Building and said, "This is where the Khalil Agha Secondary School was."

I told him, "The square's features have changed a number of times in recent years, starting with the bold decision of some governor to knock down Fishawi's and the group of old buildings next to it. In the middle of the square there used to be a clock, which then became a fountain, which was modified and then surrounded by a garden. In the same spot, thirty years ago, was the station for horse-drawn buses that went to al-Darb al-Ahmar and then on to al-Husayniya."

Naguib Mahfouz pointed to the old buildings of the ministry of religious endowments to the west of the mosque and said, "This used to be al-Bab al-Akhdar, which was a large vaulted passageway that led to a cramped *hara* which was an abode of the dervishes and holy fools of al-Husayn. You'd find them sitting on either side of the street."

I for my part recalled 'Maréchal 'Ali,' the holy fool who used to wear a military uniform with numerous insignia of rank on his shoulders while his chest was decorated with old medals interspersed with a few Pepsi Cola caps. In his hand he held a stick with which from time to time he would push people aside. Mahfouz laughed; he remembered him well.

From al-Husayn Square we crossed into a place from which Naguib Mahfouz drew the inspiration for one of his most beautiful novels, *Midaq Alley*.

However, we came to Midaq Alley from the direction of al-Azhar, and thus had to pass first along al-Sanadiqiya Street. Filth covered the ground, the refuse of small stores and houses.

Mahfouz said sadly, "This street and its lanes used to be swept twice every day and sprinkled with water. I still remember the celebrated 'municipal mule,' the yard for the carts, and the mule stables. It was close to Bayt al-Qadi."

Mahfouz pointed to some of the buildings that had been erected in the thirties. He spoke of these old houses surrounded by gardens reaching as far as Midaq Alley, a very narrow alley not exceeding twelve meters in length and five in width. It being a Sunday, the café was closed, as were three stores on the other side of the street. He said, "I remember that there was only one café in the alley. I don't remember that house." At the top of the alley was a herbalist's in front of which sat three old men. Mahfouz asked, "Is the bakery still there inside the alley?"

The oldest man replied, "Certainly. It seems you know about the old days."

Mahfouz climbed the stairs leading to the bakery. These stairs were recent, erected over the dirt footpath that he describes in his novel. He contemplated the bakery where Zayta, the man who created the deformities of crippled beggars, lived. I whispered to one of the three old men, "It's Naguib Mahfouz, the great writer."

After a moment, he replied, "Is he the one who showed the alley in the movies?"

I nodded and he said, "Welcome" and returned to his silence.

We left the alley and the café where Mahfouz would come and sit with his friends in the old days; the idea of *Midaq Alley* was born at one such moment. In just a few days, at this same spot, the novel came into being, scene after scene, incident after incident, until it was complete and bestowed fame on this narrow, forgotten place. I remember that one day I went with an Orientalist who wanted to see Midaq Alley. The Orientalist stood for a while and looked at the alley, then said, laughing, "If Naguib Mahfouz could write this huge, wonderful novel about this narrow, limited place, what could he have done with a street like al-Azhar?"

The Markets

On to al-Hamzawi market with its little stores belonging to herbalists and perfumers, which still keeps its old site and its original form, that of the Egyptian store of the nineteenth century where there was no barrier between seller and buyer. If this market had been situated in any European country, huge sums would have been spent to preserve, restore, and bring tourists to it. Then we went on to the goldsmiths' market. Mahfouz stopped at the entrance to Salihiya Lane. Above the ancient doorway rose the minaret of al-Salih Nagm al-Din Ayyub, one of the oldest, and most unusual, minarets in Cairo, since it is crowned with an incense burner. This feature is considered representative of the first form of the Egyptian minaret at the time when it was starting to acquire its unique character.

Mahfouz stopped for a few minutes in front of a closed door and asked, "Is this place still a café?"

A passerby answered, "Yes, but today is Sunday."

He said, "It's the strangest café. A long narrow passage with the chairs arranged along each side in such a way that the seated customer touches the one opposite. Or so it was in our days anyway."

We returned to al-Mu'izz li-Din Illah Street and he pointed, smiling, to an old, collapsing house and said, "In this house a number of very beautiful girls used to live, and certain prominent male members of the community would come and sit and raise their eyes and wiggle their eyebrows at the girls and preen their mustaches. That's how flirting was done in the thirties and forties."

We continued across Suq al-Nahhasin, the coppersmiths' market, where Mahfouz pictures Ahmad 'Abd al-Jawad's store in the *Trilogy*. I noticed that his look lingered on certain places and that he slackened his pace in front of others, usually raising his head to contemplate and see. I did not want to disturb his memories with questions.

He passed in front of the historic Qalawun complex, the Bimaristan or hospital, the baths, the mosque, and the mausoleum, as well as the mosques of al-Nasir Qalawun and Barquq, their lofty minarets towering high above us. I said to Mahfouz, "You describe the location of Ahmad 'Abd al-Jawad's family's house in the *Trilogy*, but there's no house in the place you describe; it is, in fact, the palace of the Amir Bashtak."

Mahfouz agreed with me. We passed in front of the famous Sultan bathhouse. "It's still there?" he asked.

"And working too," I remarked. "Most of the bathhouses of al-Gamaliya are still working."

We reached the public fountain of 'Abd al-Rahman Katkhuda. Mahfouz stopped for a few minutes and pointed to al-Tumbukshiya Lane: "This side was all a market belonging to merchants from the

Levant. They used to sit in front of their stores wearing high yellow turbans, smoking waterpipes, and displaying *nuql*—apricot fruit leather, hazelnuts, almonds, and coconuts."

Then he pointed to the remains of a spacious old building and said, "That was the house of al-Muhaylimi. They were an important family, and a number of them took part in the 23 July Revolution."

I said to Mahfouz, "Now we're going to make our way to Bayt al-Qadi Square. We can go via Qirmiz Passage or the Bayt al-Qadi neighborhood passage."

He said, "I came here a week ago and went via . . . ."

I said, "In that case, let's take the other passage."

The *Kuttab*

We started walking through the *hara* of Bayt al-Qadi. Naguib Mahfouz said, "We used to call it the *Hara* of the Kebab-seller."

We went through the old, historic passageway where the family of Ahmad 'Abd al-Jawad took refuge during the Second World War from an air raid, after which the hero of the *Trilogy* breathed his last. The street is crooked. Mahfuz pointed to some tall houses and said that they were as they had always been and hadn't changed. Suddenly, he hastened his stride, arriving before me at the corner where there is an old, historic public fountain. I caught up with him. He seemed tired from his efforts.

He said, "This is the *kuttab* where I learned. The fountain still survives but the *kuttab* unfortunately has disappeared. It was on the upper floor, at Number 9."

He indicated the collapsed upper story, went in at the door, and returned to say that the stairs were still there and just as they had been but they now led nowhere. At the same moment an old man approached us repeating, "Who are you? Who do you want?"

I told him, "We're visitors." However, he kept repeating, "Who are you? Who do you want?"

I realized that he couldn't hear and thought of Shaykh 'Abd al-Samad in Mahfouz's *Trilogy*. We left the *kuttab* and our steps led us back again to the Bayt al-Qadi neighborhood, and the place where Naguib Mahfouz was born.

The Old House

Mahfouz's stride lengthened. He directed himself to the side leading to Qirmiz Road. He said, "I remember that our house was Number 8."

I looked at the house standing at one side. I said, "This one is numbered '8'."

Muhammad 'Abd al-Rahman, the photographer, said, "The numbers of houses don't change."

The house itself had changed, however. The house in which Naguib Mahfouz was born had disappeared. It had consisted of three stories—a vertical rather than a horizontal house; *Fountain and Tomb* contains a detailed description of it. The house that is there now, however, consists of two stories, the first of which is occupied, the second of red brick and unfinished. The house is ugly. Mahfouz seemed to feel regret and sorrow. He said, "The windows of our house were of turned wood and the house looked out over Qirmiz Road on one side and Bayt al-Qadi Square on the other. The square was full of trees. I would stretch out my hand and grasp the leaves of the trees. They were of the sort we call 'pasha's beard.'

He walked around the sole remaining tree, next to the public lavatory that occupies the middle of the square and which was built not so long ago. There used to be a trough next to it for donkeys and mules to drink from, which has now disappeared. "I don't know what kind of tree this is," he said, "but it's certainly not pasha's beard. Next to our house, on the square, was the home of Dr. 'Abd al-'Aziz. It had a grand entrance and contained a clinic, after which one came to a large garden inside the house itself. On the other side of Qirmiz Road was the house of the Sukkari family, which occupied this whole area. These houses weren't there. Next to the Sukkari house was a lodging house for dervishes. When I was young, the lane consisted of the huge house, like a palace, and next to it a house where the Sufis lived."

He was silent for a few moments. Then he said, "I used to watch the gang leaders as they came back to the Gamaliya police station from their battles on the empty tract, and from a small room on the roof I used to watch the demonstrations of the 1919 Revolution—the demonstrations by the women of the city's traditional classes—and the firing. This was when problems started with my mother: she would pull me away from the window and I wanted to watch, especially the shooting."

He pointed to the gate of Bayt al-Qadi, the 'house of the judge,' after which the square is named and said, "I often saw the demonstrations and the British soldiers confronting them here. I saw so much."

He turned round to cast a glance at the square, and at Judge Mamay's historic open second-floor reception area that dominates it. He pointed to two tall buildings and said, "Those were built when we were here. They caused a lot of fuss because they were so high according to the standards of our day."

While we were passing beneath the gate of Bayt al-Qadi, he said, "A man who sold toffee used to sit here. His name was al-Shabkhurli."

Mahfouz let out one of his loud, ringing laughs. "Can you give me any clue as to the meaning of that name? Al-Shabkhurli!" And we left Bayt al-Qadi Square, where Naguib Mahfouz was born, in house number 8.

We passed Khan Ga'far Elementary School and the Egyptian Club Hotel, where Mahfouz saw the first movie shows in Egypt, and found ourselves in the streets around the Shrine of al-Husayn, were the Mosque of Our Master al-Husayn is situated. Opposite is the historic public fountain of 'Uthman, above which is Bayn al-Qasrayn Elementary School. I studied there for a number of years.

Mahfouz contemplated the school's façade at length. Then we moved on to Fishawi's café, which was demolished in 1969, and of which only remnants remain. In this café Mahfouz had spent long evenings of conversation and longer hours smoking a waterpipe, seeking inspiration for the events and heroes of his novels when he was a government employee at the Mausoleum of al-Ghuri working on the ministry of religious endowments' Good Loan program. This time too he smoked a waterpipe, though the waterpipe of long ago was a far finer affair and the tobacco came in numerous forms and categories. In grieving accents that reflected his nostalgia for the old days, he said, "Oh my! It was a time of . . . ."

I don't know what was passing through the great writer's mind or what distant images he was calling up. I do know that this place brought him great inspiration and that there was no other area to which he was ever as attached as he was to al-Gamaliya, al-Husayn, and here; that even though he lived in other parts of Cairo—al-'Abbasiya and Nile Street—he never reflected these areas in his works with the same strength that he pictured al-Gamaliya; and that the *hara* remains the center of his world.

The *Hara*

In 1924, when Mahfouz was twelve years old, the family moved from the old house on Bayt al-Qadi Square to the house in al-'Abbasiya that his father had bought for one thousand pounds.

Mahfouz continued to be attracted to al-Gamaliya, frequenting the Midaq Alley café, Fishawi's café, and the store of one of his friends, who was a merchant in al-Ghuriya.

In the mid-fifties, he got married and moved to Nile Street in al-'Aguza—to a small apartment on the ground floor looking out over the Nile. He never severed his links to al-Gamaliya, and his nostalgia for the older parts of Cairo remained strong, even overwhelming; that old world, and those ancient *hara*s, became in effect the heart of all his works. He was able to reflect their spirit powerfully and truthfully and to immortalize them.

I recall that I traveled to Morocco two years ago and sat on the airplane next to a Moroccan who taught at the Université Muhammad V. He was wearing the well-known Moroccan dress—white mantle with hood—and was a likeable man who lightened the tedium of the five-hour journey for me with continuous conversation. He was returning from a visit to Cairo, where he had spent his vacation. The primary motive for this visit had been to visit the Cairo of al-Mu'izz li-Din Illah, to see the places of which Naguib Mahfouz had written and the roots from which the characters of whom he had read in the *Trilogy* had sprung. How happy he had been with the visit!

A few weeks ago, the French Cultural Attaché invited me to dinner with a number of my colleagues on the occasion of the translation of some of our works into French. There we met with a number of the French literary figures who had undertaken these translations and who were working at the French Centre d'études et de documentation économique, juridique et sociale that has recently been established in Cairo. One of these, a novelist with an excellent knowledge of Arabic, told me that he had rented a room in the Husayn Hotel that looks out over al-Husayn Square and neighbors the famous Khan al-Khalili district; he had spent two months in the area, studying it stone by stone and experiencing it through the numerous characters he came to know there, the works of Naguib Mahfouz ever in the back of his mind.

To the Core

The twelve years that Naguib Mahfouz spent in al-Gamaliya penetrated to the core of his soul and are powerfully reflected in the world of his novels, whereas the suburb of al-'Abbasiya, where he spent his whole youth and his early manhood, appears as a solely secondary place, the journey to which starts in al-Gamaliya, as in the *Trilogy*, when we find Kamal, one of its heroes, seeking to visit the palace of the Shaddad family. Al-'Aguza and Nile Street are not reflected in his works at all. The modern streets and skyscrapers did not attract him, and I believe that it was simply a place to live, sleep, and work. It is the same for me: I lived in the *hara*s of al-Gamaliya for thirty continuous years until, when I married, the housing crisis forced me to take up residence in Hilwan and I left al-Gamaliya in body, though never in heart or soul. I have to confess that I am still unable to communicate with Hilwan. I am incapable of making relationships there, and I am incapable of feeling it; nor am I willing to take on the task of exploring it. A constant feeling that my residence there is temporary and that one day I shall return with my family to al-Gamaliya accosts me.

The *hara* in which Naguib Mahfouz lived in the twenties of this century was different from the one I lived in in the mid-seventies. Older Cairo was, in Mahfouz's day, a population center for the middle classes, big businessmen, and important officials. The *hara*s of al-Gamaliya had a strange social makeup. In one, we might find a palace with a lavish garden, while next to it we might find a middle-class house occupied by a businessman's family, and next to that a huge tenement occupied by dozens of poor families. The *hara* embraced all different social levels, and vestiges of this setup still remain in the Tablawi Road *hara* at Qasr al-Shawq where I lived. There one found the celebrated Musafirkhana Palace, the guest palace of the Muhammad 'Ali family, in one of whose rooms Khedive Isma'il was born. The palace still stands to this day,[8] but is used as a museum and a base for some painters. Other large houses still standing in the *hara* are that of the Shams al-Din family, from whom the shaykh of the Ahmadiya Marzuqiya order of Sufis is chosen; the house is located next door to the tomb of Sidi Marzuq. Also in the same *hara* are modern houses occupied by members of the middle class and old houses occupied by poor families. In the *hara* of al-Darb al-Asfar, there were, until the start of the fifties, a number of large houses with surrounding gardens, of which the oldest were the Suhaymi house, still standing and used as a museum, and the house of Mustafa Ga'far, which the Antiquities Department has taken over for its offices. The rest of the houses have fallen down.

The houses with gardens began to fall down in the thirties when the big families started to leave al-Gamaliya for Cairo's modern quarters. Some of the *hara*s have now become receptacles for the lowest classes of society and the hand of neglect has spread its fingers over the whole area. I remember that our neighborhood, al-Tablawi Road, used to be swept and sprinkled with water twice a day. The sweeper would come in the morning and at noon and would sweep the garbage next to the walls, and the garbage cart would come and remove it. Then the sprinkler cart would come. Now, though, what sorrow and grief I experience when I see the sewers overflowing, making entry to the old mosques and historic houses and just walking around difficult. Most of the *hara*s of al-Gamaliya were paved with stone, just like the old quarters of Paris. Now, cultural short sightedness has afflicted the officials of the Cairo Governorate and they have exchanged the stones for asphalt, which soon develops cracks and potholes. This is what happened in al-Tablawi Road, for example. And all this is not to mention the changes to some of the landmarks of the area, of which the most obvious example was the demolition of the old Fishawi's café, that stupid decision that destroyed one of the loveliest and most ancient of Cairo's cafés, leaving only remnants.

Let us return to the dialog with Naguib Mahfouz.

Reality and Symbol

In the literary works of Naguib Mahfouz the *hara* appears on two levels: one realistic, the other symbolic. We find the first level in Mahfouz's realist works—in *Midaq Alley* and *Khan al-Khalili*, and later in the *Trilogy*: *Palace Walk*, *Palace of Desire*, and *Sugar Street*. Here we meet with a *hara* whose features and characteristics are clearly defined, especially if we compare them to the reality. In these novels, Mahfouz maintains the landscape of the real Gamaliya. If one who follows the movement of the characters in the novels compares them to the real place, he will find an astonishing faithfulness to its topography and landmarks, so much so that the *Trilogy*, *Khan al-Khalili*, and *Midaq Alley* may truly be considered accurate reference sources for the landmarks as they were at the time when the events took place, not counting those landmarks that have since disappeared, like Si 'Abduh's café, which was below ground level and had in its center a fountain surrounded by a little balustrade. Here it was that Kamal 'Abd al-Jawad, the hero of the *Trilogy*, used to meet with Fu'ad al-Hamzawi. I have followed the movements of the characters as traced by Mahfouz on the ground and found a precise match between the description and the features of the place, and if we go today to Midaq Alley, we will find the café, the barbershop, and another closed shop. The people of the alley say that a fat man used to sell sweet semolina pastry in the alley and that he is the one who appears in the novel as 'Uncle Kamil.' The *midaq*, or dirt footpath, itself is still there, and likewise the bakery.

In this realist phase, the *hara* was a faithful reflection of the place as Mahfouz knew it.

The second, symbolic level at which we find the *hara* treated by our great writer appears in *Children of the Alley*, *The Harafish*, *Fountain and Tomb*, and numerous short stories. Here the *hara* becomes a mixture of reality and dream, a distilled reality, as we find in *Fountain and Tomb*, and this private *hara* has an independent existence and its own vocabulary and recurrent symbols. We find the houses, the *liblab* tree, the café, the passageway, the ruined lot, and the sense of serenity, for here lurk the men of God, those ever free to devote themselves to His remembrance, who neither remove the veil nor manifest themselves, but whose mysterious prayers echo over and over again, sometimes in Turkish and sometimes in Persian. The empty tract, however, is the end of all of this—open and running to the ends of the earth, inspiring feelings of nothingness; and at the horizon the domes and minarets appear, mulberry trees growing in their corners.

In Naguib Mahfouz's *hara*s, the days follow one another, gravid with their secrets, and characters appear and characters depart, sometimes disappearing forever. Quarrels break out, heads are broken, gang leaders issue declarations of war, and gang leaders are defeated. Generation displaces generation, lives come to an end, and the walls of the *tekke* remain high, the voices of the dervishes echoing from behind them. Here Mahfouz's *hara*s seem transparent, containing in miniature all that life holds and reflecting the features of mankind in its various states. They are, to be brief, a distillation of our world and our mortality created by our great writer with poetry, a relaxed sensibility, and an amazing and admirable love for the heart of our ancient Cairo.

Al-'Abbasiya and the Café

Al-'Abbasiya has expanded and is no longer how it used to be in the twenties and thirties. Then, the desert started at the end of al-Sarayat Street and al-'Abbasiya was divided into two sections. East al-'Abbasiya was where the palaces surrounded by verdant gardens were situated, and despite the change in the landmarks, the picture drawn of it by Mahfouz's pen in Part Two of the *Trilogy* is still the one that, for me, defines the area. I cannot go there without feeling the caress of zephyrs from that distant past when Kamal 'Abd al-Jawad left his house in Bayn al-Qasrayn on his way to the palace of the Shaddad family, his heart beating, his emotions surging because he was on his way to the house of his beloved, 'Ayda Shaddad. She lived in a house on al-Sarayat Street, in whose garden the ethereal vision of her first appeared to him, throwing his emotions into turmoil; and it was on this street that Kamal stood beneath a tree watching the lighted window in the Shaddad family's palace on 'Ayda's wedding night, shaking with cold and pain. It was an experience of love in which pain and passion mixed that affected me greatly. I talked about it with Mahfouz many times, asking about how 'Ayda looked in real life and what her character was like. She was older than Mahfouz and were she alive today she would be on the threshold of her eighties.

When I asked about the 'Ayda whom he loved in real life, his face softened and his features appeared to sink into a sea of memories, memories that were now long past and hard to access. That love that had swept over Naguib Mahfouz at the beginning of his youth, that love that was still the greatest experience of his life, was now almost fifty years old. This relationship moved me deeply, so much so that it drove me, in my early twenties, to love someone similar and live out a comparable experience, in which love existed for the sake of love with hope of neither consummation nor a shared life.

Naguib Mahfouz lived his adolescent years in al-'Abbasiya from 1924 until after his marriage in the fifties. He continued to visit al-'Abbasiya once a week, on Thursdays, when he would have lunch and spend the whole day with his mother. Then, at six o'clock, he would make his way to 'Urabi's café where he would find the friends of his childhood. It was in this café, starting at the end of the sixties, that I used to visit with Mahfouz.

The Old Café

In the first half of the twentieth century 'Urabi's was one of the best known of Cairo's cafés. Its owner was one of the best-known gang leaders of the city. Mahfouz describes him as being of impressive appearance, a man made to be a leader, whose influence was increased by the fact that the chief of the al-Zahir police station had once come to him to seek protection. I only knew 'Urabi through Mahfouz and when I started going to the café, 'Urabi had already been dead for a number of years. The café once contained magnificent antiques, but its area has now been reduced to a narrow rectangle looking onto al-Gaysh Street. In this café I met Mahfouz's old friends and beheld with them a completely different person from the Mahfouz I had come to know at the literary symposium at Café Riche every Friday evening.

At Café Riche, Mahfouz appeared to listen more than he talked, taking part in the discussion in a measured way. He seemed to be interested in getting to know the new young writers, sometimes engaging them in conversation. Most of the time, however, he listened. The literary symposium at Café Riche came to a strange end when the owner redid the place and decided to make Friday the weekly day off. It seems the man preferred to avoid the headache—many of the discussions that took place there touched on political subjects. Mahfouz's literary symposium then moved to a café-restaurant on the Nile.

The Thursday meetings at 'Urabi's café, in contrast, were distinguished by their liveliness, with our great writer's laughter ringing out as he exchanged sarcastic jokes and biting comments with the friends of his childhood. I quickly became a member of this intimate company. Mahfouz would leave at eight thirty, but his old friends would insist that I stay and spend the evening with them at the café, or at the house of one of them in al-'Abbasiya, and it was not difficult for me to recognize among them a number of the characters of whom I had read in the great writer's novels.

Karnak Café Was Born Here

I witnessed the birth of the novel *Karnak Café* in 'Urabi's café in al-'Abbasiya. One day we saw someone with white skin and white hair and of medium height. His eyes were strange, seeming to be turned toward the outside. His fingers were fine, pointed at the ends like the talons of a bird of prey. When he entered, a strange silence fell, and the waiter hastened to bring a waterpipe, which he placed next to him, setting in front of him a chess set on which those present started playing with him.

It was natural that the stranger should attract our attention. Mahfouz leaned toward me and asked me, "Who is that?" I didn't know him, but I signaled to the waiter and whispered to him, "Who's that?" "It's Hamza al-Basyuni, the former director of the military prison," he replied.

Mahfouz's eyes widened and he took to observing the man discreetly. I still remember how Hamza al-Basyuni looked, the way he held the waterpipe and bent over the chessboard, and the atmosphere of gloom that his presence created in the café. He had just left prison after serving his sentence following his arrest after 1967. The following week he did not appear, and Mahfouz's friends told numerous stories that they'd heard about him and about the military prison. A few days later I read in the press the news of Hamza al-Basyuni's death in an automobile accident on the Cairo-Alexandria road.

On the afternoon of that Thursday on which Naguib Mahfouz beheld the executioner of the military prison, the novel *Karnak Café*, which appeared years later, was born.

Memories

About seven years ago,[9] Naguib Mahfouz severed his connection with 'Urabi's café, and the weekly Thursday gathering fell into oblivion. It was a problem of transportation: Mahfouz does not own a car and uses taxis, and it became difficult to find a taxi to take him from al-Nil Street to al-'Abbasiya. Moreover, his mother had died at the beginning of the seventies and his 'Abbasiya friends themselves stopped coming to the café, some departing this life, others kept at home by sickness. In despair, our great writer said, "Imagine! I can't even pay my respects to the dead because of the transportation situation. Often I have to send a cable."

Mahfouz was, and still is, loyal to those he has known all his life. His dearest friends to this day are those whom he knew and who knew him in his early boyhood—Mukhtar and Fu'ad Nuwayra (brothers of the artist 'Abd al-Rahman Nuwayra), 'Abd al-Hayy al-Alfi, and Dr. Adham Ragab, all of whom I used to see at 'Urabi's café. When I go to Café Riche early in the morning, I find our great writer carefully reading the obituaries in the newspapers and marking the names of some of the deceased; then he writes cables of condolence.

The authentic Egyptian values are embodied in Naguib Mahfouz: loyalty, the paying of compliments, and solicitude for ancient acquaintances. Dropping the weekly Thursday gathering with his lifelong friends hurts him, without a doubt. However, work and time—that time that obliterated the true, the hidden, hero behind the greatest of his literary works and made him immortal—are unconquerable forces.

The Riffraff

Last Thursday,[10] before he left for Alexandria, Mahfouz called his friend the artist Bahgat 'Uthman, as he does every week, at exactly eight o'clock, and the two of them made their way together to an evening with 'the Riffraff,' whose gatherings have gone on uninterrupted since they started in the early forties. I remember that Mahfouz used to leave 'Urabi's café in al-'Abbasiya after the Thursday meeting with his old friends, make his way to a nearby kebab-seller, and buy a kilo of kebab from him, and this is what he would take with him to his Riffraff friends on the Pyramids Road, where the group's meetings took place at the house of the writer Muhammad 'Afifi—a celebrated kilo of kebab this, that didn't change in thirty years. Previously, he used to bring a kilo of *basbusa* as well, but he stopped doing so when he contracted diabetes in the early sixties. The Riffraff protested, saying, "What fault is that of ours?"

Despite his friends' complaints, Mahfouz completely abandoned the custom of bringing *basbusa*, and, with the increased difficulty of getting to his childhood friends' evening gatherings in al-'Abbasiya, the custom of bringing kebab was discontinued too. Simultaneously, time began to take its toll on the Riffraff set, one going abroad, another departing this life for good, until Muhammad 'Afifi himself passed away, thus depriving the Riffraff of their longstanding place of assembly. The gathering moved to the house of the artist Ahmad Mazhar, an old Riffraff member. Mazhar, however, would travel on occasion and on this particular Thursday evening Mahfouz and Bahgat 'Uthman were visibly at a loss. Where, and how were they to pass the evening together? On that particular night they were the only 'Riffraff-ers' in town; the rest were either away or at work. Mahfouz thought a little and then said to Bahgat, "What do you say we go to Hilwan and surprise Gamal al-Ghitani at home? We could go out with him to a café in Hilwan. It's years since I went there."

My friend Bahgat waxed enthusiastic, started the car, and headed for the long road down "the Corniche, where gentle breezes are off their leash." After a few moments, however, Mahfouz said, "But the surprise may annoy Gamal. He may not be prepared to receive us."

Bahgat replied, "That's precisely what makes it fun."

Mahfouz, tight-lipped, said, "No. I'm afraid we'll disturb him. Let's go to Muqattam."

Bahgat complied, our great writer's reservations carrying the day, and the car set off for the Muqattam. On the way, Mahfouz said, "I remember visiting Sayyid Qutb in Hilwan after his release from prison in 1964. I found him sitting in the house with a number of men with beards. They were sitting in silence, just staring ahead. A sense of fear hung over the place and Sayyid Qutb no longer resembled the old friend I had known. I wanted to break the stridency of this heavy silence, so I made some inconsequential joke, thinking that it would cheer them up and they'd laugh, but they looked at me askance and no one smiled, not even Sayyid. I left the house in silence, conscious of the degree of the change that had overcome Sayyid Qutb, God rest his soul. After that I ceased to hear news of him until his arrest, trial, and execution were announced."

The car kept going until it reached the summit of Muqattam. Both of them thought of the late Muhammad 'Afifi, in whose house the group used to convene. Standing on the edge of the cliff, Mahfouz fell into a brown study, the cars parked around them in the dark, each with its lovers.

Mahfouz recounts, "Every now and then, some youths bent on disturbing the lovers in their seclusion would pass by. They would come up to our car and shout, 'That's enough of that!' and shine lights on us—at which they'd be greatly surprised to find two men.

That night Mahfouz was aware of a feeling of sadness, and of the passing of time, and no doubt thought of his departed friends.

As we were sitting looking out over the sea in Alexandria, in Muntazah Park, I asked him, "But what's the story behind the 'Riffraff'?"

A Long Life

In 1942, some friends—who all had won literary prizes awarded by the Arabic Language Academy—came together in a group. This group included the able novelist 'Adil Kamil, a lifelong friend of Naguib Mahfouz's who abandoned literature after producing successful works such as the novels *Mighty Millième (Millim al-akbar)* and *Sunray King (Malik min shu'a')*, 'Ali Ahmad Bakathir, Yusuf Gawhar, Husayn 'Afif, and Naguib Mahfouz. Mahfouz got to know 'Adil Kamil and Yusuf Gawhar for the first time. Time passed and Mahfouz's friendship with his fellow novelist 'Adil Kamil continued, while the others went their separate ways. Mahfouz suggested to Kamil that they meet at 'Urabi's café in al-'Abbasiya every Friday morning, and

Kamil responded by saying that he met with a group of people every Thursday evening, some of whom were acquaintances of Mahfouz's, such as Ahmad Zaki Makhluf and Amin al-Dhahabi, and suggested that Mahfouz join the group, which he did, though he did not go every Thursday.

In 1943, the literary symposium at Café Opéra was formed. 'Adil Kamil used to attend, and the Opéra symposium continued until 1962. I would go every Friday morning and we would meet with the great writer and it was, I repeat, a lively event. This and the symposium of the late Shaykh Amin al-Khawli, which was known as 'the Symposium of the Custodians' and which I also used to drop in on every Sunday evening, were perhaps the last of the great literary symposiums of Cairo. At these two salons, I got to know a number of writers; we discussed many issues, and I made a number of friendships, some of which have lasted until today. The literary climate was full of life, characterized by its vivacity. Such symposiums have disappeared now from our lives but how useful they were, especially for those taking their first steps in the world of literature. At the same time, they represented the continuity of the generations.

In 1962, the Café Opéra symposium came to an end, when the security services intervened and put a stop to it.

The Beginning of the 'Riffraff'

'Adil Kamil's group included Ahmad Zaki Makhluf, Amin al-Dhahabi, and Ahmad Mazhar. Ahmad Mazhar was an officer in the army at that time, and a friend of the novelist 'Adil Kamil. There was also a government official called Mahmud Shabana who worked at the ministry of finance.

Mahfouz became a regular member of this evening gathering.

Our great writer says, "We called ourselves the *Harafish*, or the 'Riffraff.' Some new people joined, some died. Among those who joined us soon after the group was formed was Muhammad 'Afifi, and his house on the Pyramids Raod became the meeting place for the gathering. Then the director Tawfiq Salih joined, and with him Salah Jahin and Mustafa Mahmud. Ahmad Baha' al-Din used to visit from time to time, and of course there was the painter Bahgat 'Uthman. The gathering flourished; its motto was 'Art and Laughter.' The

Palestine war of 1948 came and went and we didn't change. We commented on the war and discussed it. The revolution of 23 July 1952 took place and still the evenings continued, our motto held high: 'Art and Laughter.' The history that we were living was reflected in our conversations and comments, but nothing ever changed, until that Monday, the 5 July 1967.

Total Defeat

Mahfouz remembers that 5 July was a Monday and that the Riffraff were all invited the following Thursday to Salah Jahin's wedding celebrations. Inviting them he had said, "My wedding's next Thursday, my brothers, but it's a toss-up whether the war will start." In fact, war did break out and we didn't go to Salah Jahin's wedding.

The Riffraff's evening gatherings changed completely.

Mahfouz says, "The topic of the gatherings had been art, laughter, and politics. It changed, and politics became the sole subject around which our conversations turned. Before, we used to laugh till our sides ached. After 5 July we were incapable of laughing at all."

Alexandria

At Délices in Alexandria, which Mahfouz used to frequent every day to read the morning newspapers and where he would meditate in the diffuse light reflected from the waters of the sea that stretched to the horizon, the great writer picked up a box of medication, a medication named Nicotic Acid, and he said, "Can you believe it? I've been looking for this in the pharmacies for the last week without finding it, though it's a very important medication for people with diabetes. It protects them from side effects. It's cheap. A box costs seventeen piasters, which is why it's so rare, or, more accurately, why it's nowhere to be found."

The Left-over Apartment

Naguib Mahfouz visits Alexandria regularly in the summer months, when he stops work due to an eye allergy. It is the only city that he visits outside Cairo; he has nothing to distract him there from the sea and his meditations. He was introduced to Tawfiq al-Hakim's literary symposium in the forties, when he visited it at Petro's Restaurant, which was knocked down a few years ago. The restaurant occupied a beautiful site next to the Sidi Bishr bathing cabins, and Tawfiq al-Hakim would hold his meetings in its outer courtyard; they were attended by a number of the literati and politicians of Alexandria and Cairo.

Mahfouz would say, "I didn't know any pashas before I started attending Tawfiq al-Hakim's symposium after the Revolution. I would sit on the edge of the group, looking at them from afar. Sometimes they would look at me suspiciously and stop talking, as though they thought I was one of the July generation. They were all opposed to the application of the agricultural reform law or had had their lands sequestrated. Some had been detained or imprisoned. One of the regulars at Tawfiq al-Hakim's symposium in Alexandria was Ibrahim Pasha Farag, God grant him health."

Until the beginning of the seventies, Mahfouz didn't have an apartment in Alexandria; he would stay in a pension. Then he adopted the custom of renting an apartment in a building close to San Stefano. The rent was only thirty pounds a month. Later it happened that the owner of the building built another story, and there was a bit of leftover space on which he built a small apartment consisting of two rooms and a small parlor. Being religious, and the father of girls, the man wanted to let this on a permanent basis, as he hated the thought of renting it to families with adolescent boys; so he thought of Naguib Mahfouz, who was also a father to two young girls. Mahfouz said, "I was surprised one day when the man asked me to go to the ministry of culture. He was calling from Alexandria and he told me about the apartment that he'd built on the remaining space, on the 'leftovers' of the place. He was asking me if I was willing to rent it. I dashed out of the office and went to Alexandria and I signed the contract then and there. Naturally, without that apartment, it would have been hard for us to go to Alexandria. Summer rents are astronomical now. The apartment that we used to rent for thirty pounds now rents for more than five hundred, to look no further."

The Iron Regime and a Morning Chat

We agreed to accompany Mahfouz on his daily itinerary along the coastline of Alexandria, on the basis that we should meet the following day in front of Casino San Stefano. He said that he might be one, or perhaps two, minutes late, as his strict disciplined slipped when he was in Alexandria since he was not tied to any particular work. The following day we waited. Our appointment was for half-past seven, and at half-past seven exactly we saw him coming along a road that runs down toward the sea. Laughing, I said, "Definitely, discipline is slipping."

He was wearing a straw hat to protect him from the sun and holding the morning press—three daily newspapers and the magazines that had come out that day. He would put off reading them until he was in the café. This was the starting point for his daily walk along the Alexandria corniche. Pointing to Casino San Stefano, he said with a laugh, "We used to come here in the twenties. It had two sections for swimming. The section on the left was designated for the men and youths, that on the right for the women and children. Because I was little, I used to swim with the ladies. In those days, the women were as large as the Casino itself, because obesity was the fashion, and the swimsuits were high and full of ruffles. It was an amazing sight!"

Mahfouz walked for half an hour. There were few pedestrians, the automobiles raced by at high speed, and here and there the white spume from the waves streaked the blue sea with horizontal lines. Then the search for a taxi began and he made his way to Délices, where he sat in a quiet corner. Over there, a man and a woman were sitting in a distant corner—an early tryst. Naguib Mahfouz sat in his usual place, starting on his in-depth reading of the newspapers, and likewise the magazines. At nine thirty, he left the café; always the same precise habits, the same internal clock that never got the time wrong. After we had finished reading the newspapers, Mahfouz said, "Did you see the serial *The Age of Love ('Asr al-hubb)*?"

"I wasn't able to watch it all," I replied, "but I saw three episodes."

Admiration appeared on his face.

"I really enjoyed watching it," he said. "The directing was strong, and so were the actors, especially Samiha Ayyub, who played the role of 'Mrs. 'Ayn,' and Salah al-Sa'dani, and the rest of the cast. What really impressed me, though, was the faithful adherence to the spirit of the literary text."

"But it got a raw deal because of the World Cup matches," I said.

Like any spontaneous conversation, this one moved from topic to topic. He said, "I watched those matches. It's soccer at a high level. I became so absorbed in viewing that I'd shout out loud from enthusiasm and stand up and cheer. Those matches revived my old love of soccer."

There was silence between us. Then I asked him, "Have you seen the Arabic translation of *Ulysses*?"

"Has it come out?" he asked.

"A week ago, in Cairo," I answered. "The translator is Dr. Taha Mahmud Taha. It took him eighteen years to complete. It's an important cultural event."

"Certainly," he said.

"Especially as there are so many distractions these days," I said. "It makes the completion of a project like that an admirable thing. When did you read *Ulysses*?"

"At the beginning of the forties," he replied. "I read it in English. It was easy to get hold of any foreign novel in Cairo those days. Now, when I make my rounds of the bookstores every Friday, I don't find new books."

"That may be because of the import laws, which treat books like any other commodity," I said.

He made a grimace of regret. As he got ready to leave, I asked him for his telephone number in Alexandria.

He said, "That telephone has been a great source of problems for me. Can you imagine, it's been out of order the entire year? A week ago, a relative of mine introduced me to an employee at the telephone department. He came and I agreed to pay whatever he wanted in return for his restoring the line, but when he took a look, he found that the line didn't fall within his jurisdiction. It seems the telephone company workers have divided the districts up into jurisdictions, and none of them will encroach on another's area. The worker left without telling me the name of the colleague in whose jurisdiction my telephone falls."

He looked grave for a moment and then he said, "The worst disasters are the ones that make us laugh, as they say. I read that King Fahd had called Reagan and exerted pressure on him to restore the water to West Beirut, which was under siege; cutting off the water supply is a savage and inhumane thing to do. I thought King Fahd might contact Reagan to intervene to have the line restored to my phone."

With this, we left Délices for the light-drenched streets of Alexandria, where all was bustle and it was almost midday.

At ten thirty, Mahfouz went to Tawfiq al-Hakim's literary symposium at Casino Champs Elysées. There were a number of discussions, some cultural, some political, and at exactly one o'clock he left. He has formed the habit of taking lunch at the Pastroudis restaurant, close to Glym. They make him a special meal of boiled meat and vegetables—a diabetic's diet. He said, "They treat me with a solicitude no other customer receives. One day the manager of the place told me, 'Salim al-Qabagi sends you his greetings and has told us to make sure you're comfortable.' He was a fellow student at the Husayniya Secondary School in al-'Abbasiya in the twenties and now, following the departure of their foreign owner, he owns the Pastroudis restaurants."

Mahfouz fell silent for a little while, gazing at Alexandria's sea that reaches to the edges of the world. Then he uttered a single exclamation: "This world!"

With Mustafa Amin for the First Time

An important transformation in Naguib Mahfouz's life was brought about by a water pipe! A pipe in his house was leaking and had to be changed. This meant workers coming, the noise of the floor being dug up, and the removal and changing of the pipe, making it unpleasant to stay in the house. Our great writer returned from his daily itinerary, which took him through Cairo from al-Nil Street and across October Bridge, then through al-Gazira and over Qasr al-Nil Bridge, then across Tahrir Square, and brought him, at eight o'clock precisely, to a café in the Downtown area; you could set your watch by Mahofuz's entering the café, and you could set it again when he ordered his coffee. Mahfouz's relationship to the watch is matter to be discussed elsewhere, but he has always been known for his extreme punctuality, as everything in his life takes place according to a very strict schedule. This starts with his going through the newspapers from eight to nine every morning, then paying his bill, then leaving the café and taking a taxi back to his house. This is his morning routine; it hasn't changed since he retired in 1972, bringing an end to his government service and his relationship to the world of employment.

On this particular hot day, as I sat with our great writer in Café Riche, I noticed that he was a little agitated. When the clock drew close to nine, he prepared to get up, but then told me he would stay a little longer, and he told me with great worry about everything that was going on with the burst pipe and how the house was turned upside down. Our conversation moved on to the scarcity of skilled workers and how high their fees were, and he said, laughing, "Can you believe it? That pipe cost me more than my father paid for the whole house in al-'Abbasiya?" (in other words, more than a thousand pounds). The hands of the clock turned and reached half-past nine, at which point I made a suggestion: "What do you say to walking with me to my office at Akhbar al-Yawm?"

He thought a little, pushed his glasses up, and said, "I've never been to Akhbar al-Yawm."

"Now I'm inviting you," I said. "Come and we can spend a while visiting the publishing house, and then one of my colleagues can take you back home in his car."

He looked at the ground for a few moments and then said, "Why not?"

Thus we left Café Riche and made for Akhbar al-Yawm.

The Press in the Old Days

Naguib Mahfouz loves a good joke. He's fun to be with. He excels at producing a joke out of ordinary talk, and when he makes a sarcastic comment his loud, pure laughter rings out as though it will never end.

In the forties he used to stay out late in al-Husayn with his old friends and would get into a form of witty punning repartee called *qafya* with several opponents at a time and defeat them all. Only one person could get the better of him, and that was 'Uncle Ibrahim,' the wandering book vendor, well known to the older residents of the Husayn district. He was short, fat, wore a *gallabiya*, and constantly shook his head as he walked along carrying his collection of religious and popular traditional works. He would be seen at different hours of the night and day in the cafés of al-Husayn, especially al-Fishawi's. Uncle Ibrahim would sit facing Mahfouz and his companions and play *qafya* with them and defeat them all. Dr. Adham Ragab, Mahfouz's lifelong friend, says, "Naguib Mahfouz loves a good joke! In Ramadan in the late twenties and the early thirties, he would go with us to the old Fishawi's, where there were professional jokesters who would call out shameless sexual jokes to one another, and woe betide the butt of their repartee! Naguib Mahfouz would stand up to them with a strange capacity to create ideas and dress them up as jokes that made these people the target of everyone's laughter. His voice was stentorian and the speed with which he could come up with an idea was amazing. He was so good he could take on twenty at a go with joke after joke till he'd silenced them all. This made us, his boyhood comrades, into his personal claque. He was a colossus of the joke, so much so that he could make his opponents laugh at themselves."

What Dr. Ragab didn't mention was that Uncle Ibrahim the bookseller was the only one who could trump a joke from Naguib Mahfouz, and that they remained friends all the same. Whenever he went to Fishawi's, Uncle Ibrahim would come and sit with him, up to the day he died in the sixties. This hidden side of Naguib Mahfouz's character is not known to many, especially among those who sat with him in the literary symposiums, since he excelled at erecting an invisible barrier between himself and others. This aspect is, however, reflected in his novels, and it's enough for one to refer to the pages of the *Trilogy* and the evening gatherings of Ahmad 'Abd al-Jawad and his salons.

On the way to Akhbar al-Yawm, we spoke of the press in the old days. I mentioned pages from the book by the great journalist Mustafa Amin, *From Ten to Twenty (Min 'ashara ila 'ishrin)*, about the press in the second decade of the century, when slanging matches were carried on through the newspaper headlines—one newspaper, for example, said of one of the Wafd Party's big writers that his mother was poor and had nothing to support her but handouts and charity, and that she lived in al-Faggala, in a dark room that cost just sixty piasters a month, all of which was lies. Similarly, there were vulgar references to the wives, mothers, sisters, and aunts, paternal and maternal, of the leaders of the Wafd. One day *al-Kashkul*, a government-aligned paper, printed the headline "Al-Nahhas Pisses." Mahfouz laughed and said, "You've reminded me of a magazine called *al-Mitraqa* (The Mallet), which was printed on coarse brown butcher's paper. Its owner had a small shop on al-Khalig Street. He was a Wafdist and against the Constitutional Liberal Party. On the first page he would publish a headline like 'So and so, of the Constitutional Liberals, was arrested walking in al-Mahatta Square'"—here Mahfouz laughed—"as though a person's membership of the party were itself a criminal charge. Or he would write on the obituaries page 'Praise be to God, so and so, a Constitutional Liberal, has died.'"

We laughed together, and I was reminded of the stories my great friend had told me of the offers he had had to work in journalism, but which he had refused out of dedication to literature.

We reached the Akhbar al-Yawm publishing house.

The First Encounter

For the first time, Naguib Mahfouz entered Akhbar al-Yawm. I suggested to my friend Muhammad 'Abd al-Rahman that he seize the opportunity and take some pictures of the great writer. Because Muhammad 'Abd al-Rahman was considered a master of the portrait, he promptly invited Naguib Mahfouz to his private studio, which is attached to the photography department. I whispered in his ear that the man suffered from a sensitivity to light, especially in the summer, and Muhammad 'Abd al-Rahman did indeed complete his work rapidly, and put six films containing about one hundred pictures of Naguib Mahfouz in front of us in his office. I told Mahfouz, "He's taken more than a hundred pictures of you." Mahfouz showed his surprise. "But it only took a few minutes. Was he taking photographs behind my back?"

It would have been unnatural to have Naguib Mahfouz on the second floor and Mustafa Amin on the ninth and not have them meet, for each represents the peak of artistic achievement in the field in which he works; they also both belong to the same generation—are the same age in fact—and have lived through the same events. This gave rise to Mahfouz's enthusiasm for following the memoirs of Mustafa Amin when they were published under the titles *From One to Ten (Min wahid ila 'ashara)* and *From Ten to Twenty*. We went up to the ninth floor together.

The 1919 Revolution

Mustafa Amin said, "This encounter ought to have taken place thirty-eight years ago. Do you remember? I sent you a message with a female journalist who worked on *Akhbar al-yawm* asking if we could publish two stories of yours a month."

Mahfouz nodded and said, "If that had happened, my whole life might have changed."

Then Mahfouz asked, "When will you finish writing *From Twenty to Thirty*?"

Amin replied, "I'm writing the memoirs now and hope to finish them, if I should live. Afterward I'll write *From Forty to Fifty*, then *From Fifty to Sixty*. But will I live long enough for that?"

I took note of the disturbing tone in Amin's voice when he said "if I should live" and "will I live long enough?"

He said to Mahfouz, "I read your story *Satan Preaches (al-Shaytan ya'iz)* and I saw the movie. It's a first-class political story, but it hasn't received enough critical attention."

Mahfouz kept silent, as he does when listening to someone talking about one of his stories, and I suggested that he look at Mustafa Amin's rare collection of photographs of the 1919 Revolution. We moved to the end of the room, where the collection was.

Demonstrations in Black Wraps

One might say the collection was a rare and living museum of the events of the 1919 Revolution. We stood while Mustafa Amin showed us one picture after another, and our great writer immersed himself in looking. Pictures of the demonstrations; people wearing *gallabiya*s, barefoot;

women's demonstrations, the women wearing their black wraps and shawls, the men urging them on.

Amin said, "See. There isn't a single man harassing a woman. There's no indecent behavior."

Mahfouz asked him, "Did you see the demonstrations by the women of the popular classes wearing their black wraps?"

Amin nodded, saying "I did. I did."

The pictures follow one another. Demostrations in front of the old Shepheard's Hotel; the House of the Nation surrounded by police; a British soldier guarding a streetcar; an old taxi; an indigent martyr lying dead on the street in a popular neighborhood.

Old Cairo: Reality and Invention in the World of Mahfouz

The great novelist of Arabic, Naguib Mahfouz, said, "My love for and attachment to the old parts of Cairo is unequalled. Sometimes one may complain of a certain aridity of the soul—you know, those moments every author goes through—but when I walk in that area, images flood my mind's eye; most of my novels came to me as living ideas while I was sitting in this area. It seems to me that there has to be some link to a specific place, or a specific thing, that is the starting point for one's feelings and sensations. For me, al-Gamaliya is that place."

The area to which Mahfouz is so attached is historic Cairo, the area regarded as the basis of the city and from which the city expanded and ramified in the centuries following its foundation in AD 969. Mahfouz was born in Bayt al-Qadi Square, in the same area of Bayn al-Qasrayn that became a stage for the events of the greatest of his literary works, *The Cairo Trilogy*. He lived there until he was twelve, when he moved to the nearby district of al-'Abbasiya, but he has never cut his links to historic Cairo. He gave the names of its streets and neighborhoods to five of his most important novels—*Khan al-Khalili*, *Midaq Alley*, and the *Trilogy*, which consists of *Palace Walk*, *Palace of Desire*, and *Sugar Street*. These names exist even in our day, and in these places the events of the novels unfold. To what extent then has he been able to embody historic Cairo in his works, and does the real Cairo match the Cairo that appears in the novels? I shall focus on the *Trilogy*, the largest and most important of Mahfouz's works, relying on my own experience of the place, since I lived in historic Cairo for more than thirty years and got to know the same streets and neighborhoods that Naguib Mahfouz had known.

Palace Walk

We are confronted with historic Cairo in the first pages of *Palace Walk*, through the eyes of Amina, wife of Ahmad 'Abd al-Jawad, as she stands at the window that looks out over the road, waiting for her husband. The window of turned latticework was located opposite the public fountain of Bayn al-Qasrayn, above the junction of al-Nahhasin Street, which slopes to the south, and Bayn al-Qasrayn Street, which climbs to the north. To Amina's left, the road looks narrow and twisty and is enveloped in a darkness that increases in its upper reaches, where the windows of the houses project. In its lower reaches, it is edged by the lights thrown on it by the lanterns of handcarts and the incandescent lamps of cafés, and of a few small stores that stay open until daybreak. To Amina's right, the road is enveloped in darkness, as it is devoid of cafés and contains large stores that close their doors early. There is nothing, therefore, to attract the eye except the minarets of Qalawun and Barquq, which loom like giants passing their evenings beneath the brilliant light of the stars.

Such is the picture of the road as it appears in the first passage devoted to its description. How does it appear in reality? The place can easily be identified from Mahfouz's description: it is that part of Bayn al-Qasrayn Street (currently named al-Mu'izz li-Din Illah Street, after Cairo's founder) where a group of important monuments stands. If we look at the road as we walk along it from north to south, we will find the following Islamic monuments (arranged in order of their locations):

- The Mosque of Barquq
- The Mosque of al-Nasir Qalawun
- The Mausoleum of al-Mansur Qalawun

- The Baths of Sultan Qalawun
- The Hospital of Qalawun.
- On the left hand side and facing these, we find:
- The House of Prince Bashtak
- The Ottoman-style Fountain of Bayn al-Qasrayn
- The beginning of the street leading to Bayt al-Qadi Square
- The Tomb of al-Salih Nagm al-Din Ayyub
- Al-Nahhasin Street.

The first observation to strike us here is that the area is utterly devoid of residential properties, the closest of which are situated in al-Khurunfish, to the north, and in the Salihiya *hara*, to the south. Naguib Mahfouz located the house in which most of the *Trilogy*'s events take place opposite the Bayn al-Qasrayn public fountain. The fountain exists indeed, but opposite it stands the huge Mosque of Barquq. In other words, the house in the novel occupies the place of the mosque in reality and stands in a position where no occupied houses are to be found. Similarly, he describes the minarets of Barquq and Qalawun through Amina's eyes but, for her to see these, the house would have to be situated on the other side of the road; and if the house were indeed correctly located on the other side, the window could not by any means face the Bayn al-Qasrayn fountain. At the same time, we find that the author's description of the road matches reality in terms of its being crowded on the left and empty of traffic on the right. The description, however, once again becomes removed from the reality of the place when Amina looks first at the Bayn al-Qasrayn fountain, then at the turning into the *hara* of al-Khurunfish, then at the doorway of the Sultan bathhouse, and finally at the minarets. For anyone to see all these things, he would have to be standing exactly in the middle of the road and not behind a window situated opposite the Bayn al-Qasrayn fountain.

In chapter 7, the author says, "When al-Sayyid Ahmad Abd al-Jawad reached his store, situated in front of the mosque of Barquq on al-Nahhasin Street . . . ."[11]

In reality, we find the Bayn al-Qasrayn fountain opposite the Mosque of Barquq and next to it the Palace of Prince Bashtak, and there are no stores in this area. On the contrary, the shops are situated to the south, about three hundred meters away, in al-Nahhasin.

In chapter 12, Mahfouz describes the movements of Yasin 'Abd al-Jawad, saying:

> He headed toward the Goldsmiths Bazaar and then to al-Ghuriya. He turned into al-Sayyid Ali's coffee shop on the corner of al-Sanadiqiya. It resembled a store of medium size and had a door on al-Sanadiqiya and a window with bars overlooking al-Ghuriya.[12]

In reality, as in the novel, we find the order of the streets through which he moves to be Goldsmiths' Street, al-Ghuriya, and al-Sanadiqiya. No café bearing the name of al-Sayyid 'Ali is to be found in the area of al-Sanadiqiya now or has existed there for the past hundred years, and if we take the café in the novel, no one sitting there could see al-Ghuriya from al-Sanadiqiya, since it's far from the former and divided from it by al-Azhar Street, which in 1918, when the events of the novel took place, was a narrow corridor; this was widened starting in 1930.

In chapter 21, Mahfouz, describing Umm Maryam's house, refers to "a window overlooking Hammam al-Sultan,"[13] whereas in reality we find that there are no houses in front of Hammam al-Sultan, or the Bathhouse of the Sultan. What we find there instead is the Tomb of al-Salih Nagm al-Din Ayyub. The Hammam al-Sultan confronts us once more when 'A'isha looks out at it:

> She stood there this morning with her eyes wandering from Hammam al-Sultan to the ancient building that housed the public cistern. Her young heart pounded while she waited for "him." Then he appeared in the distance. He turned the corner, coming from al-Khurunfish . . . .[14]

If we take it that (as in the novel but not in reality) the house stands opposite the Bayn al-Qasrayn fountain, it would be difficult for anyone situated there and looking out of the window to see the Sultan bathhouse and the fountain at the same time; one's field of vision cannot comprehend both at once.

We note, by tracing the movements of the characters in the imagined reality of the novel, that the author does not maintain accuracy in his description of the details and does not allow the actual features of the place to restrict his imagination. In contrary fashion, however, when he draws general features, he is more precise. Thus, in Chapter 28, when Yasin crosses al-Gamaliya Street, then sees 'Atfat Qasr al-Shawq, the description is general and more or less accurate, as 'Qasr al-Shawq' is the name applied to a street that branches off the main street of al-Gamaliya, and it is this that the author treats as an *'atfa*, or turning. 'Atfat Qasr al-Shawq in real life, however, is located at the end of Qasr al-Shawq Street, beginning at 'Abd al-Rahman Katkhuda Elementary School. Similarly, when Amina goes to visit the mosque of Our Master al-Husayn with Kamal, the general description appears to be correct when compared to the real place. They leave the house and pass by first Qirmiz Road, then Bayt al-Qadi Square, dominated by the Gamaliya police station, then Khan Ga'far Secondary School, and then Khan Ga'far Road at the point where a side of the mosque of al-Husayn looms. The description here is accurate and the imagined place matches reality exactly, the landmarks mentioned by Mahfouz—the police station, the Khan Ga'far school, and Bayt al-Qadi Square—existing to this day.

The general description in chapter 40, when the family moves from Bayn al-Qasrayn to al-Sukkariya, next to the 'Mitwalli' Gate is of the same sort (and here we note that Mahfouz uses the popular name for this huge gate that still exists to this day as one of the four, out of the original eight, surviving old gates of Cairo). And when Ahmad 'Abd al-Jawad takes his sons to Friday prayer with him at the mosque of al-Husayn, they follow the same route that Amina and Kamal walked before. Mahfouz does not mention the details, but they the cross Bayt al-Qadi Square and then we see them entering the mosque.

Also, at the end of *Palace Walk*, the demonstration in which Fahmi takes part moves off from al-Mahatta Square, where the main railroad station is situated, makes for the start of Nubar Street, and then approaches the Azbakiya Gardens, where Opera Square opens out; here the bullets are fired and Fahmi is killed. The reader who did not live in Cairo in the twenties will be taken aback, asking how the demonstration could have left from al-Mahatta Square and arrived at Nubar Street, which is located currently in the Sayyida Zaynab area, to the south, while Opera Square is in the center of the city. How, the reader will ask, could the demonstration pass Nubar before crossing Opera Square? Here Mahfouz appears to be unfamiliar with the layout of the streets in Cairo. The truth, however, is the opposite, for the name Nubar used to be applied to Ibrahim Pasha Street (later named al-Gumhuriya Street), and at the start of King Faruq's reign he gave the name of his grandfather Ibrahim Pasha to Nubar, and gave the name Nubar Pasha to another, smaller, street that starts at Lazughli Square and ends at al-Mubtadayan Street, and was formerly called al-Dawawin.

We also note that in the first part of the *Trilogy* the movements of the characters take place within the area of historic Cairo; these movements expand suddenly when Yasin goes with his wife to the theater in al-Azbakiya. We are not given any description of the theater. What we are shown is Yasin at home after they return. Next the action extends to al-Mahatta Square, where the demonstration begins. There are seventy-one chapters in the novel, and the events in these take place as follows:

- forty in the house of Ahmad 'Abd al-Jawad;
- twelve in 'Abd al-Jawad's store, which is half a kilometer from his house;
- eight in the streets of the Gamaliya area—no character ventures farther than three kilometers from the house (the distance Fahmi travels to go to al-Mahatta Square);
- three in the house of Zubayda the singer, a kilometer from Ahmad 'Abd al-Jawad's house;
- three in Amina's mother's house in al-Khurunfish, half a kilometer from Ahmad 'Abd al-Jawad's house;
- three in the Sukkariya house, which is about two kilometers away;
- one in the house of Muhammad Radwan, next door to Ahmad 'Abd al-Jawad's house; and
- one in the mosque of al-Husayn, which is no more than one kilometer away.

Also in the first part of the *Trilogy*, Ahmad 'Abd al-Jawad travels to Port Said, and that is the only time he travels in the entire work. However, the road to Port Said is not described, and the author mentions no details beyond the fact that Ahmad 'Abd al-Jawad leaves his house and returns.

Palace of Desire

The events of the first part of the *Trilogy*, *Palace Walk*, take place in April 1919 and those of the second, *Palace of Desire*, in July 1927, i.e., after six years have passed. The characters now have different orbits within the city of Cairo. They have grown older and each has his own relationships; consequently, their movements have to take in areas of the city not mentioned in the first part. At the start of chapter 6, Kamal, who is now an adolescent, is walking with his friend Fu'ad. They pass through Qirmiz Passage, a landmark that is mentioned several times in the *Trilogy* and that really exists; it passes beneath an old Mamluk mosque and is steeped in legend. Mahfouz, however, conflates it with another passageway that is situated beneath the House of Prince Bashtak, this latter having a number of twists and turns, unlike the first. If we take the location of Ahmad 'Abd al-Jawad into consideration, it would appear that Mahfouz has the second passageway in mind. However, he gives it the name of the first, which is farther from the house.

Kamal and his friend arrive at Ahmad 'Abduh's café, which is underground. This café existed until the thirties, and it would seem, from what Mahfouz has said about it and from the memories of long-term residents of the area, that his description is accurate. The café was destroyed and in its place to this day is the Princess Shuwaykar building complex.

In the same chapter, mention is made of the Egyptian Club, when Kamal says to his friend, "Next Thursday we'll go to the Egyptian Club to see Charlie Chaplin. Now we'll play a game of dominoes."[15]

The Egyptian Club is an old hotel that still exists near the Mosque of al-Husayn. The hotel includes an open-air courtyard in which, during the first third of this century, movies used to be shown; the first movie showing to be presented in Egypt was seen there in 1910.

In chapter 7, Ahmad 'Abd al-Jawad makes his way to "a houseboat at the end of the first triangle of streets on the road to Imbaba."[16] Houseboats are indeed to be found in this area, and some used to be employed for purposes of diversion and as places in which to spend a few hours of pleasure. Ahmad 'Abd al-Jawad will visit this houseboat a number of times.

In chapter 8, Ahmad 'Abd al-Jawad sees his sweetheart, the singer Zannuba, in the Watawit *hara*, which survives to this day next to the mosque of al-Husayn and which leads to al-Gamaliya Street. In the last century it was roofed with tree branches and bats, or *watawit*, took up residence, which is how the street got its name.

In chapter 14, Kamal goes to al-'Abbasiya. Mahfouz describes the route in general terms—al-Husayniya Street, then al-'Abbasiya Street, then al-Wayliya, then al-Sarayat Street—and all these streets exist with the same names today. The landmarks that Mahfouz describes have changed, however. At the time when the novel is set, al-'Abbasiya was a quiet suburb, full of gardens and trees, and its large villas were residences for the rich and the affluent. Things are different now: al-'Abbasiya is a popular quarter, and crowded. The villas have totally disappeared. The palace of the Shaddad family which Mahfouz describes was a real palace, though the name of the family in real life is different from that used in the novel. The palace has been destroyed, and two modern apartment blocks stand in its place.

In chapter 17, Kamal leaves with Husayn Shaddad and his sister 'Ayda and they go to the pyramids for an outing. The car sets off from al-'Abbasiya, goes to al-Sakakini, then to Queen Nazli Street (now called Ramses Street), then to al-Zamalik, then to the Giza Road, which takes them to the foot of the Great Pyramid, and then to the Sphinx. This itinerary from al-'Abbasiya to the pyramids matches reality, though Mahfouz does not describe it in detail, giving only the main landmarks.

Then, in chapter 35, Kamal goes to 'Wagh al-Birka,' which is a real place—though its name in colloquial speech is 'Wishsh al-Birka'—which was then entirely devoted to prostitution, which was legal in the twenties and up to 1949. Another street, called Tayyib Road, is connected to Wagh al-Birka. Both places are real, and they appear in the novel only after Kamal lives through a severe emotional crisis that leads him to drink and to his becoming acquainted with Woman as body, in this place situated close to al-Azbakiya Garden in the middle of the city. *Palace of Desire* consists of forty-four chapters:

- thirteen chapters that take place in the house of Ahmad 'Abd al-Jawad in Bayn al-Qasrayn;
- eight that take place in the palace of the Shaddad family in the suburb of al-'Abbasiya;
- four in Ahmad 'Abd al-Jawad's store in al-Nahhasin;
- seven on the houseboat or the road bordering the Nile;
- two in al-Sukkariya;
- two in Wagh al-Birka;
- three in Yasin's house in Bayn al-Qasrayn;
- one in Ahmad 'Abduh's café;
- one in Muhammad Radwan's house;
- one at the pyramids;
- one at the Mosque of al-Husayn; and
- one at the house of the singer Zubayda.

The area of Qasr al-Shawq (whose name the second part of the *Trilogy* bears) occupies only three chapters of the novel. There is a curious reason for this, namely that the *Trilogy* was originally one huge novel under the title of *Palace Walk*. For practical reasons, it was not possible for it to come out as a single volume and the publisher asked the author to divide it into three parts, which he indeed did, giving each part its own name.

Sugar Street

The events of the third part of the *Trilogy* begin in January 1935 and end in the summer of 1944. Time passes, characters grow older, their movements range further afield within Cairo, and new places appear.

At the beginning of chapter 4, Kamal rides the streetcar on his way to 'the House of the Nation'—the house of Sa'd Zaghlul, leader of the 1919 Revolution; the house stands to this day. Kamal leaves the marquee set up for the celebrations and proceeds to Qasr al-'Ayni Street, passing in front of the American University building in Isma'iliya (now Tahrir) Square. Ahmad 'Abduh's café appears again in chapter 6, when Kamal sits there with his friend Isma'il Latif, and in chapter 7 Yasin too sits in a café: "From this warm spot you can see people coming and going . . . back and forth from Faruq Street, the Muski, and al-'Ataba."[17] The author seems not to mention the café in al-'Ataba Square by name. Faruq Street (now called al-Gaysh Street) still exists, and al-Muski Street likewise has not changed its name.

In chapter 8, Radwan, Yasin's son, walks along al-Ghuriya, passing al-Sukkariya. He goes through the Mitwalli Gate, then turns into al-Darb al-Ahmar, which is now mentioned for the first time in the *Trilogy*. Another place linked to Radwan's movements that makes its first appearance here is the suburb of Hilwan, which is situated about thirty kilometers to the south of Cairo. There Yasin is a visitor to the house of 'Abd al-Rahim Pasha.

In chapter 15, Kamal goes to *al-Fikr* magazine and Mahfouz says, with great precision, "*Al-Fikr* magazine occupied the ground floor of 21 'Abd al-'Aziz Street." 'Abd al-'Aziz Street starts at al-'Ataba Square and still bears that name, but the building that Mahfouz specifies (and this is the only time he mentions an address with such precision) does not exist, and no magazine has its offices on the street.

Kamal goes to a brothel in 'Atfat al-Gawhari, which is a turning off al-Muski Street; this street does not exist in real life.

In chapter 20, we find Ahmad Shawkat and his brother 'Abd al-Mun'im at Cairo University, in Giza. Then once again, in chapter 25, we find Ahmad Shawkat in his office at the university, where he makes the acquaintance of his colleague 'Alawiya Sabri, a relationship that will lead to his visiting her house in the suburb of al-Ma'adi; al-Ma'adi is situated about fifteen kilometers south of Cairo. In what is the third and final reference to that institution in the entire *Trilogy*, we also find Kamal at Cairo University. In chapter 30, Kamal walks on Fu'ad Street, which is under blackout because of the war, and Mahfouz describes the crowds and the British occupation troops; Fu'ad Street is now named 26 July Street. During his walk, Kamal is compelled to take refuge in a *café dansant* that really existed and was removed in the late fifties.

In chapter 36, the family takes shelter in Qirmiz Passage, Kamal having to carry his father. As I have indicated earlier, the passageway referred to by Mahfouz in the novel is another passageway, situated beneath the historic House of Prince Bashtak. That the family took shelter there during the air raid confirms this earlier identification, since the family's house, as described by Mahfouz, is closer to the latter than it is to Qirmiz Passage.

At the start of chapter 40, we find Kamal with his friend Riyad in the Khan al-Khalili café, which was put up on the site of Ahmad 'Abduh's café, but above ground: "From its doorway, which opened out to al-Husayn, this small café, like a corridor with tables lining the two sides, extended back to a wooden balcony that overlooked the new Khan al-Khalili."[18]

Here Mahfouz provides a glimpse of one of the changes that have taken place in the area. The café that he describes is a real café that existed, as described by the author, until 1969, when it was demolished and a modern building was put up in which the same café was reopened, though naturally with a different design. Mahfouz, however, refers to the café as 'Khan al-Khalili' whereas in reality its name was and still is Darwish's café. It still exists in its new quarters.

Kamal also goes to Ewart Hall at the American University, where he watches Budur, the sister of the 'Ayda whom he loved when he was in the flower of his youth. The hall is mentioned just once. It still exists, and its entrance opens onto al-Shaykh Rihan Street. One other place is mentioned just once—the Tea Garden at the zoo, where Ahmad Shawkat meets his woman friend Sawsan Hammad; the rockery there is a real place and still exists.

Kamal meets Budur one more time, in Ibn Zaydan Street, and he walks with her to al-Galal Street and then on Queen Nazli Street. Neither of the first two streets exists in real life.

At the intersection of Sharif and Qasr al-Nil streets, Kamal unexpectedly runs into his friend Husayn Shaddad. They go to Café Ritz. This was a real café situated opposite the Egyptian National Bank, but it was destroyed in the late forties.

We note therefore that the places in Cairo that appear in the third part of the *Trilogy* are more numerous, in keeping with the characters' movements within the city. We note too that the places visited by the family of Ahmad 'Abd al-Jawad, the pivot of the novel, are limited and, in the first part of the *Trilogy* when the family is cohesive, do not exceed the area of historic Cairo. Then, in the second part, the orbit of movement widens as the characters develop and advance in age, while in the third part the rhythm of life speeds up, as do the characters' movements, and their numerous displacements within the city described above follow as a result. It also follows that new places appear.

Sugar Street consists of forty-five chapters, with the following *mises en scène*:

The house on Bayn al-Qasrayn	12 chapters
The house on Sugar Street	12 chapters
The open street	8 chapters
Cafés	4 chapters
Cairo University	3 chapters
Hilwan	3 chapters
al-Fikr magazine on 'Abd al-'Aziz Street	2 chapters
Ahmad 'Abd al-Jawad's store	1 chapter
al-Insan al-gadid magazine in Ghamra	1 chapter
The ministry where Yasin works	1 chapter
The suburb of al-Ma'adi	1 chapter
The brothel	1 chapter
Qirmiz Passage	1 chapter
Ewart Hall	1 chapter
The Tea Garden	1 chapter
al-Nagma Bar	1 chapter
The Gamaliya police station	1 chapter

Within the novel, time advances and a wider area of the city is shown. Via Mahfouz's descriptions, the novel records the landmarks of Cairo—many of which have now changed—starting with the house of Ahmad 'Abd al-Jawad, which may be considered an archetype of a middle class family dwelling in historic Cairo. Such homes have disappeared completely now, to be replaced by multistory buildings. Mahfouz even records the cafés, some of which have disappeared, and the names of the streets that have changed. And he describes means of transport that have become extinct, such as the *sawaris*, which is mentioned a number of times. The *sawaris* was a horse-drawn bus; these buses were owned by a Greek, and they remained in existence until the early fifties. In addition, Mahfouz mentions certain signs of the development of the city, such as the introduction of water mains. He describes the broad outlines of the city of Cairo accurately but abandons this accuracy when he descends to the level of detail. There can be no doubt, however, that he has been able, through his concentration on the internal life of the characters, to embody a Cairene way of life that lasted for a long period and traces of which still survive in our lives today.

Names of streets occurring in the Trilogy, with their current names:

Old Name	*Current Name*
Bayn al-Qasrayn Street	al-Mu'izz li-Din Illah Street
al-Mahatta Square	Ramses Square
Nubar Street	al-Gumhuriya Street
Isma'iliya Square	al-Tahrir Square
Fu'ad al-Awwal Street	26 July Street
Queen Nazli Street	Ramses Street

Part Three

Scattered Gatherings

The Gathering on the *Autobiography*

TUESDAY

Farah Boat

What beautiful creation is this?

What refined literature?

What quintessence, what nectar? What pure, thrilling, refreshing honeycomb conducive to every intimation of beauty?

Admiration, bedazzlement, and a deep attention to the lessons Naguib Mahfouz offers us with a manifest modesty concealing a rare mastery.

Questions follow one another in quick succession, accompanied by the diverse impressions aroused by this work of literary nonfiction with which Mahfouz has surprised his readers and admirers. For the first time in many years, a published work of literature has become the center of people's conversations, comments, and impressions, reviving memories of those fertile days of the sixties when the novels of Naguib Mahfouz were published in serial form on Friday mornings, each installment becoming a topic of discussion and the object of admiration and meditation. In *Echoes of an Autobiography*, the great builder is transformed into a skilled jeweler, fashioning from words, letters, and punctuation marks pieces of rare prose resembling rubies, emeralds, and coral. They scintillate, they are full of music and poetry. Some of them contain all of human wisdom. Others embody the courageous confrontation of humankind with the eternal, with life and death.

At the weekly meeting with the great writer, which embraces the chosen few of his intimate friends, we put to him a number of questions that aim to shed light on the circumstances surrounding this work, unique in modern Arabic literature. Here it must be pointed out that these companions lived the experience of the writing of this work: Mahfouz—who usually did not talk about what he was writing—cast out signals week after week and said he was writing a few meditations on scraps of paper and who knew what might come out of them? His signals were modest and obscure and we had become accustomed to not pursuing them with further questions, for he would say only what he wanted to say. The situation was different now, however, after the appearance of *Echoes of an Autobiography* and all the admiration and questions that it had given rise to. The previous Tuesday, in the place where we usually met, I and my friend the novelist Yusuf al-Qa'id had asked everything we could think of, and he had answered us with a frankness that was both complete and, in some aspects, surprising to us.

It was natural to ask, first, when Mahfouz had started to think about writing *Echoes of an Autobiography*.

For a few moments he stared in front of him, at an unknown point in time and space. Then he looked at us, and we reminded him that he had told us one day about a series of meditations that he was writing: were these what had now been published?

He answered quickly, "Absolutely. The truth is I hadn't thought of publishing them. It never occurred to me. After the operation was carried out in London, I returned to Cairo in poor health. I had a desire to write but I had no particular topic. I started to write down some ideas, any ideas. Then I thought of rereading these with the aim of polishing them, in case something might be made of them. I started by taking each 'meditation-ette' and rewriting it carefully. But as far as publication was concerned, I was very scared to take it to the readers, so much so that my friend Zaki Salim demanded that he read it so he could give me his opinion, and likewise my friends in Alexandria; but I was very afraid. I was so afraid, I flung it at the publisher.

Here we reminded him of what he'd said to us more than once about wanting to show us a work he'd written that was giving him problems, and his voice rose a tone.

"You're right. You're right. I remember that well. It's the only work that I've written and wanted to show you before it was published. I intended to show it to more than one friend. The title itself only materialized after I'd finished it. I'd put a tentative title of *Meditations (Ta'ammulat)* but I found that much of what it contained was inspired by my life. I also found, however, that it wasn't exactly a life story. At this point, I thought of the word 'echoes' *(asda')* on the basis that 'echo' allows a degree of freedom, so that the writer cannot be held accountable for the details. That's how the title *Echoes of an Autobiography* came into being."

From Mirrors to Echoes

We reminded him of a similar situation that he had experienced in the sixties: during our meeting with him at 'Urabi's café (now vanished) on al-Gaysh Square he had spoken to us of not having a subject for a novel and that he had thought of inviting a number of the friends he'd come across over the course of his life and writing about them. That was how *Mirrors* came about. Was there a similarity between the two situations? He responded immediately.

"No. *Mirrors* was a different matter. I had thought I would write a history that turned on some of those whom I'd met in my life—Sayyid Qutb, or Mansur Fahmi, for example—but I discovered that I knew very little about these people. I mean, I couldn't write a chapter about Sayyid Qutb, or Mansur Fahmi, or Muhammad Mandur. I couldn't do history."

"Were you thinking of writing about the real people under their own names?" I asked.

"Yes. But my knowledge of them was very limited and the available information was extremely sparse. I couldn't become a historian, so I wrote about them as a writer, as a novelist. A few lines from real life are there just as the kernel, but the rest of the story is made up."

"That caused a misunderstanding when *Mirrors* was published," I said.

"Exactly. Given that I didn't write people's original names and wrote in the form of a novel, the original inevitably got forgotten. I wanted the novel to be regarded as a creative, fictional work, but I know that some people tried to deduce from it real things that had no basis in reality.

"Let's return to *Echoes of an Autobiography*," I said. "If *Mirrors* is to be considered a novelistic treatment of certain characters drawn from life, then *Echoes of an Autobiography* is different, because the writer and his subject are the same person."

"Right. In each piece, the original is either an incident that cropped up in my life, or a moment, or a thought—a 'meditation-ette.' All these things, without a doubt, derive from me."

"Didn't you draw up any plan for the work?" I asked. "Didn't you make a blueprint for *Echoes of an Autobiography*, so that one particular piece should come before another?"

"Absolutely not, which is why you'll find that some of the pieces are very recent while others are very ancient; I included them just as they occurred to me. There is absolutely no historical order. For example, I remember that the first piece is about the Revolution, when I'm on my way to school, and the second is about my grandmother's death, when I was grown up; I was an adolescent at the time. In other words I was coming and going in my memory without planning. I was like someone who can't find a topic to write about and is trying to fill in his time. I wasn't feeling very well when I wrote it. I was sick."

However, we reminded him that he always used to tell us when he was working on this book that if it found a topic, it wouldn't be a novel—or, as I put it to him, "You have a sort of predisposition against going into a novel with a preexisting concept."

"Right. In other words, if I came upon a topic now for a novel, I wouldn't be able to do it. The continuity, and the linking of beginning to end—I'd be incapable. A novel needs one to be able to sit down and think. Yes indeed. I have a desire to write that isn't dimmed or exhausted the way it was before *Children of the Alley*. Last January I finished twenty-two short stories. I only published one of them: "The Rose Garden" *(Hadiqat al-ward)*. The desire is still strong in me but, on the other hand, I don't have a topic for a novel now, and there's nothing on the horizon."

"Why?" I ask. "Has your relationship to reality changed?"

"I was accustomed to write about society. Take for example the opportunist. Whenever I think about such a character I think of Mahgub 'Abd al-Dayim and I say to myself, 'But I've written about him.' For me, society no longer provides fundamentally new things. What have changed in society are the specifics of the opportunism: bribes now are calculated in the millions rather than in terms of a pay raise.

"We regard Mahgub as innocent compared to what goes on nowadays," I say. "He was trying to rise in an extremely class-conscious society. But the way people try to rise these days is different."

"From my perspective, they're the same in essence. It's an aberrant way to try to get ahead."

Mahfouz falls silent for a little and we return to our discussion of *Echoes of an Autobiography*.

Wisdom

We tell Mahfouz that the new work contains a measure of wisdom, universal wisdom, and of the essence of human experience. He listens to us—modestly as always when listening to praise—repeatedly murmuring, "Ah, ah," or nodding his head. We ask, "Was that intentional or is it a sort of inner dialog?"

"Of course I'm talking to myself. When someone writes at the age that I am now, he has behind him all he has lived through in his long life and all the experiences he has acquired. Naturally, it's different from when I was writing in the twenties."

We note that the book contains an overwhelming anxiety about death."

"Yes. That's true."

"And sex too."

"And what?"

"And sex."

"Yes. Sex. Perhaps."

And his pure laugh rang out. Here we were reminded of the contents of his library: even though he retains few books, it is noticeable that Persian literature occupies an important place among those. When we entered his house on the day that he received the Nobel prize, the collected works of Hafiz al-Shirazi were open on his desk. Might it be said that he has been influenced by Persian literature, especially in view of the symbolic Sufi expressions that remind us of Persian poetry?"

"Yes. My favorite poet is certainly Hafiz al-Shirazi. I put some of his poetry into *The Harafish*, and some from Sa'di too."

We remarked that it was the first time that his readers would be reading something by him in which he himself was the hero. Mahfouz agreed with us. Then we reminded him of his earlier statement that he would never write an autobiography, and he replied, "As far as my autobiography is concerned, I dictated that to Gamal and it came out as *Naguib Mahfouz Remembers*. The intellectual and mental aspects I gave to Raga' al-Naqqash and I believe his book will be published by al-Ahram next December. There are crumbs and areas that neither Gamal's nor Raga''s questions zoomed in on. So I said I'd write about them myself. Thus *Echoes of an Autobiography* complements the other two works, meaning that if anyone wants to know about me, he should read all three—*Naguib Mahfouz Remembers*, Raga''s book, and *Echoes*."

"Wouldn't you agree that the title doesn't do justice to the work? The word 'echoes' is no guide to its contents at all."

"To tell you the truth, this caused me some perplexity. I decided that *Meditations* was too big for the work. I mean, am I supposed to be Descartes? And then, to be frank, it's not an autobiography, just 'echoes.'"

We told Professor Naguib that it was perhaps the first autobiography of its type in the literature of the world.

He gave a quiet smile.

"Were you aware," we ask, "that you were standing at the intersection of poetry and prose when you were writing *Echoes of an Autobiography*?"

"Perhaps. The book was a real puzzle to me. I'd look at it and not find a short story, or a novel, or poetry. What was one to make of that? It was this perplexity that lay behind my fear of presenting it for publication."

"Are you still afraid, Professor Naguib?"

"Indeed. The hardest thing I know is to face the reader. I've had moments when I almost tore *Echoes of an Autobiography* up."

"We can't picture that. What a loss it would have been for Arabic literature!"

He shakes his head in silence.

I tell him that in the end literature is all texts. It can't be divided up into short story, poetry, novel. Could this concept be applied to *Echoes*?

"To a great extent."

"Are you a believer in the role of the unconscious in literary creation?" we ask.

"It has the most powerful role. Of course the unconscious plays a big role. There are some who attempt to surrender to it completely and to do away with the mind, but the creative writer is never free of the unconscious."

"We had the impression," we commented, "that your reading has declined a great deal in the recent period. However, *Echoes of an Autobiography* proves that you are completely up on the latest writings in the field of the prose poem, modern poetry, and new experiments in literature."

Mahfouz told us that he had stopped reading almost completely in 1988. "I've read all the generations—Yusuf Idris, Amal Dunqul, al-Qa'id, El-Bisatie, Al-Wardani, Abu Rayya—but I haven't read prose poems. If there's any resemblance, we might say that it's a general mood."

"Professor Naguib, you have taught us a great deal, a very great deal, through *Echoes of an Autobiography*."

He let out one of his pure laughs, which sparkled over the billows of the Nile. Then he said, "My dear people, spare my blushes!"

August 2001

Farah Boat

The Million Pound Gathering

This took place on the evening of the Tuesday before last. I returned to my house at eleven o'clock after our weekly meeting with Naguib Mahfouz, an appointment we have not missed once since the summer of 1977. I was worried about what I'd been hearing and was thinking of a number of parties to whom I was close.

We had learned from Naguib Mahfouz that he was in a state of tension, for Ibrahim al-Mu'allim, the publisher, had come to him two days previously and offered to buy all his works and publish them using modern methods—on compact discs, via the Internet, and with other methods that he did not fully understand. He said al-Mu'allim had offered him a huge sum, one without precedent in the history of publishers and publishing—a million pounds, to be paid in full, at one go.

We were loud in our approval, until I noticed the Master's discomfort and patent worry. We asked him the reason and he said that after he had agreed he'd remembered that he'd signed a contract, through his usual publisher Salah al-Sahhar, with a friend of the latter's who worked for an institution in Abu Dhabi.

"Abu Dhabi? Who exactly in Abu Dhabi, Professor Naguib?"

After thinking for a little, Mahfouz answered, "A project at the Electronic Village."

I understood immediately what he meant. "No, Professor Naguib," I said. "The Electronic Village is the name of the project itself and its founder is one of the best of Arab intellectuals, Muhammad al-Siwidi."

All those present agreed with me, for they were all well informed as to the efforts of Muhammad al-Siwidi in the service of Arabic culture, from the distinguished cultural activities witnessed by the Cultural Academy, for which he had created a worthy place on the map of Arab culture, to his pioneering projects, such as putting Arabic poetry on the Internet and making it available to readers throughout the world; the number of lines of verse made available in this manner so far exceeds two million. All this was in addition to a project to establish a Web site for old Arabic literature that would provide readers and Internet users with the basic sources, among them works of more than a thousand pages, such as al-Isbahani's *Songs (al-Aghani)*, the *Lives of Noted Noblemen (Siyar a'lam al-nubala')*, biographical dictionaries, and huge lexica. I was aware of al-Siwidi's initiative in funding, in silence and without media fanfare, important cultural projects from which official cultural institutions had flinched, among them, by way of example, the printing of Dr. Tharwat 'Ukasha's huge three-volume work, *The Arts of the Renaissance (Funun 'asr al-thaqafa)*. A man of culture such as Muhammad al-Siwidi could only strive for the best for Naguib Mahfouz. There could be no doubt that the contractual arrangement had happened without his involvement. The amount the publisher had agreed to was very small compared to that offered by al-Mu'allim, in that it called for the payment of 76,500 pounds for the entirety of his works, which was a modest sum for the output of a writer of Naguib Mahfouz's stature, in terms of both its quality and its quantity.

I felt that the contract was an injustice to Naguib Mahfouz. In addition, a friend of ours had mentioned during the session that some people had started trying to make an issue out of the matter in the media. This gave me another reason for disquiet, since, if the media made an issue of it, our friend the poet Muhammad al-Siwidi would find himself in a situation he had never imagined, and he or his aides would be obliged to make clarifications. The financial rights of writers in our Arab World is an issue hedged around with sensitivities; how much more so if the writer be Naguib Mahfouz?

Late at night, and after some hesitation, I started making contacts to obtain al-Siwidi's number in London, where he was spending his vacation. In the end I was successful in contacting his private secretary, Badr, in Abu Dhabi. I hate the ringing of the telephone late at night, whether I'm at home or with my companions and friends, and I only resort to such things out of extreme necessity. Fortunately, Badr was not yet asleep. I requested him to inform our good friend al-Siwidi in London that he must call me on an important matter. Badr asked me to give him at least some hint of what was involved.

"It's about Naguib Mahfouz."

I have no idea how the contacts could have been made so rapidly, but in less than one minute the telephone rang and al-Siwidi's voice came to me across the vast distance. I related to him what had happened, and I stated my impressions and my opinion. Immediately I heard his quiet voice saying that he had initiated the project out of love for Naguib Mahfouz and that the Web site, which had indeed been put up on the Internet seven months ago, offered its services free of charge at all levels in order to disseminate Mahfouz's work on the widest scale. Al-Siwidi added, "Out of affection for Naguib Mahfouz, if another offer has now materialized that will realize greater benefit for the great writer, then I shall be the first to welcome it. I waive forthwith the contract concluded with the Electronic Village so long as those making the new offer demonstrate their seriousness."

"May I publish this statement of yours in *Akhbar al-adab*?" I asked.

"Certainly. With pleasure."

I thanked him warmly. When I mentioned the name of Muhammad al-Siwidi to the poet 'Abd al-Rahman al-Abnudi, he told me that he knew the man as well as he did himself, that he had initiated this project with the purest cultural motives, and that he would never be an obstacle in the face of a new situation that served Mahfouz's interests. Yusuf al-Qa'id affirmed the same and we started competing with one another in telling stories about Muhammad al-Siwidi as we all knew him to be. Now, with this new stand of his, he had confirmed the honorableness of his intentions past and future.

Early the next day, I called Ibrahim al-Mu'allim, the director of Dar El Shorouk. I told him I would come and see him at one o'clock in his office. He tried to find out from me why I was coming, and the reason for my haste; even though we'd been trying to arrange a meeting for months, commitments on both sides had limited our contact to the telephone, as is the case with other relationships—for one moves about less now and my work as a journalist takes up no small amount of time.

"Are you serious about the contract with Naguib Mahfouz?" I asked him.

Looking at me over the desk, al-Mu'allim replied, "Of course. But . . ."

I raised my hand in confirmation. "If you're referring to the contract that a certain party, namely the Electronic Village, has arranged, it's not a problem."

He appeared amazed. "How so?" he asked.

I narrated to him what had happened with our good friend Muhammad al-Siwidi and told him that everyone was now agreed on serving Mahfouz's interests. The important thing was the seriousness of the contract.

Al-Mu'allim pressed a bell and the director of his office came. "Please," said al-Mu'allim. "I need the envelope with the contract for Naguib Mahfouz."

Then he took a check book from his pocket and wrote in it on the typewriter, "Pay to the order of Mr. Naguib Mahfouz 'Abd al-'Aziz one million pounds only."

The check was drawn on the Exports Bank in Cairo and it was the first check that I had ever seen for a million pounds. True, the figure of one million has become commonplace these days, but a mere half century ago, before the July Revolution, there was only one person in Egypt whose wealth was to be counted in the millions and that was Ahmad 'Abbud Pasha. Now the wealth of a number of people in Egypt is reckoned in the billions. It's easy for me to pronounce the word 'billion' but very difficult for me to imagine it, and the same goes for 'million,' as far as I'm concerned, even though, as I say, a million pounds has become a very commonplace sum in the business world in Egypt.

Ibrahim al-Mu'allim said, "I'm ready to go to Naguib Mahfouz any time you choose to sign the contract and hand over the check, once the original contract has been rescinded."

"I suggest next Tuesday," I said, "at our weekly appointment."

"Agreed."

On Thursday morning, I phoned the exquisite poet and good friend Muhammad al-Siwidi in London and informed him of Ibrahim al-Mu'allim's seriousness and readiness, and the same morning he phoned our friend Mahmud Khidr, his legal advisor, and instructed him to travel to Cairo and take whatever steps he saw fit to ensure Naguib Mahfouz's best interests, without referring back to him on any detail.

On Tuesdays, the day of our weekly appointment, I usually leave my office at five thirty. Mahmud Khidr arrived and we set off for the Farah Boat that was moored on the Nile in Giza. Ibrahim al-Mu'allim had preceded us. Everything took place in an atmosphere overflowing with affection for Naguib Mahfouz and with a wonderful sense of idealism whose source were the rare nobility of Muhammad al-Siwidi and the ambitious plans of a veteran publisher who has set an example for the conduct of the relationship between creative artist and publisher. In this way, a million pounds went into Naguib Mahfouz's bank account in return for the works that he had spent seventy years producing. It was the first million pounds I ever heard about or saw and I am totally confident that they were the fruit of totally honest effort. They were Mahfouz's million.

Glossary of Names

'Abbas Mahmud al-'Aqqad (1889–1964) Journalist, poet, and literary critic.

'Abd al-Aziz Fahmi Lawyer and political figure.

'Abd al-Hadi Abu Rayda Philosopher.

'Abd al-Hakim 'Amir, Field Marshal (1919–67) General who commanded the Egyptian army during the Suez Crisis and Six Day War. Relieved of all duties after the 1967 defeat; committed suicide.

'Abd al-Karim Saqr Football player.

'Abd al-Rahman al-Abnudi Poet who writes in Upper Egyptian dialect.

'Abd al-Rahman al-Sharqawi Novelist, author of *Egyptian Earth*.

'Adil Kamil Novelist, part of Mahfouz's inner circle, al-Harafish. Died in 2006.

Ahmad 'Abbas Salih Novelist.

Ahmad Amin (1886–1954) Scholar and intellectual historian; wrote extensively on Islamic culture and thought.

Ahmad Baha' al-Din Columnist, editor of *Sabah al-khayr*.

Ahmad Hasan al-Zayyat Editor and publisher of *al-Risala*.

Ahmad Lutfi al-Sayyid (1872–1963) Writer, editor, and educationalist. One of the architects of modern Egyptian nationalism.

Ahmad Mazhar Legendary actor, known as the Knight of the Silver Screen; a member of Mahfouz's inner circle, al-Harafish.

Ahmad Nuwayra Neighbor of Mahfouz in al-'Abbasiya.

'Ali Ahmad Bakathir Yemeni writer whose novel *Wa islamah* was made in the 1960s into a major film.

'Ali 'Isa Ninth-century Arab astronomer who measured the earth's circumference.

'Ali al-Kassar Actor of the 1940s and 1950s, who usually played Nubian characters.

'Ali 'Uqla Syrian writer; became head of the Arab Writers' Union in 1979, following the Union's boycott of Egypt.

Amal Dunqul (1940–83) Poet.

Amin 'Uthman (1900–46) Minister assassinated by revolutionaries, including the young Anwar Sadat.

Anwar al-Mu'addawi Literary critic, the first to write about Mahfouz.

Asmahan (1918–44) Famous singer of Syrian Druze origin; sister of singer Farid al-Atrash.

'Atif al-'Iraqi Professor of Arab philosophy.

Badr al-Dib Novelist.

Barlanti 'Abd al-Hamid Actress of the 1940s and 1950s, married to Field Marshal 'Abd al-Hakim 'Amir.

Boutros Boutros-Ghali Egyptian diplomat who served as the sixth secretary general of the United Nations between 1992 and 1996.

Dawud Husni (1870–1937) Composer.

Fathi Ghanim (1924–99) Novelist and political writer.

Fu'ad Nuwayra Mahfouz's neighbor in al-'Abbasiya.

Gamal Abd al-Nasser (1918–70) Army officer, leader of the 1952 Revolution. Second president of Egypt, nationalist, pan-Arab leader.

Hafiz al-Shirazi (720–796) Persian poet.

Hasan Nasir Businessman, member of Mahfouz's inner circle, al-Harafish.

Husayn Higazi Football player.

Husayn Rushdi Pasha (1863–1928) Prime minister of Egypt between 1914 and 1919.

Ibn Rushd (1126–98) Known to the West as Averroes. Andalusian-Arab philosopher, physician, and polymath.

Ibn Sina (980–1037) Known to the West as Avicenna. Persian philosopher, physician, and polymath, who wrote in Arabic.

Ibrahim Aslan Novelist, author of *The Heron.*

Ibrahim Pasha Farag Wafdist member and friend of Mahfouz.

Ibrahim Tal'at Wafdist member.

Ihsan 'Abd al-Quddus (1918–90) Journalist, novelist, and short-story writer.

'Imad al-'Abbudi Businessman, part of Mahfouz' inner circle, al-Harafish; nicknamed al-'Umda by Mahfouz.

'Imad al-Din Adib Egyptian journalist. Former editor-in-chief of *Asharq Alawsat* newspaper.

Isma'il al-'Adili Novelist.

al-Jahiz (781–869) Iraqi prose writer of the early Abbasid period.

Jurji Zaydan (1861–1914) Journalist, publisher, novelist, scholar, and nationalist intellectual.

Kamal Abu al-Magd Leading attorney and intellectual.

Kamal Salim Film director.

Layla Murad (1918–95) Singer and actress.

Luwis 'Awad (1915–90) Intellectual and writer.

Mahmoud Al-Wardani Columnist and novelist.

Mahmud Amin Sulayman Columnist.

Mahmud al-Sa'dani Columnist.

Mustafa al-Lutfi al-Manfaluti (1876–1924) Writer and poet.

Mansur Fahmi Professor of philosophy in the 1920s who later became secretary of the Arabic Language Academy.

Mayy Ziyada Palestinan author.

Mohamed El-Bisatie Novelist.

Muhammad 'Abd al-Halim 'Abd Allah Novelist.

Muhammad 'Abd al-Wahhab (1900–91) Singer and songwriter, and a pioneer in the development of modern Arabic music.

Muhammad 'Ali (1769–1848) Regarded as the founder of the modern Egyptian state; the dynasty he founded ruled Egypt until the revolution of 1952.

Muhammad Farid (1868–1919) Nationalist leader, writer, and lawyer.

Muhammad Hasanayn Haykal Leading journalist, once editor of *al-Ahram*, and a leading commentator on Middle East affairs for over fifty years.

Muhammad Mandur Critic, reformer, and politician.

Muhammad al-Muwaylihi (1858?–1930) Journalist and prose fiction writer.

Muhammad Naguib (1901–84) First president of Egypt. Served as president from the declaration of the Republic on June 18, 1953 to November 14, 1954.

Mukhtar Nuwayra Mahfouz's neighbor in al-'Abbasiya.

Mulla Sadr al-Din al-Shirazi (c. 1571–1640) Persian philosopher who led the Iranian cultural renaissance in the seventeenth century.

Munira al-Mahdiya Singer of the early twentieth century.

Musa Sabri Journalist, columnist, and editor; former editor of *al-Akhbar*.

Mustafa Amin Journalist and editor of *Akhbar al-adab*.

Mustafa Hamam Poet.

Mustafa Kamil (1874–1908) Journalist and political figure.

Mustafa Mahmud Scientist born in 1923.

Mustafa Nagi Chairman of the Egyptian National Cultural Center.

Mustafa Sadiq al-Rafi'i Novelist.

Naguib al-Rihani (1891–1949) Innovative director and comic actor of the 1930s and 1940s.

al-Nahhas Pasha (1879–1965) Served as Egypt's prime minister five times, between 1928 and 1952; Wafd party leader.

Niyazi Mustafa (1911–86) Film director.

Nur al-Huda Lebanese singer of the 1930s and 1940s.

Qut al-Qulub al-Dimardashiya (1899–1968) Novelist and patron of the arts. Founded a prize for literature of which Mahfouz was a recipient. It was his first ever prize.

Raga' al-Naqqash Columnist; author of a collection of interviews with Mahfouz.

Rashad Rushdi The first Egyptian to head the English department at Cairo University after the end of the British occupation of Egypt.

Sa'd Mikkawi Composer.

Sa'd Zaghlul (1859?–1927) One of Egypt's most prominent nationalist leaders. Served as prime minister from January to November of 1924.

Salah Abu Sayf (1915–96) Film director, considered the godfather of realism in Arab Cinema.

Salah Jahin (1930–86) Composer, lyricist, cartoonist, poet, and actor. One of the most enduringly popular figures in Arab art.

Salama Musa (1887–58) Socialist essayist.

Sayf Wanli Painter of the early twentieth century.

Sayyid Darwish (1892–1923) Singer and composer, considered the father of Egyptian popular music.

Sayyid Qutb (1906–66) Author and Islamist; the leading intellectual of the Egyptian Muslim Brotherhood in the 1950s and 1960s. Executed in 1966.

Shaykh 'Ali Mahmud Reciter of the Qur'an and religious songs in the early twentieth century.

Shaykh Amin al-Khawli Intellectual; died in the 1960s.

Shaykh Hasan al-Banna (1906–49) Social and political reformer, founder of the Muslim Brotherhood. Assassinated in 1949.

Shaykh Mustafa 'Abd al-Raziq Professor of philosophy; onetime grand shaykh of al-Azhar.

Shaykh Mustafa al-Maraghi Former grand shaykh of al-Azhar.

Shaykh Zakariya Ahmad Composer of the first half of the twentieth century; a friend of Mahfouz.

Shukri 'Ayyad Literary critic, writer, and university professor.

Sonallah Ibrahim Novelist.

Taha Hussein (1889–1973) One of the most influential writers and intellectuals of his generation and figurehead for the modernist movement in Egypt.

Tariq al-Bishri Leading historian and Islamist intellectual.

Tawfiq al-Hakim (1898–1987) Playwright and novelist. One of the most significant figures of twentieth-century Arabic literature.

Tawfiq al-Tawil Philosopher.

al-Tayyib Salih Sudanese novelist.

Tharwat Abaza (1927–2002) Writer and columnist.

Tharwat 'Ukasha Former minister of culture.

al-Titsh Football player.

Umm Kulthum (1904?–71) Singer, songwriter, and actress, known as the 'Star of the East.' Still recognized as the Arab world's most distinguished singer of the twentieth century.

Yahya Hakki (1905–93) Novelist.

Yasin Sirag al-Din Political figure; head of the Wafd party.

Yusuf Abu Rayya Novelist.

Yusuf Gawhar Member of Mahfouz's inner circle, al-Harafish.

Yusuf Idris (1927–91) Novelist, short-story writer, and playwright.

Yusuf al-Qa'id Novelist.

Yusuf al-Siba'i (1917–79) Novelist, appointed minister of culture in 1973. Assassinated in 1979.

Zaki Nagib Mahmud Philosopher.

Zaki Salim Egyptian professor of philosophy.

Notes

1 Starting from this date and up to the present our meetings have taken place on the same floating restaurant.
2 Naguib Mahfouz, *Fountain and Tomb*, trans. Soad Sobhi, Essam Fattouh, and James Kenneson (Boulder and London: Lynne Reiner Publishers, 1998), 25–26.
3 *Fountain and Tomb*, 36.
4 Naguib Mahfouz, *Mirrors*, trans. Roger Allen (Cairo: Zeitouna/The American University in Cairo Press, 1999), 179–81.
5 *Fountain and Tomb*, 57–60.
6 Naguib Mahfouz, *Miramar*, trans. Fatma Moussa Mahmoud, edited and revised by Maged el Kommos and John Robenbeck (Cairo: The American University in Cairo Press, 2005), 1.
7 *Mirrors*, 98–101.
8 The Musafirkhana Palace was destroyed by fire in 1998.
9 That is, in 1981.
10 That is, on a Thursday in 1988.
11 Naguib Mahfouz, *The Cairo Trilogy*, trans. William Maynard Hutchins, Olive E. Kenny, Lorne M. Kenny, and Angele Botros Samaan (Cairo: The American University in Cairo Press, 2005), 41.
12 *The Cairo Trilogy*, 77.
13 *The Cairo Trilogy*, 142.
14 *The Cairo Trilogy*, 147–48.
15 *The Cairo Trilogy*, 607.
16 *The Cairo Trilogy*, 616.
17 *The Cairo Trilogy*, 1037.
18 *The Cairo Trilogy*, 1218.